W9-ANR-095

June L. Wright and
Daniel D. Shade, Editors

Young Children: Active Learners in a Technological Age

A 1993–94 NAEYC Comprehensive Membership benefit

National Association for the Education of Young Children, Washington, DC

Photo credits: Subjects & Predicates, p.7; June Wright, p. 16; Hildegard Adler, pp. 21, 124; BmPorter/Don Franklin, pp. 25, 145; Edmark, pp. 27, 32, 123; Jane Davidson, pp. 45, 85, 91, 155, 157, 163; Suzanne Thouvenelle, p. 59; Dwight Bachman, pp. 65, 88, 100, 104, 169; Nina Pratt, p. 72; Cy Jones, pp. 96, 100, 138; courtesy of America Tomorrow, Inc., pp. 111, 119; SLR Images, p. 127; Thomas A. Hoebbel, p. 129; Elena Gomez (University of Maryland Photo Outreach), pp. 155; Jazy Graphics, p. 173.

National Association for the Education of Young Children
1509 16th Street, N.W.
Washington, DC 20036-1426
202-232-8777   800-424-2460

The National Association for the Education of Young Children (NAEYC) attempts through its publications program to provide a forum for discussion of major issues and ideas in our field. We hope to provoke thought and promote professional growth. The views expressed or implied are not necessarily those of the Association. NAEYC wishes to thank the editors and authors, who donated much time and effort to develop this book as a contribution to our profession.

Library of Congress Catalog Card Number: 94-068838

ISBN Catalog Number: 0-935989-63-3

NAEYC #341

Editor: Carol Copple; *Cover design:* DeAnn Cobb; *Book design and production:* Jack Zibulsky, Penny Atkins, and Danielle Hudson; *Copyediting:* Betty Nylund Barr.

Printed in the United States of America

Contents

About the Editors

June L. Wright is an associate professor of early childhood education and computer education at Eastern Connecticut State University where she directs the Computer Discovery Project, investigating young children's learning styles, parent–child relationships, and integration of the microcomputer into the curriculum. A member of the NAEYC Children and Technology Panel, and Chair of the Technology and Young Children Caucus, Dr. Wright also represents the United States on the Early Childhood/Elementary Computer Education Working Group of the International Federation of Information Processing (IFIP). Her publications include *Logoworlds* and *Exploring a New Partnership: Children, Teachers and Technology*.

Daniel D. Shade is the director of the Technology in Early Childhood Habitats (TECH) program, a research and teacher training project at University of Delaware. His major professional contributions have been in the areas of developing a theoretical foundation for the use of computers with young children, and the application of developmentally appropriate practice to young children's software evaluation with his colleague Susan Haugland. Dr. Shade has published numerous articles on topics related to the use of computers with young children and served as editor of the *Journal of Computing in Childhood Education*. He is a member of the NAEYC Children and Technology Panel.

About the Contributors

Patricia Adkins Ainsa is a professor of early childhood education at the University of Texas at El Paso, with 15 years of experience in higher education and 5 years in elementary and special education. She has directed computer literacy grants and parent training projects and has presented workshops in the United States, Mexico, Peru, France, Belgium, England, and Scotland. Her computer-related publications comprise books, journal articles, and software packages, including *Computergarten, Rainbow Keyboarding,* and, the most recent, *Teacher Workshop-Technology*. Dr. Ainsa serves as an editor for *Computing in Early Childhood Education*.

Michael M. Behrmann is an associate professor of special education at the George Mason University Graduate School of Education in Fairfax, Virginia, where he is director of the Center for Human Disabilities and oversees graduate training in assistive and special education technology. Dr. Behrmann is also the director of the Assistive Technology Resource Consortium. He heads federally supported research projects and state-funded technical assistance projects for people with severe disabilities and for service providers in early childhood special education. Dr. Behrmann's research focuses on assistive technology, instructional applications of technology, and using technology and multimedia in teaching. In addition to writing several books and articles, he edited the *Handbook of Microcomputers in Special Education* and *Integrating Computers into the Curriculum: A Handbook for Special Educators*.

Elizabeth R. Beyer is a program associate/technology consultant at the Erikson Institute for Advanced Study in Child Development. At three inner-city public schools in Chicago, she manages educational technology teams composed of teachers, computer coordinators, school administrators, and parents. Prior to working at Erikson, Ms. Beyer was a senior consultant at a Chicago-based firm, where she focused on the design, development, and implementation of corporate training. She founded The Technology Alliance, a volunteer organization for business executives seeking to help public school teachers incorporate new computer technologies into their classrooms.

Bonnie Blagojević is a preschool teacher and director of The Sharing Place in Orono, Maine. She is a freelance writer and co–list owner of Early Childhood Education on Line, an Internet discussion group.

Mario R. Borunda is dean of the graduate school at Wheelock College in Boston, Massachusetts. After teaching elementary-grade children in Honolulu and Los Angeles, he co-founded the Center for Urban and Minority Education and did extensive research in higher education. He is particularly interested in issues of race and racism in communities of color and in promoting the interests of people of color in institutions of higher education.

Barbara T. Bowman, who joined with two other faculty members in 1966 to found the Erikson Institute for Advanced Study in Child Development, currently serves as its president and teaches courses in early education and administration. She has directed training projects for Head Start teachers, caregivers of infants at risk for morbidity or mortality, and teachers of mathematics and computer education. Ms. Bowman is a past president of NAEYC and is currently on the NAEYC Technology and Young Children panel. She has served on numerous national and state commissions, including the National Research Council, the National Academy of Sciences, and the Early Childhood Education Task Force of the National Association of State Boards of Education.

Sue Bredekamp is the director of professional development at the National Association for the Education of Young Children, where her major contributions include developing and directing a national, voluntary accreditation system for early childhood teacher education, and researching and writing NAEYC's position statements on early childhood teacher education, developmentally appropriate practice, and appropriate curriculum and assessment. Her professional experience includes teaching and directing early childhood programs, serving on the faculty of a four-year college, and working in the Head Start Bureau at the Administration for Children, Youth and Families. She represents NAEYC on the Technology and Young Children panel.

Cynthia Char is a senior associate at Education Development Center (EDC), a nonprofit research and curriculum development corporation, where she has worked on several projects involving multimedia and young children's use of interactive technologies. She has also been directing a variety of research and materials design efforts at EDC involving curriculum, computer software, and multimedia. Dr. Char's prior professional experience includes conducting media-related research at the Bank Street Center for Children and Technology and at Harvard University's Project Zero. She is a member of the NAEYC Technology and Young Children panel.

Douglas H. Clements is a professor of early childhood, mathematics, and computer education at the State University of New York at Buffalo. Previously a kindergarten teacher, he has conducted research and published widely on the learning and teaching of geometry, computer applications in mathematics education, the early development of mathematical ideas, and the effects of social interactions on learning. Through a National Science Foundation (NSF) grant, he has co-developed "Logo Geometry," an elementary geometry curriculum software based on the Logo computer program, and is currently working with colleagues on two new NSF projects. He is a member of the NAEYC Technology and Young Children panel.

Jane Ilene Davidson is a master teacher at the University of Delaware Laboratory Preschool and a lecturer in the Department of Individual and Family Studies. Her writings include *Computers and Children Together in the Early Childhood Classroom,* and *Emergent Literacy and Dramatic Play: Natural Partners.*

George E. Forman is a professor in the School of Education at the University of Massachusetts at Amherst. His books, *The Child's Construction of Knowledge* (with David Kuschner) and *Constructive Play* (with Fleet Hill), extend the theory of Jean Piaget to early childhood education. Dr. Forman has also written on early symbolic development (*Action and Thought*) and the educational value of computers (*Constructivism in the Computer Age,* co-edited with Peter Pufall). A former president of the Jean Piaget Society, Dr. Forman has also been a research psychologist at Harvard University's *Project Zero.*

Susan Haugland is a professor of child development at Southeast Missouri State University in Cape Girardeau, Missouri. In 1985 she co-founded (with Daniel Shade) KIDS (Kids Interacting with Developmental Software). Initially, KIDS focused on establishing a theoretical framework for computer integration and a systematic method for software evaluation that was congruent with developmentally appropriate practices. Since 1988 the KIDS project has been conducting in-depth research on the effects of microcomputers on young children's development. Dr. Haugland continues to direct the KIDS project, which evaluates software with Daniel Shade's TECH project at the University of Delaware. She is also the director of the Center for Child Studies, an NAEYC-accredited early childhood laboratory serving 150 children, ages 6 weeks to 6 years. She has published two books and numerous professional articles on a variety of early childhood issues.

Charles Hohmann, an educational psychologist, has directed curriculum development at the High/Scope Educational Research Foundation since 1972. During this time he has been heavily involved in training preschool and elementary school teachers in a variety of national and international projects. Dr. Hohmann has developed mathematics and science learning activities for programs serving preschoolers, school-age children, and adolescents. In addition, he conducts workshops for educators throughout the United States on various topics, including computer learning for young children. He is the author of *Young Children & Computers* and serves on the NAEYC Technology and Young Children panel.

Elizabeth A. Lahm is coordinator for the Early Childhood Special Education Technology Project at the Center for Human disabilities at George Mason University in Fairfax, Virginia. She also serves as vice president of the technology and media division of the Council for Exceptional Children and chair of the special education interest group of RESNA, an interdisciplinary association for the advancement of rehabilitative and assistive technologies. Her primary professional interests are technology in early childhood special education and software features and design.

Ceasar L. McDowell, a 1991 W.K. Kellogg National Leadership Fellow, is assistant professor of education at Harvard University, where he teaches courses in educational technology and in the nature of community. His research and teaching interests include the use of mass media in promoting democracy, educating urban students, organizing urban communities, civil rights history, peacemaking and conflict resolution, and testing and test policy. As president of the Civil Rights Project, Inc. (CRPI), the nonprofit educational partner of Blackside, Inc. (producers of such television documentaries as "Eyes on the Prize," "Malcolm X," and "The Great Depression"), he is involved in its launching of a nationwide public dialogue initiative on issues around poverty, using community settings and electronic/communications media to facilitate the discussion.

Gwendolyn G. Morgan is a child care quality consultant for Work/Family Directions Development Corporation, the development arm of Work/Family Directions, a management and consulting firm addressing work and family issues with large corporations. She is also on the faculty at Wheelock College in Boston, Massachusetts, where she heads the new Center for Career Development on Early Care and Education and directs a series of one-week seminars for child care directors, family child care leaders, licensors, resource-and-referral staff, and other policymakers. She has been a consultant or staff member to a number of child care policy research studies, including Project Connections (in 1981 and 1982), the first national study of child care resource-and-referral. She is a member of the NAEYC Technology and Young Children panel.

Daniel Murphy is the director of the Prevention Services Network in Kenosha, Wisconsin. His professional experience with at-risk families and youth includes 12 years at Head Start. He is currently finishing a second graduate program in adult and continuing education, in which he is focusing on the family's role in the moral development of children.

Teresa J. Rosegrant is associate professor of early childhood education at George Mason University in Fairfax, Virginia. For a number of years she was a public school kindergarten teacher in Arlington County, Virginia. She has served as a member of the National School Readiness Task Force, Educational Goals in the Year 2000, and the board of the National Academy of Early Childhood Programs. She has been a consulting editor for NAEYC and a member of the Technology and Young Children panel. She coedited, with Sue Bredekamp, *Reaching Potentials: Appropriate Curriculum and Assessment for Young Children, Volume 1.* In addition, she is coauthor of two software programs, *Talking Text Writer* and *Listen to Learn.*

Suzanne Thouvenelle is director of research and development at MOBIUS Corporation in Alexandria, Virginia. She has been actively involved in research related to the use of technology with young children in classroom and child care settings. Among her primary interests are equity of access to technology and support for children in the U.S. whose native language is not English. Additionally, Dr. Thouvenelle is involved in research on technology applications that support authentic assessment of children's learning. She is a member of the NAEYC Technology and Young Children panel.

Preface

The past decade has been a time of increased focus on the role of early childhood education in our society. With a sense of urgency and commitment, early childhood educators have struggled to specify what constitutes high-quality care and education. We have seriously considered the importance of learning styles and teaching strategies. We have sought valid, "authentic" means of assessing growth and development, in order to prevent the use of curricula based on inadequate evaluation and academic principles.

In the midst of such concern over defining meaningful education for young children, a newcomer—the microcomputer—has appeared in the early childhood environment and raised further issues for early childhood educators. The appropriateness of the computer in early childhood environments was not universally accepted in the 1980s and still is not in the 1990s. Knowing that young children construct knowledge through manipulating objects and moving in space, early childhood educators were very skeptical of the value of computers for young children. Often-asked questions included, "What will happen to children's development if symbolic representation takes place on a two-dimensional medium—the computer screen?" Other questions focused on how social relationships would be affected and whether emotional expression would be encouraged.

Beginning in the mid-1980s, clusters of early childhood researchers and teachers gathered to study the computer's impact and contributions to early education and to discuss with software developers what they had observed when young children used computers and how these experiences might lead to meaningful interaction between children and microcomputers. Early software for young children seemed to be little more than electronic ditto pages. Furthermore, early reports of the kinds of software being introduced into the schools revealed that children from advantaged home backgrounds were being offered software that would promote higher–order thinking skills, while children from lower-income families were being "remediated" with drill-and-practice software. Many people noted the potential for learning through play presented by open-ended software and argued its appropriateness for all children.

A number of educators and parents noticed the above disparity and realized that if children *did* benefit from early opportunities to use microcomputers, then another kind of illiteracy was occurring: the illiteracy of children who had no opportunity to explore this new tool or who had the opportunity but were exposed to inappropriate software. By 1990 there was a keen awareness of the growing lack of equity in computer access and use, and of early childhood professionals' confusion about whether and how to use the new technology in the experiences that they offered young children.

Wheelock College's Center for Career Development in Early Care and Education, working with Work/Family Directions, sponsored an invitational symposium to stimulate critical thinking on the use of computers with young children and to build connections among practitioners, researchers, software designers, and early childhood experts. The steering committee that planned the symposium was led by Gwen Morgan and included Cynthia Char, June Wright, Andrea Genzer, and Patricia Day.

The symposium, which was supported by the IBM Funds for Dependent Care Initiative, met on August 1 & 2, 1991. It was named *In Search of Future Microworlds*, a phrase intended to convey the potential for developing "microworlds" (Papert 1980) in which children would be empowered to build their own intellectual structures, a concept dynamically portrayed in *Mindstorms: Children, Computers, and Powerful Ideas* (Papert 1980). The goal was to share information, examine it from different perspectives, and identify action that would enhance the appropriate use of computers with young children. Much of the material in this volume was stimulated by the interaction of the participants during the symposium. Believing that the ideas and reflections that were shared at the symposium should be available to others, the participants offered to put their thoughts into writing, and this plan was encouraged by the NAEYC Governing Board.

As a result of that decision, what follows is a discussion of how children interact with the computer, what criteria should be used to provide high-quality experiences, the need for professional development opportunities, the roles the microcomputer can play in the early childhood years, and how early childhood professionals can influence technological developments in our society.

The dialogue continues among people who are concerned about the role of the microcomputer in education. The NAEYC Technology Panel and the Technology and Young Children Caucus (TYCC) meet annually to continue discussing the issues raised in this book. Interested individuals are encouraged to join the caucus (by contacting either of the editors). We take seriously the recent warning about the manner in which the microcomputer, the "children's machine," will offer powerful learning environments:

Will such alternatives be created democratically? Will public education lead the way or, as in most things, will the change first enhance the lives of the children of the wealthy and powerful and only slowly and with much effort find its way into the lives of the children of the rest of us? (Papert 1992, p. 6)

Our technological age is an exciting time, one that invites all of us to be lifelong learners! Please join us in our quest for future microworlds!

—*June L. Wright and Daniel D. Shade, Editors*

Young Children as Active Learners

June L. Wright

Listen to the Children: Observing Young Children's Discoveries with the Microcomputer

There are two aspects to providing occasions for wonderful ideas. One is to be willing to accept children's ideas. The other is providing a setting that suggests wonderful ideas to children—different ideas to different children—as they are caught up in intellectual problems that are real to them.

—Eleanor Duckworth in *The Having of Wonderful Ideas,* 1987

Listen to the children and you, too, will have wonderful ideas. You will hear insights that go beyond what you expected. You will observe actions that cause you to rethink what young children can do and understand. You will wonder what else young children can think and do that you never noticed before.

The rare opportunity that experimenting with microcomputers has given us is a chance to focus on children as they explore a new medium. Because the medium is new and different, we are cautious, concerned, even skeptical. Therefore we observe more carefully, and from that observation emerge special insights that add to our understanding of how the young child reasons and what the young child seeks to invent. As we listen and question, we discover more often than not that *we* are the learners.

Among early childhood educators, a network of keen observers have emerged who have looked beyond the immediate fascination the computer holds for children and beyond the potential for teaching specific skills and concepts to intuit and analyze why children are fascinated and what processes are involved in the learning that occurs. Weir and colleagues (1982) call the microcomputer "a window into a child's thinking process" as they describe the powerful role of the microcomputer in our ongoing effort to understand how children learn. In her study of children's learning styles, Solomon (1986) notes that styles are more readily recognized at the computer because the flexibility of the computer and the different paths it offers allow learning processes to go further and become more explicit. The ability to identify children's learning styles is dependent upon creating an open-ended environment in which children

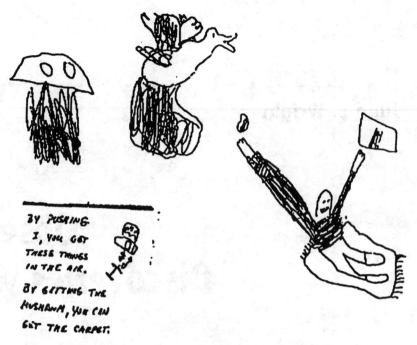

BY PUSHING
I, YOU GET
THESE THINGS
IN THE AIR.

BY GETTING THE
HUSBAND, YOU CAN
GET THE CARPET.

- BY PUSHING
8, YOU CAN
FIND THE
NUMBERS.
- BY PUSHING
0, YOU CAN
CLIMB THE
BEANSTALK.

Figure 1. *Some children have a clear idea about what they would like computer programs to do. Five-year-old Timmy articulated his ideas in this sketch.*

can explore what this new plaything has to offer and choose which paths they prefer to take.

Damian (age 4½) was delighted when two visitors stopped at the computer corner to see what he was doing. He began systematically choosing each of the programs, demonstrating how it worked, and moving on to the next program. As the visitors watched the programs, they asked him to use one to create an animal or build something. "Oh," Damian said in a disappointed tone, "I know how to do that, but I'm the only one in the class who knows how to run all the programs. Don't you want me to teach you?"

(Metro Delta Head Start, Baltimore, MD)

Part I—Young Children as Active Learners

Timmy (age 5) participated in a research study using a new piece of software. He and his dad were asked to find the animals hidden in the park and write a story about them. Then they were asked to tell the researcher what they liked about the software. Dad said, "The digitized animals that moved and looked real!" When asked how they would like to change the program, Timmy replied, "I'd like some more animals—new ones I wouldn't recognize."

The next day, Timmy arrived at school with a diagram in hand. He found the researcher and explained that he had a new idea for another program he'd like her to put on the computer (see figure 1). He sure hoped she could do it because kids would like to play with it!

(Center for Young Children, College Park, MD)

The challenge that Damian defined for himself was to master the functioning of all 11 programs in the package and become the class tutor. Timmy's self-defined challenge was to come up with new ideas for what programs he'd like to use on the computer. Software designers often comment that the computer interface should be "transparent" so that it will not interfere with the child's interaction with the program; however, these children chose to focus on how to design a program and an interface. These pioneers had paths of their own that they wanted to explore. As Duckworth suggests, they defined "intellectual problems that are real to them." Are we willing to acknowledge and respond to their taking the initiative?

Young children in charge of the action

Much has been written about the strengths and shortcomings of using technology with young children. The purpose of this chapter is to let the children speak for themselves. The following interview was done by Mary, a teacher, with a 4-year-old girl at the end of a year with computers in the classroom. It captures the child's sense of mastery and self-assurance.

Mary: I have a friend who has never used computers. What do you think I should tell her?

Lydia: That they're fun—you can play games and make pictures and choose what you want.

Mary: How does the computer know what to do?

Lydia: I push the buttons and I tell it what to do. It talks to me, and so I tell it what to do.

Mary: Is it hard or easy to use the computer?

Lydia: It's very, very easy; I know what to do.

Mary: Do you like to use the computer alone or with a friend?

Lydia: With a friend so I can talk to her.

Mary: Is there anything else I should tell my friend about computers?

Lydia: That they sing, too, and I sing with them, and I can write a story if I want to.

(Windham-Willimantic Child Care Center, Willimantic, CT)

Lydia's comments reflect the philosophy, teaching strategies, and qualities of software that were chosen by her teacher, Mary, to foster a sense of autonomy, competence, and enjoyment (see chapter 6 for further discussion of creating the classroom environment).

While adults struggle to keep pace with the technology, its new hardware and new operating systems, children see computer technology as a normal part of their environment. Ten years ago children would look at the computer screen and wait for it to do something (a passive mode similar to that experienced when watching television). Today they announce, "My Mom (or Dad) has one of those" or "My sister (or brother) plays games on that." Unaware that they should be intimidated, young children assume that they control the machine unless they are told otherwise.

Teachers as mediators

Current interfaces empower parents and teachers to arrange welcoming screens customized for the individual child and programmed to speak to the child using familiar voices.

Amy, age 4, greeted her mother with the question, "Mom, does your computer at work say 'Hi, Gail'? It doesn't? Well my computer says 'Hi, Amy, want to play?' You should get yours fixed!"

Two years later, when her younger brother, Cheo, entered the same class, Amy quizzed her mother at home, "Does the computer say 'Hi, Cheo' now?" When told that it did, she observed, "I knew Gwen (her teacher) would know how to fix it!"

(Center for Young Children, College Park, MD)

Although software is increasingly easy to use, it is much harder to convince teachers of that fact than it is to involve the children.

An instructor of a college language and literacy course was introducing her graduate students to the potential for recording voice with graphics to create a narrated slide show. She invited one of them to come and record part of the story. Because there were no volunteers, she modeled recording with the mike and tried again . . . still no volunteers. She then called up a different set of pictures and ran the narrated slide show. "Who do you think told this story?" she asked. "It sounded like a child," commented one teacher. "Right, it was a 6-year-old," replied the instructor.

(Eastern Connecticut State University)

It is interesting to note that a similar situation in an undergraduate course had a very different response. Two of the students volunteered to participate and created a dialogue to accompany the pictures. The current college generation is much more at ease with the microcomputer. They are more like Amy in their perception of the machine: they view it as just another part of their world, and they assume that they can be in control of it.

Although Wendy is a newcomer to the use of computers with young children, she is teaching the children in her family child care home that they are "good computer operators." Wendy is interested in having the children in her care be aware of their own environment and the world beyond.

Tyron: I'm going to the world to see the people.

Wendy: What city do you live in, Tyron?

Tyron: Mt. Vernon.

Wendy: What do you need to put in the city of Mt. Vernon?

Tyron: The police car . . . and the bus . . . and the ambulance for taking people to the doctor.

(Tyron selected the vehicles from the menu bar and placed them in his city.)

Wendy: I like this city of Mt. Vernon we live in, and I like it to look just like you're makin' it.

(Tyron then chose some people from the menu bar, each of whom said "Hello" in a different language as he placed them on the screen.)

Tyron: Hola! (repeating what the computer voice said)

Wendy: What language is that, Tyron?

Tyron: Spanish. . . . (again repeating what the computer said) Jambo.

Wendy: Jambo . . . What language is that?

Tyron: Hmm . . . Africa.

Wendy: That's an African language; it's called Swahili.

Tyron: Hello . . . that's North America.

Wendy: North America—good for you . . . that's called English. . . .
"Melente?" Miss Wendy doesn't know that language—we're gonna
have to find out. Miss Wendy has a job to do.

(Rise-N-Shine Family Child Care Home, Mt. Vernon, NY)

This exchange demonstrates a family child care provider's commitment to providing children in her care with a comfortable
way to represent their surroundings (the city)—through which
they make frequent walking field trips—and her interest in encouraging the children to feel at ease with the characters in the
computer scene who speak many languages. For this caregiver,
computer programs that represent many cultures and languages
help prepare her children to play together in unity, or *umoja* (in
Swahili). She believes that the computer may be one way to
open the world to her children, a goal that reflects the thoughts
of John Dewey, who reasoned that a "long-term goal of American
education is not only to help children develop personal integrity
and fulfillment but also to enable them to think, reason, and
make decisions necessary to participate fully as citizens of a
democracy" (Bredekamp & Rosegrant 1992, p. 17).

**Especially for children who do not have computers at home, developmentally
appropriate computer experiences in the family child care setting are beneficial.**

A *multiple intelligences perspective*

The theory of multiple intelligences identifies a number of
separate human capacities, ranging from musical and linguistic intelligences to interpersonal and intrapersonal intelligences (Gardner 1993). This theory suggests that if we look
directly at the functioning of all intelligences, we will have a
multifaceted view of children, avoiding the limitations of our
customary lenses that focus primarily on linguistic and logical-
mathematical understanding. Such a view could lead to more

Table 1. *The Seven Intelligences*

Intelligence	End-States	Core Components
Logical-mathematical	Scientist Mathematician	Sensitivity to, and capacity to discern, logical or numerical patterns; ability to handle long chains of reasoning
Linguistic	Poet Journalist	Sensitivity to the sounds, rhythms, and meanings of words; sensitivity to the different functions of language
Musical	Composer Violinist	Abilities to produce and appreciate rhythm, pitch, and timbre; appreciation of the forms of musical expressiveness
Spatial	Navigator Sculptor	Capacities to perceive the visual-spatial world accurately and to perform transformations on one's initial perceptions
Bodily-kinesthetic	Dancer Athlete	Abilities to control one's body movements and to handle objects skillfully
Interpersonal	Therapist Salesman	Capacities to discern and respond appropriately to the moods, temperaments, motivations, and desires of other people
Intrapersonal	Person with detailed, accurate self-knowledge	Access to one's own feelings and the ability to discriminate among them and draw upon them to guide behavior; knowledge of one's own strengths, weaknesses, desires, and intelligences

intelligence-fair assessment in our schools and further realization of the cultural influences that are present in children's learning styles. (The seven intelligences identified by Gardner are described in table 1.)

It has been my experience that insights into children's interactions with the microcomputer can be sharpened by the application of this *multiple intelligences perspective* (Gardner & Hatch 1989). We will use this paradigm as a framework to focus our thinking about children's use of the microcomputer and to help us recognize the power of multimodal symbolic representations. In their discussion of young children as "masters of change," Tsantis and Keefe point out that "advances in multimedia computer technology are vastly expanding the range of functions to combine pictures, voice, music, animation, full-motion video and massive data storage in highly engaging interactive applications which provide multisensory appeal" (1992, p. 277). One of the exciting potentials of the microcomputer, and possibly one of the reasons for its widespread appeal, is its ability to provide various kinds of experiences that are often overlooked but that could offer children with diverse intelligences an opportunity to learn and express themselves in different ways.

Young children as artists and storytellers

One of the recurrent scenarios that emerge as children create computer images is a new sense of control resulting from using such attributes as the "fill" feature in paint programs. The ability to change the background color with one click leads to dramatic play centered on time passing—children delight in changing their screens, trying to maintain the same atmosphere on two separate screens, and reflecting day and then night in the stories they tell.

Bobby (age 4): I made it day; when you turn on the light, it's morning.

John (age 4): But let's make it night. The builders are making a building at night. You see, they got flashlights!

Children also discover the ability to overlay colors and often portray their feelings in a more serious way.

Mitch (age 5) drew his house, with windows and a door. He drew a path for himself and his brother. Then he covered it all up with red. As he drew he told the story of how his father was building them a new house, how it caught on fire, and how he put a path there so he and his brother could get out if it happened to the next house his dad built. (a true story)

Clara (age 3) drew what she called her house. She always covered it with red. After several days, her teacher asked her mother if she knew why all of Clara's houses were covered with red. Her mom decided to talk to Clara about it and learned that Clara had been watching all the fires in the TV news report. Clara was afraid that her house would burn down.

(Center for Young Children, College Park, MD)

What the children are doing on the computer parallels Dyson's (1990) reports of children in their play becoming fluent and inventive users of a variety of symbols—gestures, pictures, and spoken and written words—to represent or symbolize their world. Their verbal, intrapersonal, interpersonal, and visual intelligences blend in unique ways to form their own unique modes of expression.

Skilled pretenders use even the most unlikely software to invent imaginative stories and to convey feelings.

Mary's parents are separated. When using the calculator on *KidDesk*, Mary typed a series of six numbers, saying, "That's my Dad's phone number." She then carried on an imaginary conversation with her Dad, telling him she was coming to visit today. When she was done she typed another series of numbers explaining, "This is Mom's number. 'Mom, I am going to eat dinner at Dad's house.'"

(Preschool class, University of Delaware Lab School, Newark, DE)

A word of caution

In spite of the powerful opportunities for symbolic representation, the computer as an artistic medium requires careful monitoring. It does indeed have rich capabilities for appreciating and creating art with hundreds of discrete colors (Tsantis & Keefe 1992). But, as Kay so accurately points out, it is often too easy in the media world to choose convenience over quality. "We replace high-resolution photographic representations of great art with lower resolution video disk images that distort both light and space" (cited in Skolnik & Smith 1993, p. 6). The result, he declares, is "recognition, not reverie." When convenience triumphs over quality, he continues, then we have "junk learning." The same can be said when exquisitely illustrated picture books are replaced with cartoon-based CD-ROM talking books, when poorly written literature is mass produced to create 30 interactive storybooks for a computer reading series, or when low-quality music programs are designed that offer children opportunities to compose with poor timbre and pitch. Saying that a program addresses a particular intelligence is not the same as saying that the program offers an opportunity to *enhance* that intelligence.

Young children as designers

A card-making program allowed Roland, a very shy child, to demonstrate to his teachers and the other children that he was an "expert" in identifying which pictures to choose to maximize the animation of the card being created. This visual-spatial child, often overshadowed by more verbal children, became the class guru as he helped other children choose "the best stickers" to make their cards "really move!"

Sam became the class expert in being able to eliminate any object from the story screen, using either the mouse or the arrow keys. His friend Chris, an advanced storyteller to whom inventive spelling came naturally, was delighted to learn this technique from Sam because he couldn't find space for his words. Sam, who could not spell his name, followed Chris's lead in adding his name and the title of his picture with random letters carefully placed, such as a title and an author signature. The boys had different strengths that drew them together to solve each other's problems.

In their search for ways to enhance Sam's linguistic and logical-mathematical abilities, the teachers had not noticed his visual-spatial ability. Once it was observed in the computer context, it was noted in other activities, as well, and could be tapped as a resource to scaffold his learning.

Given programs that allow them to create images using geometric shapes, some children choose to create images of houses, trains, and flying caterpillars, while others create designs, varying the size, shape, and color attributes in symmetrical or repetitive patterns, demonstrating their awareness of spatial order (see figure 2).

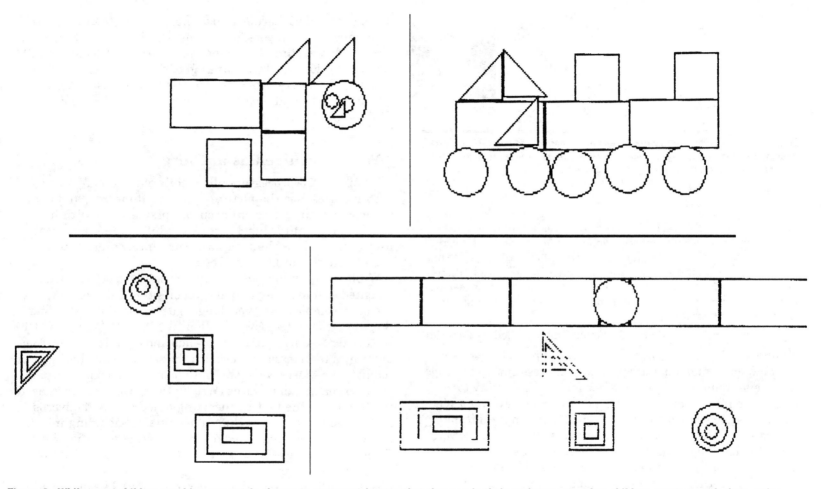

Figure 2. *While some children combine geometric shapes to represent images that they see in their environment, other children create new designs, using different shapes and varying their size and color.*

11

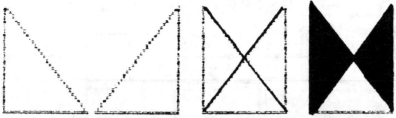

Figure 3. *In this computer drawing, the child demonstrated her spatial awareness by overlapping triangles and then filling them with color, acknowledging the newly created triangle by leaving it white.*

Tammy created an overlaid design by choosing a large white square within which she placed two overlapping triangles with opposite orientations. The placement created a third triangle that did not appear on the shape menu. Tammy filled the original triangles with color but left the newly formed triangle white (see figure 3). Knowing that this triangle did not exist, she invited her friend, Cheung, to create it.

(Center for Young Children, College Park, MD)

Tammy displayed a cognitive awareness of how she had created the new shape and a metacognitive awareness of the challenge her friend would face in solving her puzzle. The ability to overlay an infinite number of shapes, creating new shapes in the process, leads to spatial and logical mathematical thinking processes not easily observed outside this dynamic microworld. Expected learning sequences become reversed as children combine triangles to make squares on the screen and then move to the block corner to rearrange triangle blocks on the shelf labelled for square blocks. Likewise, children create scenes of cities and farms on the computer, print them out, and then move to the block corner to use their "maps" to build their landscapes. The universality of this practice was highlighted in a crosscultural summer seminar at Eastern Connecticut State University, during which this kind of mapping was reported by a family child care provider from Mt. Vernon, New York (Nashid 1994), and a child care director from Helsinki, Finland (Huhtinen 1994).

Young children as authors

Talking word processors allow children to create stories with pictures, see the pictures turned into words, and hear the words read. Young children can play around with listening to the computer label pictures, while more sophisticated users can see how their pictures turn into words, and they can use these words to create stories.

While many children enjoy typing their own stories using invented spelling, research also reports that children's stories are more complex and their language is more elaborate when they dictate the tale (King & Rental 1981). An analysis of 100 stories dictated by 4- and 5-year-olds and recorded on the computer by a teacher's aide revealed that children at this age were competent revisers when shown that they could use the computer to change their words (Wright 1989). Children increased the fluency of the text by inserting adjectives and adverbs and added substance to their story line by including initiating events, expanded climaxes, and character motivation. Some children developed a new understanding of what it means to be an author.

Elisa was delighted when the teacher printed out the story she had dictated. "Wow, the computer knows my words . . . and the printer knows my words. Can it do another copy?" When told it could, Elisa decided to write a few more chapters. Then she asked, "Can you print me six copies? . . . If you could print me 100 copies, I could sell them for 5 cents each . . . . And if the cover could be hard, I could sell them for $1 each and I could be rich!"

(Center for Young Children, College Park, MD)

There is a special sense of self as published author when the story the child sees looks so professional. The children can illustrate these books and easily turn them into class library books by inserting the pages into an inexpensive photo album.

Young children as mechanics

Many children are fascinated by the relationship of the various parts of the computer. They relish a look inside the computer to see how the mouse sends messages to the computer and its monitor. Often the best questions are asked during minor repairs and adjustments.

Teacher: Tommy, you'll need to wait while I put in the new switch box for the printer.

Tommy (age 3): So you have to connect that cord to the computer—and then to the box? And now that computer works?

Teacher: It will when the box is connected to the printer.

Tommy: So what about this (the second) computer?

Teacher: I'll connect it to the box too . . . and then the box to the printer.

(Tommy watched each turn of the screwdriver. When the teacher finished, Tommy clapped his hands in delight.)

Tommy: So now both computers will print, right?

Teacher: You're exactly right, Tommy!

(Windham-Willimantic Child Care Center, Willimantic, CT)

This 3-year-old had followed very accurately the chain of events that connected two computers and a printer to a switch box and understood the functioning of the switch box. His teachers were amazed because they knew Tommy as a very active child who seldom focused on any activity for more than three to four minutes. "He understood that?" asked one teacher in amazement. But here was something that interested Tommy. They realized that they had just observed one of those special moments that could help them identify kinds of cause-and-effect relationships that would pique Tommy's curiosity. Tommy would probably do very well with the machine assembly activity, one of the assessments used in the Project Spectrum classroom, where the multiple intelligences theory is explored (Gardner & Krechevsky 1993).

Young children as logical thinkers

Papert (1980), discussing the challenge of forming all possible color combinations of assorted beads, suggests that this task is not systematically and accurately achieved until fifth or sixth grade because our culture has traditionally lacked models that allow the child to explore such complex systematic procedures. Yet 4-year-olds have been seen systematically combining the primary paint colors in a computer simulation program to build the three secondary colors so that they could create a picture with all six colors. If questioned, some children explain that they are putting the colors together in different ways. Others explain that you have to remember which colors you've made so you can be sure to mix the ones that are missing. The children are organizing their thinking from two very different perspectives, each one effective.

However, sometimes the child is very logical but in a fashion that the programmer was not expecting.

Jack enjoyed playing with the *Stickybear Town Builder* because he could drive all over the computer town and tell stories as he went. But he found that he kept running out of gas, and the game ended. So he reasoned that if he built his own town (using an advanced level of the program), he could put lots of gas stations in it and then remember to fill up his tank. Unfortunately, when he built the town and visited the new gas stations, there was no additional gas provided. That was not part of the program design, so Jack still had the same imposed time limitation.

(Reported by C. Johnson, a parent)

If we spend much time observing children, we soon recognize that the inventive young child can always think of at least one more thing that the program should do! Perhaps that is why children are such a valuable part of software evaluation teams.

Building microworlds together

While working with young children in a *Logo* microworld, Solomon (1986) observed that some children were micro-explorers, cautiously checking out each command; others were macro-explorers, putting in a random number of commands and gleefully watching the effects; and some were planners, purposefully executing a series of commands intended to bring about a specific reaction. Solomon warned that teachers could not gain this insight into children's learning styles by giving them brief exposure to a variety of programs.

At times we are tempted to "make it easy" for the children by supplying simplified microworlds. For example, it is possible to move around in a *Logoworlds* environment, directing the turtle on the screen by using the mouse. The mouse can be changed to other shapes and "stamp" images on the screen. If our purpose is to encourage the creation of designs or a picture story, this application is appropriate. However, guiding a turtle with the mouse will not help children gain increased understanding of directional turns and angles or estimation of distance. (See Clements, chapter 3, for further discussion of the potential for mathematical-logical reasoning using the Logo language.)

Papert (1980) pointed out that there is a world of difference between what computers can do and what society might choose to do with them. His own beliefs had been guided by his mentor, Jean Piaget ([1948] 1973), who believed that the long-range goal of education was autonomy. In Papert's vision, "*the child programs the computer* and in so doing, both acquires a sense of mastery over a piece of the most modern and powerful technology and establishes an intimate contact with some of the deepest ideas from science, from mathematics, and from the art of intellectual model building" (p. 5). Papert and the language he and his colleagues created (Logo) set a tone for many early investigators of the use of the microcomputer with young children (Heller, Martin, & Wright 1985; Lawler 1985; Church & Wright 1986; Solomon 1986; Clements 1987; Shade & Watson 1990). Microworlds were developed to enhance logical-mathematical and linguistic development. Robotic microworlds extend the environment to maximize the development of spatial awareness and musical representation.

In a kindergarten class that was using the Tasman Turtle (one of the earliest robots), the teacher wrote a procedure for the turtle which alternated its two horn sounds in response to a press of the "S" key. Daniel (age 5) interpreted this sequence as the turtle's speech. He reasoned that there should be more patterns of "turtle talk" and requested procedures to yield specified patterns of sound, which he defined as having various meanings. Manipulating the two sounds available, he invented a turtle vocabulary. Daniel had conceptualized the powerful potential for symbolic representation inherent in writing procedures.

(Center for Young Children, College Park, MD)

Andy and Linda were introduced to two Roamer robots at their child care setting. They were told the forward and back commands. Next, Janice, the teacher, showed them how to measure by a predefined unit how far one step forward would be. The children spent some time figuring out how many forward steps it would take the Roamer (which they decided was a farm tractor) to go from one animal pen to the next. Soon they decided to draw a road between the pens so the Roamer could move the animals. Janice had planned to teach right and left turns on the second day. "But," reasoned Andy and Linda, "our path has curves. We need to turn the Roamer like we turn our cars. How do we do that?"

(Windham-Willimantic Child Care Center, Willimantic, CT)

Young children will work very hard to solve problems that they invent. If wheel toys turn, surely the Roamer must also turn, they reason. They master commands and create solutions much more rapidly than we would predict.

Children bring the strengths of their multiple intelligences to a collaborative learning situation. One child masters the Roamer commands, another focuses on designing the roads, a third estimates the distance to be traveled. The fourth child realizes that there is no red paint for the barn. "Oh well, we have white and black; we can make grey and say it's an old barn." The child designing the road looks up and suggests, "We can write a story about 'The Old Barn.'" An onlooker adds, "I know an old barn that is down by the Connecticut River; let's make a river." Given content that intrigues them, children are able to embellish it in a way that gives it personal relevance. For these children the farm and the river are familiar places into which they can integrate their new Roamers to create a meaningful tale.

Conclusion

As facilitators of an exciting learning environment, we must consider the computer's potential for exploration and growth and select programs that will offer opportunities for children to use their multiple intelligences freely. Van Dyk (1994) observes that learning-style models provide exciting opportunities to

1. recognize diversity of needs and celebrate a diversity of gifts;

2. sensitize teachers to the reality of individual differences; and

3. encourage teachers to enlarge their repertoires of classroom teaching strategies.

By viewing interactions at the microcomputer from a multiple intelligences perspective, we have an opportunity to broaden our own perspectives on children's learning. Each child creates a unique set of images, and the observant teacher will look through this cognitive window and see the emergence of wonderful ideas.

Epilogue—Walking to the beat of a different drum

One day I watched Jordan (age 5) and his sister Jessie (age 3) as they played *Zurk's Safari*. Jessie asked her brother to "read the story, Jordan" and Jordan agreed, choosing the storybook the Lion was holding in the opening picture that served as a menu. Maya, a lost lion cub, appeared and asked, "Will you help me find my way home?" The two children immediately responded to the little cub and set out to select one of the five other creatures in the Serengeti to lead Maya home. Jessie insisted, "Jordan, it's the giraffe, 'member?" Jordan agreed to

As Jordan (5) helps his sister Jessie (3), he proudly predicts that she will soon understand how the program works "'cause I'll teach her."

try the giraffe—but that didn't work. "No. Jessie, it's not the giraffe this time; it's some other animal."

After several choices, the bird led the lion cub to the next screen. Jordan turned and explained to me, "Jessie thinks it's always the giraffe who takes Maya home because that's who did it the first time we played. She doesn't know the computer was fixed to make the story different each time. But she'll learn about the other animals 'cause I'll teach her."

Children are fascinated as they listen to the authentic beats of the different African drums; they search for intriguing creatures (bush baby, and wombat, and yak) and watch them move against the delicate watercolor paintings of their natural habitats.

We have a chance to walk with the children to the beat of a different drum, to create and explore microworlds that represent many cultures and many thinking styles, to express our beliefs and our fantasies in new forms of visual literacy and send those thoughts and images around the world. Let's travel with Jordan and Jessie to lands where giraffes and jackals lead the way and share their secrets! The children can tell us what makes technology meaningful to them—if we are listening.

References

Bredekamp, S., & T. Rosegrant, eds. 1992. *Reaching potentials: Appropriate curriculum and assessment for young children, Volume 1.* Washington, DC: NAEYC.

Church, M.J., & J.L. Wright 1986. Creative thinking with the microcomputer. In *Young children and microcomputers*, eds. P.F. Campbell & G.G. Fein. Englewood Cliffs, NJ: Prentice Hall.

Clements, D.H. 1987. Longitudinal study on the effect of Logo programming on cognitive abilities and achievement. *Journal of Educational Computing Research* 3 (1): 77–98.

Dyson, A.H. 1990. Research in review. Symbol makers, symbol weavers: How children link play, pictures, and print. *Young Children* 45 (2): 50–57.

Duckworth, E. 1987. *"The having of wonderful ideas" & other essays on teaching and learning.* New York: Teachers College Press.

Gardner, H. 1993. *Multiple intelligences: The theory into practice.* New York: Basic.

Gardner, H., & T. Hatch. 1989. Multiple intelligences go to school: Educational implications of the theory of multiple intelligences. *Educational Researcher* 18 (8): 4–10.

Gardner, H., & M. Krechevsky. 1993. The emergence and nurturance of multiple intelligences in early childhood: The Project Spectrum approach. In *Multiple intelligences: The theory in practice*, ed. H. Gardner, 86–111. New York: Basic.

Heller, R.S., C.D. Martin, & J.L. Wright. 1985. *LOGOWORLDS.* Rockville, MD: Computer Science Press.

Huhtinen, R. 1994. Conversation with author, 7 July.

King, M., & V. Rental. 1981. *How children learn to write.* ERIC, ED 213050.

Lawler, R. 1985. *Computer experience and cognitive development: A child's learning in a computer culture.* New York: Wiley.

Nashid, W. 1994. Conversation with author, 7 July.

Papert, S. 1980. *Mindstorms: Children, computers and powerful ideas.* New York: Basic.

Piaget, J. [1948] 1973. *To understand is to invent.* New York: Viking.

Shade D.D., & J.A. Watson. 1990. Computers in early education: Issues put to rest, theoretical links to sound practice, and the potential contribution of microworlds. *Journal of Educational Computing Research* 6 (4): 375-92.

Skolnik, R., & C. Smith. 1993. Educational technology: Redefining the American classroom. In *FASE special report.* Los Angeles, CA: Foundation for Advancements in Science and Education.

Solomon, C. 1986. *Computer environments for children: A reflection on theories of learning and education.* Cambridge, MA: MIT Press.

Tsantis, L.A., & D.D. Keefe. 1992. Preschool children . . . Masters of change. In *Teaching thinking: An agenda for the twenty-first century,* eds. C. Collins & J.N. Mangieri. Hillsdale, NJ: Lawrence Erlbaum.

Van Dyk, J. 1994. Learning style models: Do we really need them? Presented at the Annual Meeting of the Association of Teacher Educators, February, Atlanta, GA.

Weir, S., S.J. Russell, & J.A. Valente. 1982. Logo: An approach to educating disabled children. *BYTE* 1 (8): 342–60.

Wright, J.L. 1989. The effect of microcomputers on narrative competence in young children. In *What research tells teachers about microcomputers and young children,* Chair S. Haugland. Symposium conducted at the Annual Conference of the National Association for the Education of Young Children, February, Atlanta, GA.

**Barbara T. Bowman
and Elizabeth R. Beyer**

Chapter 2

Thoughts on Technology and Early Childhood Education

Computer technology is not a single tool but rather a continuum of tools having in common a small microchip that permits humans to expand greatly their power over the environment and over ideas. Recent changes in the quality and quantity of available technology are causing a dramatic shift in how people organize their thoughts about the world, its resources, and their relationships with one another. Comparison with earlier paradigm shifts has resulted in labeling the last half of the 20th century as the beginning of a technological revolution, similar to the commercial and industrial revolutions that came before. Among the characteristics of this new revolution are

1. access to and reorganization of knowledge systems through inexpensive audiovisual and computer hardware and software, worldwide computer networks, and interactive technologies;

2. cheaper and more instantaneous communication devices (e.g., television, telephones, satellites);

3. new symbol systems (computer programming) and the need to use old ones in new ways (e.g., word processing, multimedia); and

4. new models for understanding the world (artificial intelligence and problem simulations).

Preparing children to live harmoniously in this new technological world is a challenge for teachers who are unsure of the nature and implications of the change. Several intertwining theoretical/philosophical propositions are useful guides to how we conceptualize the role of technology in the education of young children. The first perspective stresses developmental appropriateness. Grounded in the romantic tradition of Jean Jacques Rousseau and, more recently, in the developmental theories of Jean Piaget, it emphasizes early childhood education as a time for child-driven curricula, in which children interact with authentic objects that they can understand and control directly. This perspective highlights children recognizing and constructing relationships—and symbols for these relationships—through their own actions and stresses computer hardware and software that places children in control and permits them to confront problems understandable and of interest to them.

Another perspective stems from the proponents of multiple intelligences (Eisner 1985; Gardner 1985). Their position stresses the elasticity of the human mind and the danger of valuing only empirical thinking (the kind that supports science and mathematics). They warn against devaluing abilities and sensitivities that are based on relational and affective components of thought. People with this perspective believe that computer experience should tap children's potential for imaginative, creative, and emotive as well as logical and empirical thinking.

A third view concerns the social context in which technology is to be embedded. Technology is a social phenomenon—as are all human inventions, its meaning is drawn from and created by people. Computers are not independent of social discourse, but are simply one of its forms, and children understand its meaning within the context of the values and beliefs of their communities. How we structure access to technology, then, has implications for social structure as well as for individual knowledge. This means that we must pay close attention to the opportunities that different groups in our society have to use computers in various ways, and we must ensure that the access to technology does not exaggerate the already deep divisions in our society.

Active versus passive use of computers

With the penchant that young children show for the artifacts of their community, most young American children have quickly and easily learned to use the technology that has been incorporated into their daily lives. By age 4, many children are adept at using various forms of technology: they can dial the telephone, turn on the stereo, guide computerized toys, and play video games. Even more quickly than many adults, young children seem to accept the technologies and learn to use them. But are children really technologically competent? Is their ability to turn on a computer, load a program, and mechanically follow the program instructions sufficient, or is something more expected? What do young children understand about the underlying process that makes these activities possible?

One end of the computer-use continuum may be described as passive, the metaphor of "drone" or "robot" being appropriate. In this sense, computer knowledge is procedural, and people who know how to access this knowledge can use built-in applications. Examples of such applications are computer-

By age 4, many children are adept at using various forms of technology: they can dial the telephone, turn on the stereo, guide computerized toys, and play video games.

assisted instructional formats and data bases. Passive use requires little knowledge of the operation being performed by the computer or skill in selecting from among options.

At the opposite end of the continuum, computers are active agents, extending the users' abilities, enabling them to create new problems and to devise new solutions. When used actively, the tools help the user to accomplish personal goals and objectives, as when one uses a calculator to solve mathematical problems; engages in creative writing on a word processor; creates a computer program; or, in the case of young children, makes a picture by using a paint or drawing program. In these instances the user must, at minimum, have a vision and understand the potential of the tool and, at best, be able to engage the tool to both stimulate and reflect upon the mental task being performed.

Bangert-Drowns (1993), in describing educational software programs along this continuum, refers to one end as encompassing "tutorials" that give the learner precise information or directions on how to perform specific skills; problems and solutions have already been programmed in, and the user follows the program's lead. The other end comprises "tools" that help to amplify mental effort, assisting the user's thought process. Examples of using amplifying tools range from performing mathematical functions using a hand-held calculator, to programming software such as *Logo*, to creating multimedia presentations.

Passive computer use has had high priority in schools, particularly for children judged to be at risk for educational failure—poor and minority children. With educators driven by the wish to raise low scores on standardized tests, drill-and-practice programs have enjoyed considerable popularity and are predicated on the belief that children must master basic skills before moving on to higher-order thinking, in which computers provide "rich discovery environments" (Piller 1992). Such practices, however, deny children the benefit of using computers to extend and enrich their own thinking. As tools for mental amplification, computers may serve a variety of purposes—from saving time, to clarifying the user's thinking, to supporting analogs for the act of thinking. The real educational benefit for children lies in their using technology actively, creatively, to solve new problems (Bangert-Drowns 1993). In this chapter we will confine our attention to active use of technology.

Children often show facile use of tools (symbol systems) with little understanding of the concepts being represented. For instance, a 3-year-old may parrot the statement "Grandma went to Florida yesterday" with little understanding of time and space that such a statement is meant to reflect. As the child develops and continues to interact with objects and people, she becomes more capable of forming mental images when they are not present and constructs her own notions of time, space, and distance (such as "Florida is far, far away—that means we couldn't get there real quick"). Adults often have to observe children closely to understand what they mean by what they say. At the same time, using words helps young children construct increasingly complex understanding of the concepts that the words represent.

Similarly, adults must make sure that as children use computers they are making meaningful connections between the symbol system of computers and the ideas that the symbols represent. Learning "computerese" is a necessary but not sufficient activity. Children must understand the relationship between what is being represented and real ideas and objects. For instance, when a young child creates a picture using a computer, he must not only know how to make the computer respond but also grasp the relationship between the pictures created and real objects. The child must recognize that the picture is not precisely the same as the object itself but can be used to "stand for" that object. Equally important, we want the child, by manipulating the picture, to gain an increasingly complex understanding of the objects being represented. To accomplish these tasks, the child must be active. She must construct relationships for herself of the different levels and types of meanings, which is best done when children interact with responsive systems that give feedback and encourage further investigation—when they engage in active computer use.

Developmental considerations

The connection between concrete objects and symbols is aided as children represent their own thoughts in play, appreciate the graphic representations of objects and ideas of others, and learn to use language to stand for and clarify both objects and thought. As children begin to understand the process by which other people symbolize experience, they become able to shift from learning from their own direct experience to learning from representations conveyed by others. Thus, children establish meaning as they construct relationships between television pictures and real people, between pictorial representations on the computer and concrete objects, between the programmable toy car and the real car.

In addition to understanding the process of symbolizing objects and ideas, young children must also grasp the social system by which ideas are symbolized. This is evident as they switch from using their own idiosyncratic representations to using more of the representations of their communities. We see, therefore, that as children mature, their drawings look less like those of other young children and more like those used by their own culture (Kellogg 1970). Other people—adults and older children—mediate children's knowledge and understanding, socializing them to conventional representations and symbols. Responsive, reciprocal, social relationships and patterns of communication motivate and structure children's interactions with the objects in their environments. Even in the age of technology, it is through relationships with others—through joint activities, language, and shared feelings with other human beings—that children grasp meaning. This fact speaks to the importance of the human mediators of computer experience, who either confer on it the mantle of adventure, discovery, meaningfulness, and pleasure or that of drudgery and monotony.

Because so much of a young child's basic development is unaffected by technology, it is easy to assume that technology is an unimportant add-on rather than a force that shapes development itself. However, just as differences in cultural practices (Rogoff 1987) and language (Cazden 1991) lead to developmental differences, so, too, do the tools that people use. Literacy, for instance, has changed the way societies organize knowledge; the changes are evident when comparing literate societies to nonliterate societies. Griffin and Cole (1986) point out that the co-construction of knowledge that is possible through computer use in the international community may potentially change the framework of thought in different communities. With computers, young children can enter new realms of experience. Computer networks provide a communication tool for connecting children to all sectors of society: children can communicate with peers throughout the world (Riel 1987) and reach new teachers from worlds as diverse as the arts and sciences (Levin & Cohen 1985).

What should we teach preschool children about technology?

More to the point, how do we want to organize what we teach young children about technology so that we can achieve the social outcomes we desire? One agenda (Bowman 1990) for teaching young children about technology might include the following concepts and activities.

1. People control technology. A child would learn that technology is controlled by someone, and that someone could be the child; that technology is a tool for addressing personally relevant issues rather than a medium over which one has no control. Supportive activities would include playing with computer programs that the child can control, making videos and tape recordings with the child, and taking field trips to see how different people use technology.

2. Technology provides different kinds of things in a variety of ways. Technology can take different forms; calculators, telephones, and tape recorders accomplish different tasks and operate in different ways. Young children can learn to appreciate these differences. Many of these objects can be integrated into play areas and used in "work" areas of early childhood classrooms.

3. Technology has rules that control how it works. Although young children may not fully understand the rules that govern the various technologies, they can begin to understand that such rules exist. Objects must have a source of power—they have plugs or batteries; computers must have instructions—either built in or provided by the user.

4. Technology has languages. Interacting with computers involves learning a vocabulary ("load the disk," "attach the modem"), which young children can easily learn. Computer programs also have languages (*DOS* tells you it is listening with an "A" prompt, the Macintosh has icons, and *Logo* has a turtle) by which the user manipulates them.

5. Computer programs require different ways of organizing thinking. Some pre-programmed units (*Reader Rabbit*, for example) require children to employ a narrow set of skills (matching and rhyming strategies), while more open programs (paint programs or *KidWorks2*, for example) permit a broad range of possible strategies and outcomes.

School-related learning

Several examples may help to illustrate how computers can enhance or augment young children's school learning.

Clements (Clements, Nastasi, & Swaminathan 1993) described three 6-year-old children who worked with the *Logo* program to construct a hat for their snowman. Motivated by the goal of creating the best snowman, their discussion and actions revolved around the relative size of the drawings produced by inserting various numbers into the program. Thus, they focused their attention on a critical set of relationships: the computer had created a visual "reality" between the hat and the numbers that neither alone could show. The capability of the graphics program to place clearly in juxtaposition relationship concepts that are difficult to see together

Children not only interact with peers as they work at the computer; through computer networks they communicate with children in other communities and countries.

Thoughts on Technology and Early Childhood Education—B.T. Bowman & E.R. Beyer (such as number and size) presented children with a new opportunity for understanding. Their ability to control the relationship themselves, out of their own interest and understanding, linked this understanding of the new relationship with what they already knew, thus cementing their new knowledge in place. Such activities improved the children's estimating skills, as demonstrated by increasing scores on mathematics tests.

Similar changes have been reported in language usage as a consequence of computer activities. McNamee (1990) reported changes in children's understanding of written communication after joining a computer network with children from other states and countries. Because writing was the only tool these children had to communicate their ideas and report their findings, they began to think of their writing to each other as different from writing for a teacher. Children began to hone their writing skills because they had a real audience to consider as they collected news and contributed messages to the network.

Riel (1989) found similar benefits from the "Computer Chronicles," a student news wire service. Children from classrooms in California, Alaska, and Hawaii participated by producing "stories" to share with other children worldwide. The effect of writing to unseen correspondents was evident. Children who participated in the program made gains of three grade levels in language mechanics and two grade levels in language expression on the annual Comprehensive Test of Basic Skills.

Evaluating programs

As children develop their abilities to understand and make use of symbol systems, new opportunities occur for technology to affect their learning. Computer technology obviously offers the possibility of enrichment and extension of basic concepts beyond what may ordinarily be available in the classroom. But while it seems clear that computer technology *can* contribute positively to children's acquisition of school-related skills, the more relevant question is, Under what circumstances will it contribute?

Computers alone do not act to affect children's learning (Solomon & Gardner 1986); they act in concert with the competencies of the individual and with aspects of the social system in which they are embedded. For instance, they use other symbol systems (alphabetic literacy) within social contexts that include novices as well as those who are more expert in a domain, and they use "historically elaborated techniques, genres, and strategies" (Griffin & Cole 1986). The complexity of the interaction between the tool and its purpose and context makes simple claims of effectiveness suspect. Instead, technology's appropriateness must be judged by the task to be accomplished, with whom it is accomplished, in what institutional setting, and by which conventions and traditions.

Criteria for judging the appropriateness of software as a learning tool include the following:

1. Children can use the program without asking for help, regardless of their reading skills, when software uses graphical and spoken instructions rather than written ones.

2. Children control the software's pace and path.

3. Good software provides opportunities for children to explore a variety of concepts on several levels.

4. Children receive quick feedback, so they stay interested.

5. Good programs appeal to children's multisensory learning style by taking advantage of the capacities offered by today's computers.

6. To determine a product's appropriateness for a child's current level of development, parents have evaluated the skill list and activities as described on the packaging, viewed the product on a friend's or teacher's computer, or asked for a demonstration in a store.

7. To engage and sustain a child's interest, the software is enjoyable. It encourages children to laugh and to use their imagination to explore.

8. Children experience success and feel empowered by learning when they use the computer (Narodick 1992).

What's in the future

Scardamalia and Bereiter (1991) see computers as an integral part of the future learning process and describe three models for organizing learning experiences for children. In the first, the teacher focuses on the task, and learning is assumed to be the by-product. This is the traditional model of teaching, in which the teacher's role involves overseeing the quantity and quality of work done by the child. Classwork emphasizes activities rather than knowledge. Activities such as collecting seeds, growing plants, and experimenting with laboratory equipment are believed to result in learning. Little attention is given to assessing whether the desired cognitive process develops from these activities. Much educational software is of this type, for example, *Reader Rabbit* and *Number Munchers*.

The second model, referred to as the knowledge-based model, focuses on understanding. The teacher is responsible for setting cognitive goals, referring to children's prior knowledge, asking questions to stimulate discussion, and monitoring the comprehension process. The teacher may encourage the child's aware-

Good computer programs are enjoyable; children often laugh as they play.

ness of her own cognitive processes (Schulman 1986), but the teacher still maintains control over the learning process. Computer programs such as knowledge-based intelligence systems (Polson & Richardson 1988) are examples of this type of teaching.

In the third model, the teacher turns over control of the learning process to the child, who is encouraged to ask questions, determine his need for information, and monitor his comprehension. This model underlies the work of Scardamalia and colleagues (1984) in writing, Collins and colleagues' (1989) cognitive apprenticeship model, and Palinscar and Brown's (1984) reciprocal teaching model. Examples of this type of software and associated environments include *Logo*, the *Wizard* program, and *Computer Supported Intentional Learning Environments* (*CSILE*). This model reflects the work being done in artificial intelligence and cognitive research and embraces the idea that knowledge and skills are constructed by the learner. Furthermore, as Donaldson (1993) argued, children's own motivations and concerns are critical in shaping the learning process. Thus, the engagement of the learner with the subject of study is an essential characteristic of this type of teaching. Engaging learning experiences are framed when the learner is interested and can control the pace and type of information to be processed. There are no universal frameworks for understanding that all children use in the same way and at the same time. Rather, each child's unique experiences set the stage for her constructions and form the framework for how future information is processed (Schank 1982).

If we combine these two ideas—that a child's mental development, or "organically growing neural network," is shaped by the child's intentions and concerns and that the experiences that a child has affect the way knowledge is structured in his brain—we come to the conclusion that the best computer tool for a learning child is one by which his intentions or concerns control the way in which he experiences new information or knowledge.

Two examples of programs that seek to respond to the learner's interests and questions are the *Wizard* (McNamee 1991) and *CSILE* (Scardamalia et al. 1989). The *Wizard* program contains two sources of information: the first is obtained through access to a worldwide network of peers to whom the child asks questions and gives information, and the second is through the "Wizard" itself, of whom the child can ask questions and receive information of interest to her. The Wizard is actually a teacher, who stimulates new questions and interests and responds to questions the child has already framed.

CSILE (Scardamalia & Bereiter 1991) is another flexibly structured program. This program, designed to recognize that children can produce and respond to educationally productive questions and adapt them to their needs, provides an environment for children to control their knowledge-building process. Simply stated, *CSILE* is a networked system that gives children simultaneous access to a data base that is composed of text and graphical notes that the children produce. *CSILE* also provides children a means of searching for and commenting on one another's contributions. This program has been used extensively in grades 1 through 6.

One popular way of incorporating *CSILE* into the elementary classroom begins with introductory lessons on a topic of interest that may incorporate videotapes or browsing of reference material. After the initial introduction to the topic, the children are encouraged to produce a list of questions as goals of future study. These questions are entered into the communal data base, and the collaborative learning process begins. Children do research and enter the answers to their own and their peers' questions; they ask and answer additional questions; they add graphics to the data base as further explanations and examples of subject matter. Children have a choice of several different statuses for the information they enter: private notes are not accessible to other children; public anonymous notes and public named notes make up the bulk of the community data base. Together the children, motivated by their own intentions and concerns, support each other's knowledge-building process.

Open-ended programs such as these open new vistas for young children. Through the use of technology, traditional knowledge and skills can be presented in radically different ways, thus deepening and expanding children's learning process. New software applications—responding to differences in children's interests, their learning style, and their preferred modalities—offer alternative ways of organizing information, thus increasing the likelihood that children will learn the software and use it appropriately.

Because recent technological thinking has the appeal of innovation, it is important not to fall victim to a pendulum swing away from other forms of human thinking, such as relational, emotional, and certain forms of artistic thought. Although all of these styles of thinking are integral to nurture development in children, certain types of thinking are more consistent with technologies. Linear and sequential organization of ideas, expression of symbolic and abstract thought, and discrete categorical systems are among those most consistent with this new generation of educational technology. While linear organization of experiences provides rich opportunities to expand and create new knowledge and understanding, it is not the only way. Within the arts, for instance, there are many different ways of organizing and representing experiences that are no less valuable because the idea is expressed by personal sound, or graphics, or movement. It is important for children to learn to grasp the meaning of experience through their emotions, their sensory perceptions, and their bodies. Technological tools are one step removed from this personal experience.

Predictions of the educational needs of citizens of the 21st century stress the importance of flexible intelligence, rapid shifts in thinking as contexts differ, and lifelong ability to learn new ways of solving problems. This vision endorses teaching children to be active users of technology rather than mere reactors to it, a vision wherein technology does not simply entail putting the same old thing inside a box rather than on a piece of paper, a blackboard, or a slate but is a tool for their thinking.

Young children share their community's perceptions of the place of technological objects in the social world and the individual's relationship to them. There is probably nothing inevitable about the way technology is integrated into the social fabric of our society; it has potential for different formulations. Young children can learn either that technological skills are "socially desirable" and expected of them or, conversely, that such knowledge is exclusive and more available to some people than to others. In contemplating the social context of technology, teachers must be mindful that institutions tend to duplicate current power relationships among people. They must consider the effect, for example, of offering middle-class children opportunities to play with technology and to use it as a resource for their thinking while providing few such opportunities for children of low-income families. Similarly, technology can be used primarily as an individual and autonomous activity, or it can encourage cooperation through networking and collaborative activities. Children may learn to regard television as "the single truth" or as simply one perspective among many; children may regard computers as tools for individual use or as instruments in joint problem solving. The choice is ours to offer.

References

Bangert-Drowns, R. 1993. The word processor as an instructional tool: A meta-analysis of word processing in writing instruction. *Review of Research in Education* 63 (1): 69–93.

Bowman, B. 1990. Technology in early childhood education. In *Technology in today's schools*, ed. C. Warger, 129–41. Alexandria, VA: Association for Supervision and Curriculum Development.

Cazden, C. 1991. Contemporary issues and future directions: Active learners and active teachers. In *Handbook of research on teaching the English language arts*, eds. J. Flood, J. Jensen, & D. Lapp. New York: Macmillan.

Clements, D., B. Nastasi, & S. Swaminathan. 1993. Young children and computers: Crossroads and directions from research. *Young Children* 48 (2): 56–64.

Collins, A., J.S. Brown, & S.E. Newman. 1989. Cognitive apprenticeship: Teaching the crafts of reading, writing, and mathematics. In *Knowing, learning and instruction: Essays in honor of Robert Glaser,* ed. L. Resnick. Hillsdale, NJ: Lawrence Erlbaum.

Donaldson, M. 1993. *Human minds: An exploration.* New York: Penguin.

Eisner, E.W. 1985. *The educational imagination: On the design and evaluation of school programs.* New York: Macmillan.

Gardner, H. 1985. *Frames of mind.* New York: Basic.

Griffin, P., & M. Cole. 1986. *New technologies, basic skills, and the underside of education: What's to be done.* San Diego, CA: University of California Press.

Kellogg, R. 1970. *Analyzing children's art.* Palo Alto, CA.: Mayfield.

Levin, J.A., & M. Cohen. 1985. The world as an international science laboratory: Electronic networks for science instruction and problem solving. *Journal of Computers in Mathematics and Science Teaching* 4 (2): 33–35.

McNamee, G.D. 1990. Learning to write in an inner city setting: A longitudinal study of community change. In *Vygotsky and education,* ed. L. Moll. Cambridge: Cambridge University Press.

Narodick, S. 1992. Software as a learning tool. *Mac's Place*: 58.

Palinscar, A.S., & A.L. Brown. 1984. Reciprocal teaching of comprehension-fostering and comprehension-monitoring activities. *Cognition and Instruction* 1 (2): 117–75.

Piller, C. 1992. Separate realities: The creation of the technological underclass in America's public schools. MACWORLD (Special edition): 8–21.

Polson, M.C., & J.J. Richardson. 1988. *Intelligent tutoring systems.* Hillsdale, NJ: Lawrence Erlbaum.

Riel, M.M. 1987. The intercultural learning network. *The Computing Teacher Journal* 14 (7): 27–30.

Riel, M. 1989. Telecommunications: A tool for reconnecting kids with society. Paper presented at the International Symposium on Telecommunication in Education, Jerusalem, Israel, 21–24 August.

Rogoff, B. 1987. Specifying the development of a cognitive skill in its interactional cultural context. In Social processes in early number development, eds. G. Saxe, S. Guberman, & M. Gerhart. *Monograph of the Society for Research in Child Development* 52 (2).

Scardamalia, M., & C. Bereiter. 1991. Higher level of agency for children in knowledge building: A challenge for the design of new knowledge media. *Journal of the Learning Sciences* 1 (1): 37–68.

Scardamalia, M., C. Bereiter, & R. Steinbach. 1984. Teachability of reflective processes in written composition. *Cognitive Science* 8 (2): 173–90.

Scardamalia, M., C. Bereiter, R.S. McLean, J. Swallow, & E. Woodruff. 1989. Computer supported intentional learning environments. *Journal of Educational Computing Research* 5 (1): 51–68.

Schank, R. 1982. Dynamic memory: A theory of reminding and learning in computers and people. Cambridge: Cambridge University Press.

Schulman, L.S. 1986. Paradigms and research programs in the study of teaching: A contemporary perspective. In *Handbook of research on teaching,* ed. M.C. Wittrock, 3–36. New York: Macmillan.

Solomon, G., & H. Gardner. 1986. The computer as educator: Lessons from television research. *Educational Researcher* 15 (1): 13–19.

Douglas H. Clements

The Uniqueness of the Computer as a Learning Tool: Insights from Research and Practice

F irst grader Darius never talked aloud, was slow to complete his work, and worked in a "socialization group" to "draw him out of his shell." After the computer arrived, Darius spent nearly 90 minutes with the machine his first day. Thereafter, his teacher noticed that he was completing seatwork without prompting and then would slide his seat over to the computer and watch others program in *Logo*. Soon after, he would stand beside the computer, talking and making suggestions. When others had difficulties, he was quick to show them the solution. Others started getting help with *Logo* from him. In brief, Darius moved up from the lowest to the highest reading group. He began completing twice as much work each day as he had previously. He participated eagerly during class discussions and—as a "crowning achieve-

Time to prepare this material was partially provided by National Science Foundation Research Grant NSF MDR-8954664, "An Investigation of the Development of Elementary Children's Geometric Thinking in Computer and Noncomputer Environments." Any opinions, findings, and conclusions or recommendations expressed in this publication are those of the author and do not necessarily reflect the views of the National Science Foundation.

Figure 1. *The person at the door will ask the child to find a "fripple" with certain attributes (in speech as well as in written text). If the child clicks on a fripple without those attributes, an announcer intones, "That fripple is not exactly the one the customer wants!" If the fripple is correct, it bounces through the door. The program records the level of difficulty the child was on so that appropriate problems are presented in the next session.* (Thinkin' Things Collection 1, *Edmark*)

early childhood teachers use computers to maximize these benefits? What are the *unique characteristics* of these computer environments on which we can capitalize?

Learning with computers

Do children learn more—or learn better—using computers? The answer, of course, depends in large part on what kind of computer software (program) children are using. Overall, though, the picture is moderately positive. Young children make significant learning gains using computer-assisted instruction (CAI) software (Kulik, Kulik, & Bangert-Drowns 1984; Niemiec & Walberg 1984; Lieberman 1985; Ryan 1991). This type of software presents a task to children, asks them for a response, and provides feedback. For example, figure 1 illustrates one of several activities from *Thinkin' Things Collection 1*. Preschooler Leah had played awhile; she was presented with the task of selecting a red "fripple" with big eyes and "not stripes." She had the mouse poised over one with stripes and said, loudly, "Not stripes!" Then she moved to a correct fripple. "Ha! I think . . . is *this* the right one? No! Is this one? Yes. Then I click on it." Leah is not only learning about attributes and logic but developing thinking strategies and "learning to learn" skills.

What are some of the unique capabilities of CAI?

• the combination of visual displays, animated graphics, and speech

• the ability to provide feedback and keep a variety of records

• the opportunity to explore a situation

• individualization

ment"—was given a 10-minute "time out" because he wouldn't stop talking (St. Paul Public Schools 1985)!

Are such results merely coincidences or real benefits of certain computer environments? If the latter, how can we

Computer-assisted instruction and beyond

The effectiveness of computer learning depends critically on the quality of the software (e.g., *Thinkin' Things Collection 1* goes far beyond drill-and-practice), the amount of time children work with the software, and the way in which they use it. Not surprisingly, studies indicate that CAI can be effective only if teachers consider such critical features (Clements & Nastasi 1992).

What is happening in schools? Fortunately, most primary-grade children do use computers in their classrooms. Unfortunately, these children do so only occasionally and usually only because their teachers wanted to add "variety" or rewards to the curriculum. Children use mostly drill-and-practice software; their teachers state that their goal for using computers is to increase basic skills rather than to develop problem-solving or creative skills (Becker 1990b; Hickey 1993).

According to NAEYC curriculum guidelines (NAEYC 1991), use of only drill-and-practice software—worksheets on a computer—is inappropriate. For example, many schools are buying drill-oriented integrated learning systems, or ILSs. ILSs automatically load one of an extensive sequence of lessons into each child's computer based on their previous performance. Evaluations of these systems show a moderate effect on basic skills (Kelman 1990; Becker 1992); however, one must question other aspects of ILSs, especially diminished teacher and child control. In too many cases, ILSs represent a triumph of bureaucratic efficiency—centralized control and managerial efficiency—over young children's development. Making the situation worse, some critics have reinforced this picture of computers: To be used with "young children, computers have to be converted into teaching machines presenting programmed learning" (Elkind 1987, p. 8). The most promising uses of computers have nothing to do with programmed learning. In one study (Haugland 1992), only children using drill-and-practice programs had significant *losses* in creativity. Children using open-ended software made significant gains in intelligence, nonverbal skills, structural knowledge, long-term memory, complex manual dexterity, and self-esteem. What we as early childhood educators are presently doing *most often* with computers is what research and the NAEYC guidelines say we should be doing *least often*. That is not to say we should never use very structured software, just that this type of computer use should not predominate.

Let's look at some alternatives for using computers in language arts, mathematics, and other areas.

Computers for reading and writing

Research indicates that drill-and-practice software can increase primary-grade children's reading skills. Amount of practice is important. A small number of sessions with such software may have little or no effect (Clements 1987a; Clements & Nastasi 1992); however, placing computers in kindergartners' classrooms for several months significantly increases reading skills. Placing them in the home as well yields greater gains (Hess & McGarvey 1987).

This approach, while moderately effective, is not consistent with the whole language approach, with its integrated promotion of children's reading, writing, and communication.

Are there alternatives? We might emphasize writing and publishing instead of drill. The whole language approach suggests that children write their own compositions, as opposed to merely practicing writing skills. Children using word processors write more, have fewer fine motor control problems, worry less about making mistakes, and make fewer mechanical errors. Findings regarding holistic ratings of quality are mixed but generally positive (Bangert-Drowns 1989; Clements & Nastasi 1992). Programs that adopt this whole language approach have shown significant increases on children's standard assessments (Kromhout & Butzin 1993).

Computers running word processors provide assistance to young writers. Unique capabilities of computers used for composition include the following:

• easy text entry,

• easy and more powerful editing,

• spell checkers and other tools, and

• built-in prompting.

Word processors encourage a fluid idea of the written word and free young children from mechanical concerns (Bangert-Drowns 1993), thus encouraging children to experiment and communicate with written language. When working on paper, one pair of children spent as much as 30% of their time talking about penmanship and wrote only 11 words, fewer than what either normally produced working alone. Working together on the computer, they wrote more than they did working on paper alone or together. They and their classmates were also more likely to cooperatively plan, revise, and discuss spelling, punctuation, spacing, text meaning, and style on the computer. For example, Bernardo and Dan discussed the meaning of their text:

Bernardo: That doesn't make sense: "The Pilgrims were scared of the Indians. The found the food."

Dan: Oh, yeah, I forgot!

Bernardo: "The found?" "The *Indians* found."

Dan: Oh, yeah.

Bernardo: You forgot the Indians. Now are you gonna try and go back and fit "Indians" in there? (Dickinson 1986, pp. 372–74)

Opportunities to make changes before printing support meaningful revision and creative risk-taking. Word processors with speech capability provide even more support, helping children develop an ear for written text and motivating them to write. Children prefer talking word processors (Pittelman & Levin 1985; Borgh & Dickson 1986; Lehrer et al. 1987). Talking word processors foster collaborative writing to a greater degree than do those without speech compatibility. Children tend to gather around and read a story aloud with the speech synthesizer. In comparison, less collaboration occurs in noncomputer groups of children who are telling stories. Often the illegibility of children's handwriting makes it difficult for other children to read the composition (Kurth & Kurth 1987; Kurth 1988).

Computers with speech compatibility also help promote the idea of audience by providing children with an apt metaphor of written text as conversation. This idea helps some weaker writers to claim ownership of stories even when matched with a child who has stronger writing skills. One below-average male writer turned to his controlling, more skilled female partner and said, "It's my story—you're audience. When you understand my words, you can help me fix them better."

Talking word processors allow children to take control of and experiment with language. For example, two young girls were examining a picture-word card with a colored triangle. They were unsure what the word *triangle* was and, after a brief discussion, walked over to the word processor, typed it in, and satisfied their curiosity. A girl who knew she confused *b* and *d* experimented with the talking word processor on her own (she typed *dead dird dlue,* and then *bead, bird,* and *blue*). A week later, she always chose the correct letter. In another study, a group of kindergartners discovered "magic letters." If they entered *BCD* into the computer, it said only *B . . . C . . . D.* If *BAD* were entered, it pronounced the syllable, *BAD.* That is, if a magic letter was in a string of letters, the computer would make a sound that was not a letter name but a word! This way, they discovered the fundamental distinction between vowels and consonants (Hofmann 1986). Another successful approach is a picture-word processor that allows beginning writers to compose messages by simply pressing squares of picture-words without having to spell words or use extensive eye-hand coordination (Chang & Osguthorpe 1990).

Word processing may have some *disadvantages,* too. For example, beginning writers tend to leave out spaces between words and fail to use the *wrap* feature of word processors. These problems, however, are not long lasting or insurmountable (Neufeld 1989). Perhaps the most significant problems may be misguided expectations and uses. Even good word processors may not make a large difference in composition. Effective teaching and writing strategies are more important than technology. Although more teachers are using word processing, they often make the computer software the object of instruction, teaching word processing rather than composing (Becker 1990b). Appropriate computer technology can enable children to learn better writing strategies but only if the computer is used thoughtfully, as a tool. Children

might discuss how to use the computer to make significant revisions, move text around, and so on (Bangert-Drowns 1993; Seawel et al. 1994).

The importance of *how* teachers use computers is illustrated by the results of a project in which parents taught their own children to compose with word processors (Rosegrant 1986). The computer became a "tool" or a "trauma," depending on how parents used it. For example, one day at school Jessica wrote a letter to one of her grandmothers and mailed it when she got home from school. Several days later, her other grandmother called, "demanding" her own letter. During the next session, Jessica loaded in the old computer letter, typed the second grandmother's name over the first, added a "P.S. How's your eye?", and promptly mailed out the "new" letter! Her mother joked, "My mother just got a form letter from her own grandchild!" She was, however, quite pleased with (and supportive of) her child's intelligent use of the tool. On the other hand, Jane had to write 13 thank-you letters—all virtually identical—following her birthday party. She, too, thought of using the same basic "file," altered appropriately, but her mother refused to let her take that shortcut, forcing her to type the same letter 13 times. From their experiences Jane and Jessica were left with very different impressions of writing, and of the computer's usefulness. Such effects are true for teachers, as well.

Finally, realizing the benefits of computer learning also requires much computer access and time. One group of researchers stated that if they had stopped their evaluation after a couple of months, they would have mistakenly concluded that computer learning yielded no effects. Only after one full year did the rich benefits emerge (Cochran-Smith, Kahn, & Paris 1988).

Exploring mathematics

The greatest gains in the use of drill-and-practice software have been in mathematics skills in the primary grades (Clements 1987a; Clements & Nastasi 1992). Such drill can have advantages over other media (Harrison & van Devender 1992). When a bit of computer intelligence is added, programs can give adaptive help, diagnose misconceptions, generate graded sequences of arithmetic tasks, and summarize the session for the teacher—all leading to substantial positive effects (Nicolson 1990).

Again, this should not be our only—or even our main—goal, which should be to "create a coherent vision of what it means to be mathematically literate both in a world that relies on calculators and computers to carry out mathematical procedures and in a world where mathematics is rapidly growing and is extensively being applied in diverse fields" (National Council of Teachers of Mathematics 1989, p. 1). This vision places less emphasis on rote practice on isolated computations and teaching by telling. It emphasizes discussing and solving problems in geometry, number sense, and patterns with the help of manipulatives and computers. A few projects have accepted the challenge of this vision. One such project—based entirely on problems, using problem-solving and *Logo* software—demonstrated strong positive gains in children's achievement (Kromhout & Butzin 1993).

There are many roles for the computer in such a vision. One type of program is the computer manipulative. In *Number Blocks,* for example, children have full control over a computer-image set of base-ten blocks, that is, blocks that represent our base-ten number system, with 1s, 10s, and 100s blocks. An "odometer" immediately represents children's con-

crete actions symbolically (see figure 2). Adding blocks to the block set results in increasing the odometer display in increments so that it always reflects the number represented by the blocks. Children also can type any number, with any block designated as the unit, into the odometer and see the resultant effect on the set of blocks. In this way, children can easily create models of addition and subtraction by creating several

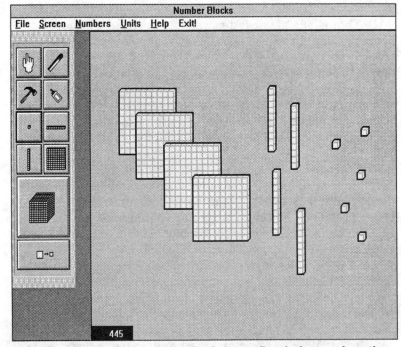

Figure 2. *A Number Blocks screen. The "odometer" at the bottom shows the symbolic representation of the number of blocks. (Screen image used with permission of Rutgers University)*

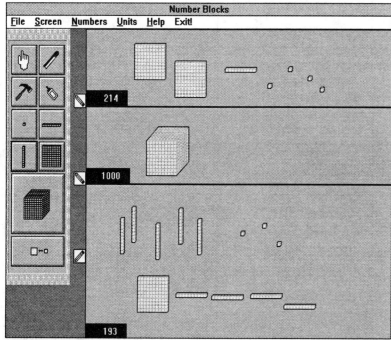

Figure 3. *Addition is facilitated by separate groups of number blocks, each with its own odometer. If the separation is erased, one odometer shows the number in the combined group. (Screen image used with permission of Rutgers University)*

groups of objects and then combining them by eliminating the separator between them (figure 3).

These computer blocks are, of course, not physically concrete. However, no base-ten blocks "contain" place-value ideas; rather, children construct these ideas while thinking about their *actions* on the blocks (Kamii 1986; Clements & McMillen n.d.). Actual base-ten blocks can be so clumsy that the ac-

tions become disconnected. The computer blocks can be more *mentally* manageable (Thompson & Thompson 1990; Thompson 1992). Also, the computer helps link the blocks to the symbols, helping children to connect these ideas. In addition, children can break computer base-ten blocks into ones or glue ones together to form tens. Such actions are more consistent with the *mental actions* that we want children to learn (Clements & McMillen n.d.).

In sum, the unique characteristics of computer manipulatives include

• offering flexibility,

• changing arrangement or representation,

• storing and later retrieving configurations,

• recording and replaying children's actions,

• linking the concrete and the symbolic by providing feedback,

• dynamically linking multiple representations, and

• focusing children's attention and increasing their motivation.

Creative uses of technology, as suggested by the National Council of Teachers of Mathematics, involve "teaching children to be mathematicians versus teaching about mathematics" (Papert 1980, p. 177). This vision gave birth to the *Logo* computing language. In *Logo*, children program the computer, for example, by directing the movements of an on-screen turtle to draw different shapes.

A class of first graders were constructing rectangles in *Logo* (Clements & Battista 1992a). "I wonder if I can tilt one," mused a boy. He turned the turtle with a mathematical command, "RIGHT 45," drew the first side, then was unsure about how much to turn the turtle at this strange new heading. He finally figured that it must be the same turn command as before. He hesitated again. "How far now? . . . Oh, it *must* be the same as its partner!" He easily completed his rectangle (figure 4). The instructions that he needed to give the turtle *at this new orientation* were not obvious initially. He analyzed the situation and reflected on the properties of a rectangle. Perhaps most importantly, he posed the problem for himself.

This boy had walked on rectangular-shaped paths and used this awareness in his drawing of rectangles on the computer. His experience illustrates several unique characteristics of programming. Research (Clements & Battista 1989; Clements & Battista 1992b) indicates that programming

- helps link children's intuitive knowledge about moving and drawing to more explicit mathematical ideas;

- encourages the manipulation of specific shapes in ways that help children view them as mathematical representatives of a *class* of shapes;

- facilitates children's development of autonomy in learning (rather than seeking authority) and positive beliefs about the creation of mathematical ideas;

- encourages wondering about and posing problems by providing an environment in which to test ideas and receive feedback about them;

- helps connect visual shapes with abstract numbers; and

- fosters mathematical thinking.

Four additional examples of children using *Logo* illustrate these benefits, especially connecting the visual and concrete with the abstract.

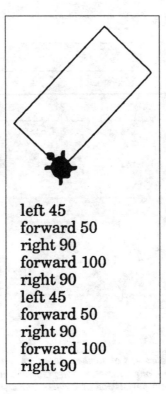

left 45
forward 50
right 90
forward 100
right 90
left 45
forward 50
right 90
forward 100
right 90

Figure 4. *A first grader expanded on his ideas about rectangles by programming the* **Logo** *turtle to draw a tilted rectangle.*

1. Three first-grade children determined the correct length for the bottom line of their drawing by adding the lengths of the three horizontal lines that they constructed at the top of the tower: 20 + 30 + 20 = 70 (Clements 1983–84).

2. Another first grader wanted to turn the turtle to point into his rectangle. He asked the teacher, "What's half of 90?" After she responded, he typed RIGHT 45. "Oh, I went the wrong way." He said nothing for a while, eyes intently focused on the screen. "I'll try LEFT 90," he said at last. This inverse operation produced exactly the desired effect (Kull 1986).

3. A preschooler discovered that reversing the turtle's orientation and moving it backward had the same effect as moving the turtle forward. The significance that the child attached to this discovery and his overt awareness of it were striking. Although the child had come to the same realization previously with toy cars, *Logo* helped him abstract a new and exciting idea for his earlier experience (Tan 1985).

4. A primary-grade teacher of a "below average" class reported that she had written some multiplication tables on the board. The children saw the pattern immediately and used the *Logo* command REPEAT to describe what they noticed (e.g., REPEAT 3 [FD 10] is the same as FD 30). She claimed that "This is the first time this has ever happened in my class. I am sure it is because of their *Logo* work. They are looking for patterns in things more than they used to do" (Carmichael et al. 1985, p. 286).

Such benefits are not always obvious to people, especially people who have not closely observed children working with *Logo*. When I first arrived at my present university, I asked the person running the educational computer lab, "What versions of *Logo* do you have?"

"We don't have *Logo*," he replied, "I just threw it out." Retaining my proper academic composure, I asked why.

"Now that we have *Dazzle Draw*, what would you want to use *Logo* for?" But, of course, the point is not the drawing, it's *thinking about doing the drawing* (Clements & Battista 1992b). A lot more thought has to go into deciding what should be easy and what should remain a struggle, in the positive sense of the word. *Logo* can be difficult, but the effort is worth it. As one third-grade boy put it, "*Logo* is very hard, but it had to be done. I liked doing it" (Carmichael et al. 1985). This boy's insight, consistent with the research, implies that newer software packages—with new pictures, "movies," and sound, and sporting point-and-click ease of use—may not always represent an improvement. In fact, children work hard and enjoy modified versions of *Logo* that support learning goals but do not compromise on what has to be done. One such version of *Logo, Turtle Math*, is tailored specifically for investigations in geometry and other mathematical topics. For example, it includes measurement tools, such as an on-screen protractor and ruler, and helps link symbols and drawings by automatically and dynamically connecting *Logo* commands to the geometric figure drawn. If a child changes a command, the figure is automatically drawn to reflect that change. Also, children can change the drawing directly by "pulling" the figure, and they can see the corresponding changes to the *Logo* commands.

Studies indicate that *Logo*, used thoughtfully, can provide an engaging context for young children's explorations of mathematics (Clements & Nastasi 1992; Wilson & Lavelle 1992). Such "thoughtful use" includes structuring and guiding *Logo* work to help children form strong, valid mathematical ideas. Children do not appreciate the mathematics in *Logo* work unless teachers help them see the work mathematically. Teachers raise questions about "surprises" or conflicts between children's intuitions and computer feedback to promote reflection. They pose challenges and tasks designed to make the mathematical ideas explicit for children. They help children build bridges between the *Logo* experience and their regular mathematics work. They allow children to use their own approaches, capitalizing on *Logo's* ability to engage people of different backgrounds and learning styles—both boys and girls (Clements 1987b; Delclos & Burns 1993). Within this context, children in preschool and primary schools can use *Logo* successfully (Clements & Meredith 1993; Easton & Watson 1993).

Another way of using *Logo* also encourages inclusion. With *LEGO-Logo*, children use the *Logo* language to control LEGO creations, including lights, sensors, motors, gears, and pulleys. Papert (1993) observed some Boston schoolchildren playing with LEGO and computers. The boys started making trucks right away, and the girls made a house. At first, the girls traded motors for things they could use to decorate their house. They were not interested in the mechanical, *Logo*-controlled aspects. Then one day a light appeared in one of the rooms in the house. The *Logo* code was simple: ON WAIT 10 OFF WAIT 10. Later there were several lights, then a lighted Christmas tree that a motor turned around. This was a soft transition. The girls found their own way into full use of *LEGO-Logo*.

Another time, two girls made a mother cat and her kitten. The kitten called its mother with a flashing light. To make the mother cat go to the kitten, the girls put on each side of her head a light sensor that sensed light in a semicircle. The cat would turn in some vague direction toward the light, back and forth, back and forth, until it reached the kitten exactly. This vague formulation wasn't an approximation; while vague, it was useful because it was interactive, that is, the sensors interacted with the flashing light. The cat always got to the kitten.

Many people, such as these two girls, who aren't comfortable with precision and exactness can find a way to acquire knowledge. They can develop their own way of appropriating mathematical and technological knowledge. With *Logo*, fantasy, technology, mathematics, science, and personal ways of knowing can come together in natural connections rather than stay separate as specialized subjects.

Young children articulate additional unique characteristics of *Logo* combined with LEGO:

- *LEGO-Logo* invites people to explore mathematics and science. Asked if *LEGO-Logo* was for boys, a 7-year-old responded indignantly, "That idea is a bit sexist. Robotics is as much for girls as for boys" (Winer & Trudel 1991, p. 50).

- Sasha, age 7, said, "If we didn't have the computer, what could we use to say that the electricity should flow and then it should stop? Where would we put our knowledge? We can't just leave it in our heads. We know it, we think it, but our programs would stay in our heads" (Winer & Trudel 1991, p. 51).

- Another 7-year-old said, "I've learnt that if something doesn't work [just] go back and check it . . ." and "if you've got problems . . . you've got to go through steps to solve it. You may decide on one way, but if it doesn't work, so you might choose another way and it will" (Lai 1993, p. 243).

Creativity and higher order problem solving

A possible concern about using *Logo* is that the turtle approach to drawing is too mechanical. Will children's creativity suffer? Studies show just the opposite result. Research indicates that *Logo* drawing allows many children to create more elaborate pictures than those that they can create by hand. It also suggests that they modify their conceptions and transfer components of this new way of thinking to their work with paper (Vaidya & McKeeby 1984). In a series of studies, creativity that children had developed with *Logo* was shown to have transferred to figural and verbal creativity off the computer (Clements & Gullo 1984; Clements 1986; Clements 1991). Further, children can use *Logo* for diverse activities, such as programming music. Children as young as 7 years of age can manipulate ideas such as rhythm, harmony, timbre, texture, and musical form. They create melodies with computational effects that would be impossible to perform with two hands, much less without expert performance skills. Computers also enhance creative musical development because children can modify and save musical ideas (Bontá & Silverman 1993).

Other types of programs, such as computer painting tools, similarly combine mathematical and artistic explorations. Every painting tool in *Kid Pix* has a large number of variations. For example, there are 20 brushes, including Splatter Paint, Galaxy of Stars, Northern Lights, The Looper, and Drippy Paint. Each tool also makes a realistic or engaging sound. Sounds include speech—the program pronounces letters in varying, real voices—and choosing to reverse an action may result in an "Oops!" (see figure 5).

Various other tools, from mirrors to motions, from outlining to filling, encourage a variety of artistic and geometric explorations. For instance, filling closed regions with color leads the children to reflect on geometric properties such as closure as the consequence of *action* rather than merely a characteristic of static shapes. Drawing rectangles by stretching electronic "rubber bands" engenders a dynamic perspective on geometric figures (Forman 1986). The power of such drawing tools lies in the possibility that children will construct new mental tools, such as spatial abilities. Art abilities also grow, as do self-esteem and confidence (Alchin 1993 reported such gains in a young child with a developmental disability).

Problem-solving computer activities motivate children as young as kindergartners or first graders to make choices and decisions, alter their strategies, persist, and score higher on tests of critical thinking and problem solving (Gélinas 1986; Riding & Powell 1987; Orabuchi 1993). The interaction of one such program designed to improve thinking in analogies was so powerful that it worked well with or without adult supervision (Klein & Gal 1992). Several studies reveal that *Logo* programming is a particularly engaging activity for young children, fostering higher order thinking (Clements & Nastasi 1988; Nastasi, Clements, & Battista 1990). Preschool and primary-grade children develop the ability to understand the nature of problems and use representations such as drawings to solve them. When given opportunities to debug, or find and fix errors in *Logo* programs (Poulin-Dubois, McGilly, & Shultz 1989), they also increase their ability to monitor their thinking—that is, to realize when they are confused or need to change directions in solving a problem (Clements & Nastasi 1992).

Jerome Bruner has shown that children encouraged to play with materials first became far more creative in solving problems with those materials (Bruner 1985). Bruner's research indicates that play is richest when the material provided has a clear-cut, variable means–end structure; has some constraints; and yields feedback that children can interpret on their own. Interestingly, these characteristics—which originally described puzzles and building blocks—fit

Figure 5. *A child's picture in KidPix. (Broderbund)*

quite well the computer environments that we have discussed . They make it possible to play with certain mathematical ideas creatively earlier than is currently believed. Such activity engenders both cognitive and affective involvement with mathematics. In the words of one child working with *Logo*, "I've thought about circles in ways I've never considered before" (Carmichael et al. 1985, p. 285).

This outcome of working with *Logo* stands in contrast to results of structured CAI activities that—because of their restrictions on solution strategies, extrinsic rewards, built-in evaluations, and lack of playfulness—may negatively affect mathematical creativity (Clements n.d.). In summary, several unique characteristics of computers facilitate young children's creativity and problem solving.

Working with computers

• allows children to create, change, save, and retrieve ideas, promoting reflection and engagement;

• connects ideas from different areas, such as the mathematical and the artistic;

• provides situations with clear-cut variable means–end structure; some constraints, and feedback that children can interpret on their own; and so,

• allows children to interact, think, and play with ideas in significant ways, in some cases even with limited adult supervision.

The social machine

Young children are capable of working together at the computer and even prefer working with one or two partners to working alone (Rhee & Chavnagri 1991; Clements, Nastasi, & Swaminathan 1993). What do children do when they interact? They seek help from each other and seem to prefer help from peers over help from the teacher (King & Alloway 1992; Nastasi & Clements 1993). Preschoolers, however, may have difficulty balancing the combined social and academic demands of collaborative problem solving (Perlmutter et al. 1986). This does not mean that teachers of preschoolers should avoid collaborative computer use, but they should be aware that the children may need additional structure and guidance. Also, young children benefit from opportunities to work alone with software (Shade 1994).

Children also engage in high levels of spoken communication and cooperation at the computer. They interact more frequently and in different ways than they interact when engaged with traditional activities, such as puzzles or blocks. Whereas in sociodramatic play there tends to be a "leader" of communication, children share leadership roles on the computer. On the computer they initiate interactions more frequently and engage in more turn taking. Only at the computer do they simultaneously show high levels of language and cooperative-play activity. Children in the primary grades collaborate more at the computer than they do when performing similar language arts or mathematics tasks with paper and pencil.

Of course, the software being used makes a difference in children's interaction with each other. In open-ended environments such as *Logo*, young children are more likely to formulate and solve their own problems and to do so in collaboration with a partner. They also are more likely to evaluate their work positively, to appear motivated, and to develop positive attitudes about learning. In contrast, externally structured environments such as drill-and-practice software may encourage children to compete with one another and to avoid the exchange of ideas. Young children using primarily drill-and-practice software may also become more dependent on teachers for help within computer and other learning environments. Furthermore, particularly for children in the early primary grades, work with drill software may foster boredom with paper-and-pencil drill tasks (Nastasi & Clements 1993). In educational computer games, children will more likely get correct answers when they work cooperatively rather than competitively (Strommen 1993).

Gains in higher order thinking from working with *Logo*, compared to drill software, may be due in part to the way children interact and the way they approach their work. In *Logo*, children more frequently exchange information and resolve conflicts by negotiating and talking through ideas. These types of social exchanges account for cognitive gains (Nastasi & Clements 1993).

For example, two children are trying to draw a hexagon with *Logo*. They have already made two sides.

Child 1: RIGHT 180.

Child 2: No! Because 180 would go (gesturing). We want it to go, shh-shh-shh-shh-shh (with gestures indicating that the hexagon can be completed by continuing the same way); we only have to repeat that five times.

Child 1: Oh, OK. But four times.

Child 2: No, 1, 2, 3, 4, 5. 'Cause that one's already there.

Child 1: 1, 2 . . . 1, 2, 3, 4, 5, 6.

Child 2: Four.

Child 1: Yes.

For these children the process of decision making involved considering the merits of different solutions.

Also accounting for cognitive gains are children's high levels of effectance motivation—the desire to control or effect change in the environment (Nastasi & Clements 1994). Computer use can enhance children's attitudes about themselves and about academic subjects such as reading (Chang & Osguthorpe 1990; Clements & Nastasi 1992; Orabuchi 1993).

The road less traveled

Teachers who use computers stand at a crossroads, facing three roads (Clements, Nastasi, & Swaminathan 1993). Those traveling on the first road use simple computer games for "rewards" or occasionally use drill software; they do not integrate computer work into their educational program. Those traveling on the second road integrate drill and other structured software activities into their programs. And those traveling on the third road use problem-solving software and tools such as word processors, *Logo*, and drawing programs to enrich children's education.

Research suggests that the first road is a meandering, useless one; unfortunately, it is the most prominent one (Hickey 1993). The second road leads somewhere educationally—integrated computer activities can increase achievement. Some teachers may use computers to provide practice, thus freeing up their time to focus on higher order goals. This is a safe and easy path. The third road takes more effort, time,

commitment, and vision (Becker 1990a), but it offers the hope of educational innovation along NAEYC guidelines.

Many teachers take the second road and return one or more years later to the crossroads, finally turning to the third road. One teacher said, "As you work into using the computer in the classroom, you start questioning everything you have done in the past and wonder how you can adapt it to the computer. Then you start questioning the whole concept of what you originally did" (Dwyer, Ringstaff, & Sandholtz 1991).

This is the route Ms. T followed. She never used computers much when they entered her school; the games seemed like a waste of time. When another first-grade teacher told her how much the children in her class were learning from a series of computer activities, Ms. T introduced them as a part of seatwork. She found that the individualized practice helped the children gain skills faster and left her with a bit more time for working with the children on comprehension and composing.

The following year, after taking an educational computer class, Ms. T decided to integrate the computer more deeply into her language arts curriculum. She showed her children word processing—only a few commands at first, then additional features as children showed the need. Her talking word processor permitted playful explorations of writing and speech sounds and was especially helpful for children with special needs. Later she used computers to provide help for "conferencing." She learned that rather than quizzing or offering unsolicited help, she should prompt children to teach each other, so she physically placed one child in a teaching role and responded to specific requests for help. She noted that some of the children were aggressive and competitive, so she closely monitored their interactions, provided them with

With open-ended software, including programming skills with Logo, children frequently exchange information and resolve conflicts by negotiating and talking through ideas.

She encouraged the children to use the computer's editing features, thereby learning to perceive text as flexible and malleable. The screen lent a public quality to writing and thus encouraged sharing. The children suggested publishing a class newspaper. They took increasingly more responsibility and were tackling problems and decisions. She suggested that they divide the responsibilities and work in pairs or teams, making suggestions about possible teammates based on her knowledge of abilities and interests. She ensured that each team included children from different gender and racial groups and that the newspaper reflected everyone's views. The computers helped manage and enable these complex tasks and allowed children of different abilities to contribute (Fisher 1990/91).

The next year, her computer-intensive language arts program was running smoothly in a fraction of the time it took the year before. Ms. T started using *Logo*. She provided a moderate amount of structure during the first activities to give children a good grasp of *Logo* and geometric shapes (Battista & Clements 1991). She then challenged the children to extend these ideas in developing projects of their own. They worked in pairs for weeks on these projects, helping each other, consulting with Ms. T, and using references. She encouraged the children to express their ideas, even when they were different from their partners', and to talk through their disagreements to synthesize ideas. They presented their projects to the class, explaining *how* they solved the problems they encountered. In addition, Ms. T wove *Logo* activities into her other mathematics units, often exploiting *Logo*'s ability to link symbolic representations, such as "FORWARD 40 FORWARD 20," to visual representations, in this case, a line segment 60 units in length. She also challenged the

children to use their new knowledge in other projects. She enjoyed seeing her children use mathematics to build something about which they cared deeply—their own designs and pictures. She was especially gratified by the motivation, interest, and success of her "low achievers."

Ms. T says she might never have started using the computer if she had seen the rough terrain. Computers sometimes were out for repair, no one in her building knew how to get a program working, and so on. But she navigated successfully and learned more than she thought she would. She understood that real differences in learning are visible only after a considerable time. Now she wouldn't teach without computers. Her path is set.

References

Alchin, G. 1993. Increasing self esteem and creativity of people with a developmental disability through the use of computer technology. *Australian Educational Computing* 8: 19–24.

Bangert-Drowns, R.L. 1989. Research on word processing and writing instruction. Paper presented at the meeting of the American Educational Research Association, San Francisco, March.

Bangert-Drowns, R.L. 1993. The word processor as an instructional tool: A meta-analysis of word processing in and writing instruction. *Review of Educational Research*, 63 (1): 69–93.

Battista, M.T., & D.H. Clements. 1991. *Logo geometry*. Morristown, NJ: Silver Burdett & Ginn.

Becker, H.J. 1990a. Effects of computer use on mathematics achievement: Findings from a nationwide field experiment in grade five to eight classes. Paper presented at the meeting of the American Educational Research Association, Boston, April.

Becker, H.J. 1990b. How computers are used in United States schools: Basic data from the 1989 I.E.A. Computers in Education Survey. *Journal of Educational Computing Research* 7: 385–406.

Becker, H.J. 1992. Computer-based integrated learning systems in the elementary and middle grades: A critical review and synthe-

Becker, H.J. 1992. Computer-based integrated learning systems in the elementary and middle grades: A critical review and synthesis of evaluation reports. *Journal of Educational Computing Research* 8 (1): 1–41.

Bontá, P., & B. Silverman. 1993. Making learning entertaining. In *Rethinking the roles of technology in education,* eds. N. Estes & M. Thomas, 1150–52. Cambridge, MA: Massachusetts Institute of Technology.

Borgh, K., & W.P. Dickson. 1986. Two preschoolers sharing one microcomputer: Creating prosocial behavior with hardware and software. In *Young children and microcomputers,* eds. P.F. Campbell & G.G. Fein, 37–44. Englewood Cliffs, NJ: Prentice Hall.

Bruner, J. 1985. On teaching thinking: An afterthought. In *Thinking and learning skills. Volume 2: Research and open questions,* eds. S.F. Chipman, J.W. Segal, & R. Glaser. Hillsdale, NJ: Lawrence Erlbaum.

Carmichael, H.W., J.D. Burnett, W.C. Higginson, B.G. Moore, & P.J. Pollard. 1985. *Computers, children and classrooms: A multisite evaluation of the creative use of microcomputers by elementary school children.* Toronto, Ontario, Canada: Ministry of Education.

Chang, L.L., & R.T. Osguthorpe. 1990. The effects of computerized picture-word processing on kindergartners' language development. *Journal of Research in Childhood Education* 5 (1): 73–84.

Clements, D.H. 1983–84. Supporting young children's Logo programming. *The Computing Teacher* 11 (5): 24–30.

Clements, D.H. 1986. Effects of Logo and CAI environments on cognition and creativity. *Journal of Educational Psychology* 78: 309–18.

Clements, D.H. 1987a. Computers and young children: A review of the research. *Young Children* 43 (1): 34–44.

Clements, D.H. 1987b. Longitudinal study of the effects of Logo programming on cognitive abilities and achievement. *Journal of Educational Computing Research* 3 (1): 73–94.

Clements, D.H. 1991. Enhancement of creativity in computer environments. *American Educational Research Journal* 28 (1): 173–87.

Clements, D.H. n.d. Teaching creativity with computers, *Educational Psychology Review.* In press.

Clements, D.H., & M.T. Battista. 1989. Learning of geometric concepts in a Logo environment. *Journal for Research in Mathematics Education* 20: 450–67.

Clements, D.H., & M.T. Battista. 1992a. *The development of a Logo-based elementary school geometry curriculum (Final Report: NSF Grant No.: MDR–8651668).* Buffalo, NY/Kent, OH: State University of New York at Buffalo/Kent State University.

Clements, D.H., & M.T. Battista. 1992b. Geometry and spatial reasoning. In *Handbook of research on mathematics teaching and learning,* ed. D.A. Grouws, 420–64. New York: Macmillan.

Clements, D.H., & D.F. Gullo. 1984. Effects of computer programming on young children's cognition. *Journal of Educational Psychology* 76: 1051–58.

Clements, D.H., & S. McMillen. n.d. Rethinking "concrete" manipulatives. *Arithmetic Teacher.* In press.

Clements, D.H., & J.S. Meredith. 1993. Research on Logo: Effects and efficacy. *Journal of Computing in Childhood Education* 4: 263–90.

Clements, D.H., & B.K. Nastasi. 1988. Social and cognitive interactions in educational computer environments. *American Educational Research Journal* 25 (1): 87–106.

Clements, D.H., & B.K. Nastasi. 1992. Computers and early childhood education. In *Advances in school psychology: Preschool and early childhood treatment directions,* eds. M. Gettinger, S.N. Elliott, & T.R. Kratochwill, 187–246. Hillsdale, NJ: Lawrence Erlbaum.

Clements, D.H., B.K. Nastasi, & S. Swaminathan. 1993. Young children and computers: Crossroads and directions from research. *Young Children* 48 (2): 56–64.

Cochran-Smith, M., J. Kahn, & C.L. Paris. 1988. When word processors come into the classroom. In *Writing with computers in the early grades,* eds. J.L. Hoot & S.B. Silvern, 43–74. New York: Teachers College Press.

Delclos, V.R., & S. Burns. 1993. Mediational elements in computer programming instruction: An exploratory study. *Journal of Computing in Childhood Education* 4 (2): 137–52.

Dickinson, D.K. 1986. Cooperation, collaboration, and a computer: Integrating a computer into a first–second grade writing program. *Research in the Teaching of English* 20: 357–78.

Dwyer, D.C., C. Ringstaff, & J.H. Sandholtz. 1991. Changes in teachers' beliefs and practices in technology-rich classrooms. *Educational Leadership* 48 (8): 45–52.

Easton, C.E., & J.A. Watson. 1993. Spatial strategy use during Logo mastery: The impact of cognitive style and developmental level. *Journal of Computing in Childhood Education* 4 (1): 77–96.

Elkind, D. 1987. The child yesterday, today, and tomorrow. *Young Children* 42 (4): 6–11.

Fisher, C.W. 1990/91. Some influences of classroom computers on academic tasks. *Journal of Computing in Childhood Education* 2 (2): 3–15.

Forman, G. 1986. Observations of young children solving problems with computers and robots. *Journal of Research in Childhood Education* 1 (2): 60–74.

Gélinas, C. 1986. *Educational computer activities and problem solving at the kindergarten level.* Quebec City, Quebec, Canada: Quebec Ministry of Education.

Harrison, N., & E.M. van Devender. 1992. The effects of drill-and-practice computer instruction on learning basic mathematics facts. *Journal of Computing in Childhood Education* 3 (3/4): 349–56.

Haugland, S.W. 1992. Effects of computer software on preschool children's developmental gains. *Journal of Computing in Childhood Education* 3 (1): 15–30.

Hess, R., & L. McGarvey. 1987. School-relevant effects of educational uses of microcomputers in kindergarten classrooms and homes. *Journal of Educational Computing Research* 3: 269–87.

Hickey, M.G. 1993. Computer use in elementary classrooms: An ethnographic study. *Journal of Computing in Childhood Education* 4: 219–28.

Hofmann, R. 1986. Microcomputers, productive thinking, and children. In *Young children and microcomputers,* eds. P.F. Campbell & G.G. Fein, 87–101. Englewood Cliffs, NJ: Prentice Hall.

Kamii, C. 1986. Place value: An explanation of its difficulty and educational implications for the primary grades. *Journal of Research in Childhood Education* 1 (2): 75–86.

Kelman, P. 1990. *Alternatives to integrated instructional systems.* Paper presented at the meeting of the National Educational Computing Conference, Nashville, TN, June.

King, J., & N. Alloway. 1992. Preschooler's use of microcomputers and input devices. *Journal of Educational Computing Research* 8: 451–68.

Klein, P., & O.N. Gal. 1992. Effects of computer mediation of analogical thinking in kindergartens. *Journal of Computer Assisted Learning* 8: 244–54.

Kromhout, O.M., & S.M. Butzin. 1993. Integrating computers into the elementary school curriculum: An evaluation of nine Project CHILD model schools. *Journal of Research on Computing in Education* 26 (1): 55–69.

Kulik, C.C., J. Kulik, & R.L. Bangert-Drowns. 1984. *Effects of computer-based education of elementary school pupils.* Paper presented at the meeting of the American Educational Research Association, New Orleans, LA, April.

Kull, J.A. 1986. Learning and Logo. In *Young children and microcomputers,* eds. P.F. Campbell & G.G. Fein, 103–30. Englewood Cliffs, NJ: Prentice Hall.

Kurth, R.J. 1988. Process variables in writing instruction using word processing, word processing with voice synthesis, and no word processing. Paper presented at the meeting of the American Educational Research Association, New Orleans, LA, April.

Kurth, R.J., & L.M. Kurth. 1987. A comparison of writing instruction using and word processing, word processing with voice synthesis, and no word processing in kindergarten and first grade. Paper presented at the meeting of the American Educational Research Association, Washington, D.C., April. (ERIC Document Reproduction Service No. ED 283 196)

Lai, K.W. 1993. Lego-Logo as a learning environment. *Journal of Computing in Childhood Education* 4: 229–45.

Lehrer, R., B.B. Levin, P. DeHart, & M. Comeaux. 1987. Voice-feedback as a scaffold for writing: A comparative study. *Journal of Educational Computing Research* 3: 335–53.

Lieberman, D. 1985. Research on children and microcomputers: A review of utilization and effects studies. In *Children and microcomputers: Research on the newest medium,* eds. M. Chen & W. Paisley, 59–83. Beverly Hills: Sage.

Nastasi, B.K., & D.H. Clements. 1993. Motivational and social outcomes of cooperative education environments. *Journal of Computing in Childhood Education* 4 (1): 15–43.

Nastasi, B.K., & D.H. Clements. 1994. Effectance motivation, perceived scholastic competence, and higher-order thinking in two cooperative computer environments. *Journal of Educational Computing Research* 10: 241–67.

Nastasi, B.K., D.H. Clements, & M.T. Battista. 1990. Social-cognitive interactions, motivation, and cognitive growth in Lego programming and CAI problem-solving environments. *Journal of Educational Psychology* 82: 150–58.

National Association for the Education of Young Children. 1991. Guidelines for appropriate curriculum content and assessment in programs serving children ages 3 through 8. *Young Children* 46 (3): 21–38.

National Council of Teachers of Mathematics. 1989. *Curriculum and evaluation standards for school mathematics*. Reston, VA: Author.

Neufeld, K. 1989. When children use word processors for writings: Some problems and suggestions. *Reading Improvement* 26 (1): 64–70.

Nicolson, R.I. 1990. Design and evaluation of the SUMIT intelligent teaching assistant for arithmetic. *Interaction Learning Environments* 1 (4): 265–87.

Niemiec, R.P., & H.J. Walberg. 1984. Computers and achievement in the elementary schools. *Journal of Education Computing Research* 1: 435–40.

Orabuchi, I.I. 1993. Effects of using interactive CAI on primary grade students' high order thinking skills: Inferences, generalizations, and math problem-solving. Unpublished doctoral dissertation, Texas Women's University, Denton, TX.

Papert, S. 1980. Teaching children thinking; teaching children to be mathematicians vs. teaching about mathematics. In *The computer in the school: Tutor, tool, tutee,* ed. R. Taylor, 161–96. New York: Teachers College Press.

Papert, S. 1993. *The children's machine. Rethinking school in the age of the computer.* New York: Basic.

Permutter, M., S. Behrend, F. Kuo, & A. Muller. 1986. Social influence on children's problem solving at a computer. Unpublished manuscript, University of Michigan, Ann Arbor.

Pittelman, S.D., & K.M. Kevin. 1985. *An exploration of the use of a speech-enhanced microcomputer-based language experience program to facilitate beginning reading instruction. Program Report No. 85-6.* Madison, WI: University of Wisconsin–Madison. (ERIC Document Reproduction Service No. ED 264 524)

Poulin-Dubois, D., C.A. McGilly, & T.R. Shultz. 1989. Psychology of computer use. The effect of learning Logo on children's problem-solving skills. *Psychological Reports,* 64: 1327–37.

Rhee, M.C., & N. Chavnagri. 1991. *4 year old children's peer interactions when playing with a computer.* (ERIC Document Reproduction Service No. ED 342466)

Riding, R.J., & S.D. Powell. 1987. The effect on reasoning, reading and number performance of computer-presented critical thinking activities in five-year-old children. *Educational Psychology* 7 (1): 55–65.

Rosegrant, T.J. 1986. *Adult-child communication in writing.* Paper presented at the meeting of the American Educational Research Association, San Francisco, April.

Ryan, A.W. 1991. Meta-analysis of achievement effects of microcomputer applications in elementary schools. *Education Administration Quarterly* 27 (2): 161–84.

Seawel, L., S.E. Smaldino, J.L. Steele, & J.Y. Lewis. 1994. A descriptive study comparing computer-based word processing and handwriting on attitudes and performace of third and fourth grade students involved in a program based on a process approach to writing. *Journal of Computing in Childhood Education* 5 (1): 43–59.

Shade, D.D. n.d. Computers and young children: Software types, social contexts, and emotional responses. *Journal for Computing in Childhood Education.* In press.

Sivin-Kachala, J., & E.R. Bialo. 1993. *Report on the effectiveness of technology in schools: 1990-1992.* Washington, D.C.: Software Publishers Association.

Strommen, E.F. 1993. "Does yours eat leaves?" Cooperative learning in an educational software task. *Journal of Computing in Childhood Education* 4 (1): 45–56.

Tan, L.E. 1985. Computers in pre-school education. *Early Childhood Development and Care* 19: 319–36.

Thompson, P.W. 1992. Notations, conventions, and constraints: Contributions to effective use of concrete materials in elementary mathematics. *Journal for Research in Mathematics Education* 23: 123–47.

Thompson, P.W., & A.G. Thompson. 1990. Salient aspects of experience with concrete manipulatives. Paper presented at the meeting of the International Group for the Psychology of Mathematics Education, Mexico, July.

Vaidya, S., & J. McKeeby. 1984. Computer turtle graphics: Do they affect children's thought processes? *Education Technology,* September, 46–47.

Wilson, D., & S. Lavelle. 1992. Effects of Logo and computer-aided instruction on arithmetical ability among 7- and 8-year-old Zimbabwean children. *Journal of Computing in Childhood Education* 3 (1): 85–91.

Winer, L.R., & H. Trudel. 1991. Children in an educational robotics environment: Experiencing discovery. *Journal of Computing in Childhood Education* 2 (4): 41–64.

The Role of Technology in the Early Childhood Curriculum

**Sue Bredekamp
and Teresa Rosegrant**

Learning and
Teaching with Technology

I n their personal experiences with technology, the authors of this chapter represent two extremes. In the early 1980s, Rosegrant conducted research on the possible benefits of using computers with young children. Her work (Rosegrant 1984) demonstrated that hardware and software could be developed to enable computers to be used effectively to help children with severe disabilities acquire literacy. This research resulted in increased access to normalized educational settings for children who had previously been denied access on the grounds that they could not learn. Subsequently, Rosegrant established and worked in writing labs with children and their

parents in Arizona and with teachers and children in Arizona and New Mexico. From her observations of children and adults interacting with computers, Rosegrant derived a conceptual framework for learning and teaching (Rosegrant & Cooper 1986; Bredekamp & Rosegrant 1992).

Bredekamp's experiences with technology and young children are probably more like those of the majority of early childhood educators today. Computers were never used when she taught preschoolers. With no firsthand experience or observation of appropriate use of computers or exposure to good-quality children's software, Bredekamp shared the negative reactions of many of her colleagues. Her primary assumption about computers was that children had more important things to do. In addition, the little experience she did have indicated that computers were essentially very expensive workbooks, the cost of which was better spent on improved staff salaries. Bredekamp's attitude about computers changed slowly, as most attitudes do, with exposure to the research but primarily through observation of groups of children engaging with good-quality software as one option in an excellent early childhood program.

Concerns of many early childhood educators about computers were clearly expressed in letters sent to NAEYC in response to a *New York Times* article on computers: "Let us not let our adult excitement with what computers can do in the adult workplace deter us from offering to children the squishiness of making mud pies, the scent of peppermint extract when making cookies, and the feel of balancing a block at the top of a tower. Children deserve to have a rich and varied childhood. The adult world of the plastic workplace comes all too soon . . . (support for lots of computer time for young children) has the potential to undo all of the good work that has been done educating the public about quality developmental education for young children" (letter to NAEYC, 1994). A similar letter stated, "I cannot think of any case in which computers could be considered developmentally appropriate for children in nursery school. Especially considering the normal length of the average preschool program. Since we agree that 3s and 4s need to have plenty of time to explore mud, sand, water, and blocks, etc., where do you fit in a computer and what would it replace?" (letter to NAEYC, 1994).

Technology and young children: The great debate

These letters reflect a strong set of beliefs about computers and young children, whereas Rosegrant's research and much more like it (see Clements, chapter 3) reflect another perspective. Reconciling these diverse perspectives is one of the major objectives of this book. Invoking the "additive principle" of education may be helpful in breaking the gridlock: education should add to, not take away from, children's understanding and experiences. None of the research cited or any of these chapters contend that computers should replace highly valued early childhood activities and materials. Rather, the work reveals that computers, although not an essential element of a good-quality program, can be used in developmentally appropriate ways that are beneficial to children (and they can be misused, just as mud, sand, water, and blocks can). An *a priori* rejection of computer technology as inappropriate does an injustice to the concept of developmental appropriateness, denying the reality that in every educational situation, a professional judgment is required to determine what is age appropriate, culturally appropriate, and individually appropriate. Computers and the myriad available software packages are far too complex and diverse for us to make a singular judgment of appropriateness or inappropriateness. Reasoning conversely, books might easily be judged as a material that is always appropriate in an early childhood classroom, when in fact teachers must constantly make judgments about which books are age appropriate, culturally and linguistically appropriate, and individually of interest, and, of course, the outcomes of these decisions change over time.

The purpose of this chapter is to challenge the dichotomous thinking about technology and young children as either wholly evil or unequivocally good. Computers are not the panacea for failing schools that many entrepreneurs think they are; they cannot replace teachers, and, like most aspects of education, their effectiveness depends in large part on teacher interaction. Likewise, computers do not spell the end of early childhood education as we know it. On the contrary, computer software developers have learned good early childhood practice in order to develop products that children will use. As is so often the case, the children evaluate the appropriateness of educational materials through their interest and persistence. In this chapter, we present a framework for conceptualizing the processes of learning and teaching and then apply this framework to decisions about the appropriateness of technology in classrooms for young children in three areas: hardware, software, and the role of the adult.

A framework for learning and teaching

From extensive observation of children working with computers, Rosegrant observed that their learning followed a recurring cycle, which she described as awareness, exploration, inquiry, and utilization. This nonlinear cycle, described more fully elsewhere (Bredekamp & Rosegrant 1992), is summarized here:

To learn something new, children must become aware, be able to explore and inquire, and then use and apply what they have learned. This process occurs over time and reflects movement from learning that is informal and incidental, spontaneous, concrete referenced, and governed by the child's own rules, to learning that is more

formal, refined, extended, and enriched; more removed in time and space from concrete references; and more reflective of conventional rule systems. (Bredekamp & Rosegrant 1992, p. 32; for a graphic description of this cycle, see table 1)

This cycle is not developmental in the pure sense of the word because the process itself does not change as the person grows; children experience the cycle of learning—and so do adults—whenever they acquire a new skill or gain new knowledge.

The majority of adults today learned to use computers as adults and may actually remember their personal experience of the learning cycle. When Bredekamp (the learner) was presented with a laptop computer, the trainer, who was already at the utilization level, gave what she thought were clear instructions that made absolutely no sense to the learner. The instruction book, also written at the utilization level, was of no help. After several frustrating attempts to apply the instruction, the learner simply took the computer home and played with it, exploring all the possible combinations and permutations without risk of error. After many opportunities to explore and discover how the machine and programs worked, the learner reached the inquiry level, at which she was able to make sense of the instruction book in relation to her own constructed understandings, some of which were adapted to make operation more efficient and to fully utilize the tool.

Children experience a similar cycle of learning, both when learning about technology and when learning with technology. While working in Pine Hill, New Mexico, at a Navajo elementary school, Rosegrant observed the learning cycle with 6- and 7-year-old children learning to write and using word processing. Early in their learning, children tended to overuse the delete function and not use other editing func-

Table 1. Cycle of Learning and Teaching

	What Children Do	*What Teachers Do*
Awareness	Experience Acquire an interest Recognize broad parameters Attend Perceive	Create the environment Provide opportunities by introducing new objects, events, people Invite interest by posing problem or question Respond to child's interest or shared experience Show interest, enthusiasm
Exploration	Observe Explore materials Collect information Discover Create Figure out components Construct own understanding Apply own rules Create personal meaning Represent own meaning	Facilitate Support and enhance exploration Provide opportunities for active exploration Extend play Describe child's activity Ask open-ended questions—"What else could you do?" Respect child's thinking and rule systems Allow for constructive error
Inquiry	Examine Investigate Propose explanations Focus Compare own thinking with that of others Generalize Relate to prior learning Adjust to conventional rule systems	Help children refine understanding Guide children, focus attention Ask more focused questions—"What else works like this?" "What happens if . . . ?" Provide information when requested—"How do you spell . . . ?" Help children make connections
Utilization	Use the learning in many ways; learning becomes functional Represent learning in various ways Apply learning to new situations Formulate new hypotheses and repeat cycle	Create vehicles for application in real world Help children apply learning to new situations Provide meaningful situations in which to use learning

Source: Reprinted from S. Bredekamp & T. Rosegrant, eds., Reaching Potentials: Appropriate Curriculum and Assessment for Young Children, *Volume 1. (Washington, DC: NAEYC, 1992), 33.*

tions, such as insert, block select, copy, move, or typeover. At this level in understanding the writing process, the children are aware that when writers write, they throw things out. In the exploration phase, the children seem to see the word processor like a Pacman gobbling up words. The story produced at this point in their understanding might be "The dog got dirty. He got in with horses. He was stinky. We gave him a bath." As the children become more inquiring writers and explore the functions of word processing, they realize that each of these sentences is an idea, and they learn to add more description, necessitating inserting text and moving blocks of text to rearrange the order. More aware of audience, the writers begin to try to interest the reader. The beginning of the story changes: "Sebastian came home and we wouldn't let him in the house. Why?" In this situation the children demonstrate the learning cycle on two levels: in learning to write and in learning word processing. Awareness of ideas or functions is followed by exploration, which leads to inquiry (*who, what, when,* and *where* questions are asked) and then utilization of the learning for a specific goal, in this case, the ability to be strategic in telling a story and attempting to interest the reader.

Most preschool-age children in America have some awareness of computers because technology is so much a part of our culture. Young children see computers in operation in the grocery store or the doctor's office, and it is highly likely that computers are part of their parents' workplace, regardless of their occupation. For some young children, computers are also a part of their home environment. Just as preschools have found the need to add the microwave oven to the housekeeping corner to stimulate more realistic play, the computer has become a part of the early childhood program because it is a part of real life. Playing with computers, like pretending

to drive a car, is part of taking on adult roles in today's dramatic play. At this awareness level, children simply recognize the broad parameters of technology and acquire an interest in learning more.

The next level of the learning cycle is exploration. At this level of learning, children observe, collect information, discover, and construct their own understanding and personal meaning. Exploration is essential to concept development. At this level, children's concepts may not reflect conventional understandings, as is apparent in examples of constructive error. Some software developers discovered the importance of exploration to learning and moved beyond "drill and practice" programs to programs in which children have many choices and can produce many different outcomes.

When children learn *about* technology, they move fairly quickly to the inquiry and utilization levels of the learning cycle. All computers have certain conventional rule systems regarding their proper use and care. Again, hardware developers became more sensitive to the need to develop tools that young children could use easily, adapting their products for children's motor skills and not depending totally on keyboard knowledge.

At the same time, some efforts to develop machines for very young children (3s and 2s), such as touch pads or touch windows, necessitate hardware that has a very short applicability period and, in fact, requires that children unlearn certain responses as they get older. These limitations raise serious questions about introducing computers with very young children as the target users; if, however, 3s or older 2s are part of a multi-age group or have older siblings, they may engage as part of the group.

Children also learn *from* technology; programs can be written for any level of learning, from awareness to utilization. The most appropriate programs are those that enable children to control their learning and to control the machine itself. When children utilize their learning to solve problems, this process usually raises new questions, and the learning cycle repeats itself.

Conceptualizing learning as a recurring cycle from awareness to utilization provides a framework for evaluating the appropriateness of what children are learning about and from technology. Attempts to teach children at the utilization level before they have had the opportunity to become aware and explore are often ineffective; because most children are at the awareness and exploration stages of the learning cycle, the most appropriate software for young children supports this type of learning. We turn now to applying this framework to three aspects of technology: hardware, software, and the role of the teacher.

Learning with machines: Issues related to hardware and software

Computers, by nature, possess certain characteristics that qualify them as good teachers of young children. Computers have the potential to be infinitely patient and forgiving, completely individualized, eminently tolerant of mistakes, and emotionally neutral. Even the best teacher cannot help but communicate an attitude of exasperation when a child makes the same mistake repeatedly. Likewise, no teacher has unlimited patience when it comes to reading the same story as often as requested. Machines can and do possess these qualities; in using technology, educators must be careful to build on rather than diminish these strengths.

The computer is an inherently powerful machine that gets stripped of its power in too many situations. The "forgiving" nature of the machine is too often limited by a program that doesn't allow the user to correct any error at any point in time. If a misspelled word stops the action or returns the user to the first step in the program, then the expensive machine is rendered impotent. Similarly, if the program promotes simple rote learning rather than exploration, a machine costing thousands of dollars has been reduced to the power of a set of flashcards.

Machines also have inherent capacity that must be evaluated carefully. One rule of thumb that is somewhat counterintuitive is that very young children need very powerful machines; the quality of graphics, sound, animation, and visuals that children need in order to learn demands the most powerful technology. Some people continue to think that because children are little, they can get by with yesterday's equipment; this error perpetuates the use of inappropriate software because outmoded hardware cannot support the newer, more challenging and interesting programs.

Computers also allow for multiple interfaces (ways of communicating and controlling the input). The technology is changing rapidly, but the computer definitely has multisensory capacities. Children can record their speech, as well as view, and they can listen. The various ways of interacting (with a touch screen, joystick, mouse, or keyboard) engage the sense of touch and employ various fine motor skills. (It is true that the smell of peppermint has yet to be produced, but then no one learning tool can or should do everything.)

Another capacity of the machine is that it can match the capacity or competence level of the user; of course, mismatches in either direction can also result. Expectations can be too high or too low. In either case, the power of the machine is diminished. One of the most difficult aspects of teaching young children is knowing how much and when to help; in helping children solve problems or develop skills, adults often err by either intruding (offering too much help and taking over) or withholding (failing to provide needed support or attention) (Bredekamp & Rosegrant 1992, p. 39). When a child addresses a problem or practices skills with a computer, for example, matching or creating patterns, the child can construct his or her own training needs; the child can ask for help or refuse it in a nonpunitive context. Of course, the machine's ability to meet children's needs for support depends on sensible software. One of the problems of the earliest software developed for children, for example, was that it was too intrusive and failed to give children enough control.

When children are exploring, they need opportunities for trial-and-error in a nonjudgmental environment. Too often, in classroom situations, children's errors (which are an important part of the learning process) are publicly displayed, and their confidence and self-esteem suffer. The computer provides a private place to practice and work out solutions without fear of failure. Especially during the primary grades, when children are expected to acquire an acceptable level of mastery of mathematical content and literacy, the computer can serve as a supportive tool for those children who have more than average difficulty succeeding.

The potentials of the hardware described must be respected if the machine is to be fully effective as a learning tool. Too often, these potentials are lost, and the culprit is the software. The characteristics of the hardware described earlier apply equally to software. Some software is not forgiving; an error (such as a typo) triggers a repeat of the entire loop of problems. Software can be designed to respect the learner. The learner should have control. The program can ask, Do you want harder problems? or it can give feedback.

One strength of the computer is its capacity for individualizing instruction. Teachers can identify those children who have

Especially in the primary grades, when children are expected to achieve a certain level of math competence and literacy, the computer can be a supportive tool for children who have more than average difficulty succeeding.

not mastered certain skills, the lack of which will haunt them later. Some examples might be understanding one-to-one correspondence in mathematics, memorizing the multiplication tables, or learning rules of punctuation. These basic skills require repetition that is not the best use of instructional time for many children. The few who need extra help can get it with specifically designed computer programs. Similarly, the advanced learner who seems to have mastered everything in the current curriculum but needs to remain with the peer group for social and emotional development can find extra challenge by moving ahead in programs that he or she controls.

In evaluating software for use with young children, no special rules are necessary; principles of good pedagogy should guide decisions. One such principle is that need should determine the use of the tool, rather than the use determining needs. So, for example, if kindergarten children want to make signs, they can employ a printing program. If third graders are writing reports, their first drafts can be done in word processing. But using word processing before keyboard skills are developed just because it is available inordinately slows down the writing process without a functional purpose. Similarly, computers can assist with displaying data in graphs or charts, but children should not use graphing capabilities if there is no data of interest or value to graph. As with so many aspects of education, professional judgment is required. Decisions about hardware and software are part of the role of the adult, a discussion of which follows.

The role of the adult

The place of computers in the school or early childhood setting is determined by the adult. Different adult roles emerge, depending on whether the setting is the classroom or the computer laboratory. For younger children, the classroom (or home) is the most appropriate setting for interacting with computers. Pulling children out of the group into a computer laboratory demands rigid scheduling and takes away the other rich options from which children may choose. In kindergarten, preschool, or child care settings, if computers are used, they should be one of many classroom activity choices. In these settings, the teacher's role mirrors the role played in many other learning situations, as described in table 1. The teacher creates the environment in which children become aware and explore, and then acts to support their exploration and inquiry in many different ways. The children and the teacher learn something new together as they engage in the process of learning. The teacher does not have to be an expert but instead is a co-constructor of knowledge with children.

In the computer laboratory, the computer can be used clinically—to address a specific identified need of a child or small group. In these settings, programs can be selected and adult support provided for children who need more time, are stuck and not making progress, need a different approach from what has been tried, or are well ahead of their peers. Obviously, taking all the children in a group into a lab and doing the same program with them as whole group instruction once again denies the power of the machine as an individual teaching tool. Similarly, providing a variety of programs may seem like the best strategy, but too much variety denies the opportunity to gain depth of experience. Well-designed software can be explored on many levels with different experiences and learning resulting. The desire to provide variety should not replace the opportunity for children to gain depth of experience and revisit programs to discover new things.

Conclusion

Technology—including video and audiotapes and, especially, computers—should not be abandoned because it has at times been misused or because mismatches have occurred in the past. The potentials of technology are far-reaching and ever-changing. The risk is for adults to become complacent, assuming that their current knowledge or experience is adequate. Technology is an area of the curriculum, as well as a tool for learning, in which teachers must demonstrate their own capacity for learning. If teachers themselves become models of exploration and inquiry, children are likely to follow. Research demonstrates that computers can make a difference in a child becoming literate or not and can support self-esteem through the process. Sometimes a child who is not imaginative or verbal during other activities will demonstrate these capabilities when using computers. Computers can be an alternative way of making sure that children experience success. All of these potentials are achieved if, and only if, adults engage in the process of decision making. Computers cannot take the place of teachers any more than teachers can take the place of computers; but together the learning environment can be improved, and computers can be a powerful tool to help children reach their full potentials as learners and decision makers.

References

Bredekamp, S., & T. Rosegrant. 1992. Reaching potentials through appropriate curriculum: Conceptual frameworks for applying the guidelines. In *Reaching potentials: Appropriate curriculum and assessment for young children, Vol. 1,* eds. S. Bredekamp & T. Rosegrant. Washington, DC: NAEYC.

Rosegrant, T. 1984. The use of microcomputers with speech technology to support beginning readers. Paper presented at the annual meeting of the American Educational Research Association, San Francisco, CA.

Rosegrant, T., & R. Cooper. 1986. *The talking text writer: Professional guide.* New York: Scholastic.

**Susan W. Haugland and
Daniel D. Shade**

Chapter

5

Software Evaluation for Young Children

Since developmentally appropriate practices were defined in 1987 (Bredekamp 1987), their importance in early childhood classrooms has become increasingly apparent. More and more early childhood educators are familiar with what constitutes developmentally appropriate practice and recognize its importance to young children's healthy development.

Computer software in a developmentally appropriate classroom should be developmentally appropriate as well; all too often it is not. Teachers who would never consider using worksheets with young children frequently select software that turns the computer into an electronic worksheet. Yet research has shown that the kind of software that teachers select may have a dramatic effect on how often children use computers and on their developmental gains in key areas, including cognitive development and creativity (Haugland 1992).

Open-ended discovery programs, frequently called *microworlds* (Papert 1980; Haugland & Shade 1990) or *simulations,* provide children the opportunity to explore an environment, make choices, and then find out the impact of these decisions on their microworld. These two types of software—open-ended and drill-and-practice—provide vastly different learning environments for young children and appear to facilitate diverse developmental outcomes.

This chapter addresses software selection and provides guidelines regarding appropriate software for young children. Although research on computer software is very limited, we highlight insights from key studies. We also review evaluation systems currently available to assist in software selection and assess the status of the hardware and software market. With technology changing rapidly, there has been a surge of software development. The key question from early childhood educators is, How much of this software meets the developmental needs of young children?

What research tells us

Two research studies have directly assessed the effects of developmental (open-ended) and nondevelopmental (drill-and-practice) software on young children. The first study (Haugland 1992) compared the effects of developmental and nondevelopmental software on preschool children's cognition, creativity, and self-esteem. For an eight-month period, three classrooms of 4-year-old children were exposed to computers for one hour, three days weekly, during self-selected activity time. Children in the fourth classroom did not have computer exposure. Of the three classrooms where children used computers, one classroom had nondevelopmental software (drill-and-practice), the second had developmental software (open-ended), and the third had developmental software reinforced with supplemental activities.

Children were assessed using a battery of assessment instruments. The children in all of the classes with computer exposure had significantly greater gains in self-esteem. Children using nondevelopmental software demonstrated signifi-

cantly less creativity; their scores dropped by an astonishing 50%. This drop did not take place when children had no computers or when they used developmental (open-ended) software. Clearly, nondevelopmental software may have a detrimental effect on children's creativity, a finding that should concern anyone using drill-and-practice software with young children.

Children exposed to the open-ended software had significant gains on measures of intelligence, nonverbal skills, structural knowledge, long-term memory, and complex manual dexterity. When computer use was supplemented with hands-on activities that reinforced the major objectives of the software, children gained in all of these areas, as well as in verbal skills, problem solving, abstraction, and conceptual skills.

The type of software the children used appeared to have a dramatic effect on their computer interactions and their developmental gains from these experiences. It is important to reiterate that this study took place over an eight-month period; these are not the results of a two-week, two-group study.

A second investigation of how different kinds of software affect children (Shade 1994) focused on children's emotional responses to developmental and nondevelopmental software. Half of the 72 children, ages 4 to 8, used the computer with a peer, and the other half used the computer by themselves. Each child was videotaped for three 10-minute sessions as she or he used software randomly selected from each of three levels of software developmental appropriateness (high, medium, and low), as defined by Haugland and Shade (1990). Children's facial expressions of emotion (e.g., interest, joy, anger, sadness) and other affect-related behaviors (e.g., self-absorption, physical exuberance) were examined as a function of the child's age, the child's gender, the presence of a peer, and the developmental appropriateness of the software. This was not the children's first exposure to computers, but it was their first encounter with this software.

Perhaps the most important outcome of this study was the discovery that, regardless of age, gender, or social condition, children expressed no negative affect (anger, fear, sadness, disgust) when they were presented with any type of software. Rather, children's facial expressions exhibited a high degree of interest, joy, and surprise to all three levels of software appropriateness. This fully replicated the earlier findings of Hyson (1985). Haugland (1992) also found that the young children in her study (reviewed previously) spent twice as much time using nondevelopmental or drill software than software designated as open-ended and discovery oriented. These findings imply that young children are not very discriminating with computer software. Like adults who surf through cable TV channels, watching anything that catches their interest, young children are drawn to the exciting potential of computer software. Being inexperienced with computers, they are just as impressed with the "happy faces" and "silly animations" of drill software as they are with the multitude of paint tools in a drawing program.

Teachers, therefore, play an important role in carefully selecting good software that offers a rich world of exploration possibilities. Just because drill-and-practice software, with its gamelike format and happy rewards, is fun to use does not mean that it is educationally sound. As NAEYC (1991) has noted, "enjoying the curriculum is an important but insufficient criterion for curriculum selection" (p. 31). If even a poorly designed software program stimulates high levels of engagement and positive affect in children, one could easily be convinced that something valuable is happening in the

Teachers play an important role in carefully selecting good software that offers a rich world of exploration possibilities.

computer center, but this is not always the case. Teachers must carefully select software in accordance with their philosophy of teaching and curriculum.

Few other research studies have assessed types of software and their effect on young children's development. Consistently, researchers have identified and documented differences based on the kinds of software children used (see Shade n.d.). Hyson (1985) noted that a drawing program tended to elicit more engagement and planning than did a program in which children counted or created a face using predesigned components. Other studies have compared computer-assisted instruction (CAI) programs to open-ended discovery software. CAI programs, formerly identified as programmed learning, have a drill-and-practice format, in which children are taught to select the correct response and are then rewarded.

Clements and Nastasi (1992) recently summarized the research in children's behavior as a function of software type. Children exposed to CAI exhibited more competitive behaviors, avoided the exchange of ideas, became more dependent on the teacher for assistance, and became bored with paper-and-pencil tasks. In contrast, children exposed to open-ended programs displayed more wondering and hypothesizing, formulated and solved their own problems, collaborated with a partner, evaluated their own work more positively, were more motivated in learning settings, and had a more positive attitude toward learning.

Although research lags somewhat behind the rapidly changing technology of computer software, the available evidence does suggest some meaningful indicators to teachers of young children. Research indicates that the kinds of software made available to young children may significantly influence their development in key areas, as well as important behaviors such as cooperation and motivation, which predispose children to learning. In addition, the research suggests that children are not discriminating in the computer programs that they will play with and enjoy; it is up to teachers to select software that fosters children's development and is integrated with the curriculum as a whole.

Software evaluation systems

In a recent survey of early childhood educators, respondents consistently expressed concerns regarding the difficulty of selecting good-quality software (Haugland & Shade 1994). The software market is booming, with many new and diverse programs emerging every month. Selecting high-quality software from this myriad of programs is a tremendous challenge. Hype on software can describe the program in a manner that is vastly different from how the program actually functions with young children. Previewing programs is not only very time consuming but cumbersome and expensive. In addition, some programs are very difficult to evaluate fairly until the true consumers, children, use the program.

Several evaluation systems are available to help educators select appropriate software. Table 1 illustrates a questionnaire that was sent to a diverse pool of evaluation systems. Eight evaluation systems responded to the survey, and the results are summarized in table 2.

It is important to select an evaluation system that is congruent with the philosophical approach of the program in which the software will be used. Fite (1993) emphasized, "in order to use computers effectively, we must ... choose quality software that supports our goals, thereby insuring that (1) the computer instruction reflects a philosophy similar to the teaching philosophy, (2) it helps children solve problems independently, and (3) it enhances a classroom curriculum" (p. 19). The philosophical approach, as well as the most important factors that each system uses when evaluating software, provide important keys for identifying the system that best meets a particular individual's or program's needs. A description of each of the software evaluation systems follows.

Children's Software Revue. *Children's Software Revue* is a relatively new publication founded by Warren Buckleitner, formerly of High/Scope. *Children's Software Revue* is based upon a philosophy of children being active learners who construct knowledge. Children's developmental competency— such as their ability to use a mouse and their reading ability—responsiveness of the program, and the program's meaningfulness to a young child provide a philosophical framework for program evaluation. Software is evaluated for children ages 3 to 12. To date, 866 programs have been evaluated, 60 of which have been child tested. To be evaluated, software is sent to a test family for two weeks or more, after which the family completes a form, rating the software on ease of use, value, and overall utility. The software review team then screens the software and compares its ratings with the family's ratings. If differences exist, another family tests the software. *Children's Software Revue* has identified six factors as being most important to good-quality software: ease of use, degree to which it is childproof, ability to educate, ability to entertain, design features, and value.

Binghamton City School District. The computer services department of the Binghamton City School District has

Table 1. Software Evaluation Systems Survey

1. How is software evaluated using your system?

2. What are the most important factors for quality programs using your system of software?

3. Is your evaluation based upon a philosophical approach? If so, please describe that approach.

4. How many programs have been evaluated to date?

5. Do you evaluate software for a particular group?

Yes   No

If so, what is the range?

6. Select and describe the five best software programs.

   a.

   b.

   c.

   d.

   e.

Table 2. Evaluation Systems

System	Number of Programs	Age Range	Philosophical Approach
Binghamton City School District Computer Services Department	1000+	5–18	All children can learn and should have access to computer technology.
Children's Software Revue	866	3–12	Children are active learners.
Florida Center for Instructional Technology Micro Education Software Evaluations	2,000	5–18	Educators' expert knowledge and experience are key in software evaluation.
Haugland/Shade Developmental Software Evaluation	500	3–8	Software should be compatible with developmentally appropriate practice and the Piagetian approach.
High/Scope Guide	514	2½–8	Children are active learners and should be in control of the computer environment.
Iowa City Community Schools	1,232	5–18	Children construct knowledge through active learning and experience.
Peak Learning, Inc., Educational Software Review Catalog	450	2–18	Children should be engaged in learning.
Technology and Learning	1000+	5–18	None

Most Important Factors			Telephone Number
• Ease of learning • Ease of use • Congruence with curriculum	• Ability to engage student interest • Ability to make use of computer capabilities		607-762-8100
• Ease of use • Extent to which it is childproof • Ability to educate	• Ability to entertain • Design features • Value		313-480-0040
• Pedagogicality • Appropriate use of technology characteristics	• Ease of use • Originality/creativity		813-974-3470
• Age appropriateness • Child control • Clear instructions • Expanding complexity	• Independence • Process orientation • Real-world model • Technical features	• Trial-and-error • Transformations • Antibias deduction	Susan W. Haugland 314-651-2952; Daniel D. Shade 302-831-8563
• Ease of use • Interactiveness • Ability to deliver on promises	• Effective use of computer's capacity		313-485-2000
• Consistency with the instruction paradigm	• Students are power users, not responders		319-339-6800
• Educational value • Ability to challenge • Learner has an active role • Role models transcend gender and race	• Complexity • Nonviolent • Handling of child's errors • Technical sophistication	• Age appropriateness • Customization • Difficulty of manuals and installation	
• Interface and ease of use • Richness and depth of content • Usefulness and effectiveness of features	• Age appropriateness and appeal • Degree of open-endedness and flexibility	• Appropriate, useful application of computer technology • Clear documentation and good support	513-847-5900

evaluated hundreds of software programs for grades K–12. Teachers and students use software and then rate it, using a simple form. Their evaluation is based upon the philosophy that all children can learn and that all children should have access to computer technology. The factors that this evaluation system finds most important in identifying quality programs are ease of learning, ease of use, congruence with curriculum, ability to engage student interest, and ability to make use of the computer's capabilities.

Developmental Software Evaluation Scale. The Developmental Software Evaluation Scale, developed by Susan W. Haugland and Daniel D. Shade, is designed to reflect a Piagetian developmental approach to learning. Young children learn best by doing, interacting, and exploring, rather than by watching and/or listening. Children are intrinsically motivated to discover, to experiment, and to learn. They are ready for and capable of learning a wide variety of skills, abilities, and concepts. The key is presenting the concepts and skills at a level that the child is ready to learn, using a method that reflects the child's interests and needs. The software is evaluated on 10 criteria, and then an antibias deduction is calculated to ensure that the software reflects our society's diversity. Software that scores 7.0 or above is considered developmentally appropriate; below 7.0 the software is considered inappropriate for young children. To date, between 20 and 25% of the software programs evaluated have met the standard for developmentally appropriate software. Software is first evaluated without children, and then—if it scores 6.0 or above (after the antibias deduction)—it is field tested with children. Software scoring below 6.0 is not field tested, to prevent exposing children to nondevelopmental software. The criteria for software evaluation are congruent with NAEYC guidelines for developmentally appropriate practices (Haugland & Shade 1990). Criteria used for evaluation are age appropriateness, child control, clear instructions, expanding complexity (the software has a low entry—i.e., is easy to access—and a high ceiling—i.e., teaches difficult, complex knowledge or skills), independence, process orientation, real-world model, technical features, trial-and-error, and transformations (children have the power to change objects and situations). The antibias deduction includes universal focus, multiple languages, mixed gender, role equity, people of color, differing ages and abilities, and diverse family styles.

Florida Center for Instructional Technology. Micro Educational Software Evaluations by the Florida Center for Instructional Technology has evaluated approximately 2,000 software programs. The software evaluations are available in print and disk versions. For the past six months, the center has stopped evaluating software and has focused on the Technology Information for Teachers (TNT) Project, providing lesson plans of highly rated software to teachers. The software is evaluated by an experienced educator who uses it in its intended context. The Florida Center believes that evaluation is a highly subjective and heuristic process, drawing on expert experience and knowledge. Evaluators are selected through a careful screening process and then are paired with a mentor for the first year. Publishers have an opportunity to comment on the process and to clear up any discrepancies in program use. Evaluations have provided critical feedback to publishers, causing revisions of actual products and helping to improve future products. Micro Educational Software Evaluations bases its software evaluations upon four factors: pedagogicality (does learning occur?), appropriate use of technology characteristics (color, graphics, sound, interaction), ease of use, and originality and creativity (is the program better than a textbook?).

High/Scope Buyer's Guide to Software for Young Children. The *High/Scope Buyer's Guide* evaluates software for children 2-½ to 8 years of age. Since 1984, more than 600 programs have been evaluated, and discontinued software is routinely omitted. The 1993 edition included 514 titles. The evaluation system is not based upon a "formal" philosophical approach. The instrument was designed before any formal association with the High/Scope Educational Research Foundation. People (adults and children) from a variety of backgrounds were observed using different software packages to help get a feeling for what worked and what didn't. The instrument is based on the belief that children are active learners and should be in control of the computer environment. Software should be designed so that children can understand the tasks and content. Software is initially screened to determine the amount, if any, of child testing required and the timeframe for the evaluation. If child testing is deemed necessary, the software is installed in one of three computers in the High/Scope preschool. After a try-out period to gauge children's general reactions, the Early Childhood Software Evaluation Instrument is used. The instrument generates quantitative scores, which are used for ratings. Factors considered most important for high-quality programs are ease of use, interactiveness, a design with children in mind, ability to deliver on promises, and effective use of the computer's capacity.

Iowa City Community Schools. Iowa City Community Schools have evaluated 1,232 software programs for grades K–12. The software is evaluated according to its compatibility with their program, which uses a constructivist approach for math and science and a whole language philosophy for reading. A variation of the MicroSIFT Evaluation Form from Northwest Regional Educational Lab is used to evaluate the software, which is previewed by teachers and/or media specialists who work at the level of instruction at which the software would be used. Factors considered most important for high-quality programs are consistency with the instruction paradigm and the presence of applications that make the students "power users," not responders.

Peak Learning Educational Software Review and Catalog. Peak Learning, Inc., publishes an *Educational Software Review and Catalog,* containing approximately 450 software programs for children ages 2 to 18. Software is evaluated for IBM-PC, Macintosh, and Apple. Peak's philosophical approach is that the program must engage the child in learning. If parents have to force their child to sit at the computer, the child will not learn as much as if he chose to be there. If the child gets frustrated, the computer experience is a missed learning opportunity. To this end, Peak asks children to review some of the software and sponsors workshops during which the reviewers can get candid, firsthand reactions to the software. Peak Learning, Inc., has identified 10 factors as most important for high-quality programs: educational value, ability to challenge users to take an active part in learning, presence of role models that transcend gender and race, complexity, a potential for being a viable and nonviolent alternative to television and arcade games, how the program handles errors, technical sophistication, age appropriate-

Several software evaluation systems call for children to give their reactions to programs.

ness, availability of customization, and difficulty of accompanying manuals and installation.

Technology and Learning. *Technology and Learning* is a professional magazine for educators that has evaluated hundreds of programs for grades K–12 over the past 11 years. The publication has evaluated software in all curriculum areas and using all platforms. Teachers and administrators with access to children and classes conduct the evaluation by "test driving" a given program with students for whom the soft-

ware is appropriate. Their evaluations are not based upon a particular philosophical approach. Reviewers at *Technology and Learning* consider the following factors most important for high-quality programs: interfacing, richness and depth of content, usefulness and effectiveness of features, age appropriateness and appeal, open-endedness, flexibility, a useful application of computer technology, clear documentation, and good support.

Software evaluation

As these reviews make clear, software evaluation is highly esoteric. Yet a careful look at each overview reveals a large number of important factors that are a part of each evaluation system surveyed. In an effort to provide a useful tool to teachers and be fair to all of the survey respondents, we have constructed a checklist for teachers to use when evaluating software for their classrooms. Although extensive rewriting of important factors was necessary to make the checklist as self-explanatory as possible, it is based on all of the evaluation systems surveyed. We have also tried to eliminate redundancy. Furthermore, we do not propose that the checklist replace any of the systems overviewed. In fact, we suggest that teachers carefully read the evaluation overviews to pick the system that best fits their teaching philosophy. Having done that, teachers can either select software from that system's recommendations or use that system's criteria to evaluate software themselves.

The checklist is extensive but is designed to be easily administered. The bulk of a teacher's time will be spent actually looking at the software program, not filling out the checklist. We cannot overemphasize the importance of two activities:

taking a comprehensive look at the program and then child testing the program if it meets the evaluating teacher's standards. Taking a comprehensive look at software means exploring everything that it is intended to do. If the software has multiple programs, then that means playing every level to completion. If the program is a microworld, then the teacher-evaluator must push the software to its limits (e.g., try every paint tool). This process is necessary to avoid the mistakes made from selecting software based on just a cursory look. It is possible to be fooled by exciting animation and graphics only to realize later that the program has no depth. A comprehensive look at the software is necessary to use the checklist. For example, one must know how gender is represented or if the software is not childproof. A teacher in this role should think of herself as a test pilot, stressing the software to its utmost limits to see where it begins to fall apart.

When child testing software, however, remember the cautions expressed earlier about children's lack of negative affect regardless of type of software and their tendency to spend more time on drill software because of its game-like design. Children like computers and are drawn to them, but children are not mature enough to be discriminating users. If you place a bowl of candy in the classroom, children will be drawn to it as well. Without supervision they will consume the entire bowl. Although a piece of candy or two will not harm children, a consistent diet of candy can lead to complex health problems. Consequently, it is essential to note what children actually do with a program, not just the fact that they like it. Several years ago at a summer camp organized by one of the authors, a language arts program based on Sesame Street characters was introduced to the children. Camp teachers and staff were excited by the children's initial positive response to the soft-ware. However, before long, teachers realized that the children—mostly boys—who were attracted to the software were drawn by the video game format of the program and that they were circumventing the educational aspects of the program to get to the "game." After several days the teachers removed the software from the classroom because the group of five to seven boys who gathered around to play that particular program every day would do nothing else. Child testing the software is important, but teachers must do so with caution. Teachers must remember that they have the final word.

Status of hardware and software

According to a report by the Software Publishers Association (1993), spending on personal computer technology in U.S. schools rose nearly 20% in the 1992–93 school year. An additional 13% increase in spending was projected for the 1993–94 school year. According to this report there are nearly 4.5 million computers in American schools, and among anticipated peripheral purchases, the report predicted that CD-ROM drives would increase by 72% during the 1993–94 year. Given this proliferation of hardware, software sales have undoubtedly increased as well.

What is not evident in this report is that we have been in the midst of a hardware shakeout for the past five years or so, best exemplified by Buckleitner's (1994) report on software releases categorized by hardware platform (IBM MPC, Mac CD-ROM, etc.). With all platforms combined, the following picture emerged for 1993: 157 (60%) educational software releases for IBM and compatibles (including Windows and CD-ROM versions); 97 (37%) releases for Macintosh (includ-

Figure 1. A Checklist for Evaluating Software for Young Children

CHILD FEATURES

- Active Learning Emphasized —
- Age Appropriate Concepts —
- Child Controlled Interaction —
- Child is Agent of Change —
- Children Can Stop Anytime —
- Children Set the Pace —
- Child Uses Independently —
- Concrete Representations —
- Concrete Reps. Function —
- Creativity (Divergent Thinking) —
- Discovery Learning —
- Engages Student Interest —
- Experimentation Is Possible —
- Intrinsically Motivating —
- Logical Learning Sequence —
- Low Entry, High Ceiling —
- Not Skill Drilling —
- Makes Learning Fun —
- Models World Accurately —
- Open-Ended —
- Operate From Picture Menu —
- Process Highlighter —
- Process not Product Oriented —
- Simple & Precise Directions —
- Speech Used When Helpful —
- Teaches Powerful Ideas —
- Verbal Instructions & Help —

TEACHER FEATURES

- Can be Customized —
- Childproof —
- Curriculum Congruence —
- Delivers on Ad Promises —
- High Educational Value —
- High Value per Dollar —
- Mixed Gender/Role Equity —
- Mult. Languages Available —
- Represents Differing Ability —
- Represents Differing Ages —
- Represents Alt. Family Styles —
- Represents People of Color —
- Supplemental to Curriculum —
- Understandable Users Manual —
- Universal Focus (all children) —

TECHNICAL FEATURES

- Animation Other than Reward —
- Aesthetically Pleasing —
- Available on Mac & IBM —
- Corresponding Sound Effects —
- Corresponding Music —
- Designed with Children in Mind —
- Digitized Human Speech Used —
- Easy Installation on Hard Drive —
- Fast Installation and Set Up —
- Max Use of Computer's Power —
- No Gratuitous Music & Sounds —
- Realistic Sound Effects/Music —
- Realistic, High-Res Graphics —
- Runs Quickly--Min. Waiting —
- Speech is Clear and Distinct —

Name of the Program: _____

Publisher: _____

Special Skills or Scaffolding Required by Children: _____

Content Appropriate for Integration into My Curriculum: _____

Age Range Indiated on Box: _____ Child-Tested (yes/no): _____

This Program is Appropriate for My Students (yes/no): _____

This Program Contains Valuable Educational Concepts (yes/no): _____

This Program Contains Powerful Ideas and Concepts (yes/no): _____

NOTES:

The above checklist has been developed from the overviews of the various software evaluation methods reviewed in this chapter. No effort has been made to compute a score based upon this checklist. Rather it is intended that as a teacher fills out the checklist, s/he will come to a general decision about the appropriateness of the program. This form may be duplicated for personal and classroom use.

---

ing CD-ROM titles); and 8 releases (3%) for the Apple II family of computers. Clearly, educators have only two platforms from which to choose—IBM and compatibles and Macintosh. With limited budgets, schools have to choose equipment that provides the most options for the dollar.

Yet a recent survey of 160 teachers of young children performed by Haugland and Shade (1994) indicated that 64% were still using Apple II computers. Adding the 24% who were using Macintosh computers raises the proportion of teachers from this sample using Apple computers to 88%. Software manufacturers seem to be concentrating on releasing software for IBMs and compatibles, making appropriate software more difficult for teachers to find for other hardware.

Furthermore, according to an analysis done by Shade and Haugland in 1993, a least 75% of the software that has been released, including new software programs and upgrades of old ones, is of the drill-and-practice nature, hence, between 20 and 25% is of the open-ended, discovery type discussed earlier. This 20 to 25% has been incrementally increasing in each of the past two years. In addition, Shade (1992) compared software scores based on the Developmental Software Evaluation Scale to award-winning programs and found that the majority of software winning awards was drill-and-practice. He concluded that most software awards are based upon quality of graphics and sound (where change has been most evident during the past 10 years). Shade continued this analysis and reported the results elsewhere (Shade & Haugland 1993).

These studies showed a slight increase in the number of awards for open-ended, discovery software—an encouraging sign despite the fact that winning an award does not always necessarily mean that a software program is appropriate for young children.

Haugland and Shade (1994) asked 160 teachers what they would like software publishers to know. Respondents indicated that they would like more software designed for young children. It appears that this wish is beginning to be fulfilled. Teachers also stated that they wanted more software in the content areas of science, problem solving, creative writing, math, and foreign language, and software that could be used in group activities and had a thematic focus. This wish suggests that teachers of young children desire to integrate computers across their curriculum rather than following the path of the integrated learning system (super-software package that provides a complete math or reading curriculum). Another major message that teachers wished to convey to software publishers was their desire to see an end to the continued production of computerized worksheets (drill-and-practice software). These responses are encouraging because they reflect NAEYC guidelines for developmentally appropriate practice.

Conclusion

In this chapter we have endeavored to present brief overviews of some of the many software evaluation systems available today. We have tried to stress the importance of the teacher's role in selecting software and have provided criteria for software evaluation, as well as current information on hardware and software production. We hope that this information will be useful as teachers endeavor to integrate computers across their classroom curricula.

Clearly, much work still lies ahead if we are to influence the production of software for children. Software evaluation systems need to conform to current developmental theory and early childhood philosophy. We advocate that NAEYC's guidelines for developmentally appropriate practice and content become the accepted theoretical basis for what we do with young children and computer software. Hardware and software manufacturers need to listen to early childhood teachers and educators and begin providing the kinds of products that teachers see as appropriate for their classrooms. Software manufacturers especially need to become cognizant of the kinds of hardware that many early childhood teachers are actually using and must continue to make products for that user base.

Finally, teachers need training in software evaluation techniques. They need to know how to select software that is developmentally appropriate and how to integrate it into their ongoing classroom curriculum. The National Council for Accreditation of Teacher Education (NCATE) has been the leader in addressing this issue by including technology training into their standards of accreditation. According to NCATE (1992), prospective teachers of young children should be trained in knowledge about the "impact of technology and societal changes on schools" and provided with "knowledge about and appropriate skills in . . . instructional technology" (p. 50). Surely the time has come to embrace these standards and prepare teachers to play a central role in determining the place and potential of computer software as another learning material.

References

Bredekamp, S., ed. 1987. *Developmentally appropriate practice in early childhood programs serving children from birth through age 8.* Exp. ed. Washington, DC: NAEYC.

Buckleitner, W., ed. 1994. *Children's Software Revue* (Newsletter), 2 (4). (Available from Mr. Warren Buckleitner, 520 North Adams St., Ypsilanti, MI 48197-2483.

Clements, D.H., & B.K. Nastasi. Computers and early childhood education. In *Advances in school psychology: Preschool and early childhood treatment directions,* eds. M. Gettinger, S.N. Elliot, & T.R. Kratochwill, 187–246. Hillsdale, NJ: Lawrence Erlbaum.

Fite, K. 1993. A report on computer use in early childhood education. *Ed Tech Review* (Spring/Summer): 18–24.

Haugland, S.W. 1992. The effect of computer software on preschool children's developmental gains. *Journal of Computing in Childhood Education* 3 (1): 15–30.

Haugland, S.W., & D.D. Shade. 1990. *Developmental evaluations of software for young children: 1990 edition.* New York: Delmar.

Haugland, S.W., & D.D. Shade. 1994. Early childhood computer software. *Journal of Computing in Childhood Education* 5 (1): 83–92.

Hyson, M.C. 1985. Emotions and the microcomputer: An exploratory study of young children's responses. *Computers in Human Behavior* 1: 143–52.

National Association for the Education of Young Children. 1991. Guidelines for appropriate curriculum content and assessment in programs serving children ages 3 through 8. *Young Children* 46 (3): 21–38.

National Council for Accreditation of Teacher Education (NCATE). 1992. *Standards, procedures and policies for the accreditation of professional education units* (49–50). Washington, DC: NCATE.

Papert, S. 1980. *Mindstorms: Children, computers and powerful ideas.* New York: Basic.

Shade, D.D. 1992. A developmental look at award-winning software. *Day Care & Early Education* 20 (1): 41–43.

Shade, D.D. 1994. Computers and young children: Software types, social contexts, gender, age and emotional responses. *Journal of Computing in Childhood Education.* 5(2): 177–209.

Shade, D.D., & S.W. Haugland. 1993. *1993 developmentally appropriate software awards.* Paper presented at the annual conference of the National Association for the Education of Young Children, November, Anaheim, CA.

Software Publishers Association. 1993. *U.S. K–12 schools spent $2.1 billion on educational technology in 1992/93; spending expected to grow 13% in 1993/94.* News release. Washington, DC: Author.

**Jane Davidson and
June L. Wright**

The Potential of
the Microcomputer in
the Early Childhood Classroom

C hildren learn by doing; therefore, our goal as educators is to create experiences that will encourage children to be actively involved with the world around them (Bredekamp 1987). Earlier chapters have suggested that the computer can offer microworlds that increase children's ability to control their environment and to represent their ideas symbolically, in word and picture. Researchers report that the microcomputer offers children another way to play (Wright & Samaras 1986), enhancing social, emotional, and cognitive development (Clements 1987; Haugland 1992).

As early childhood educators we know that children learn best when they are free to explore their environment, developing their own projects without predetermined goals set by others. We already know how to introduce activities and materials to children in a way that encourages them to experiment with various techniques. The emphasis is on the child's control of the process, thus helping each child develop autonomy. We know that a sense of personal accomplishment and self-worth is vital to every young child's development. So, using what we already know about children and teaching, we need only elaborate on the specific techniques and insights that are helpful in facilitating a playful computer environment.

This sounds easy, but to the many early childhood educators who do not feel comfortable with computers themselves, this is a large order. How will teachers, who have not grown up playing with microcomputers, become convinced that they can facilitate a playful computer environment in which children can explore this new way of learning? In *Interactions in the Classroom: Facilitating Play in the Early Years,* Trawick-Smith (1994) defines play as any activity that is self-chosen, open ended, spontaneous, and enjoyable. If children learn best when they are playing, we might also consider that teachers will learn to use the computer best when they choose a program they really enjoy and *play* with it. Teachers often move through the same stages as children when interacting with their first computer program:

- discovery—a growing awareness that what appears on the screen is what I created or selected

- involvement—motivation to achieve mastery of basic commands and sequences

- self-confidence—ability to execute a plan and to predict outcomes

- creativity—invention of solutions, design of challenges for others, and original creations

As with children, teachers also need freedom, support, and encouragement when tackling a new endeavor—getting to know the computer.

Underlying the creation of a classroom in which children playfully experience computer learning is the view that the early childhood curriculum is "as much a way of interacting with children as it is a collection of lessons or carefully constructed learning materials" (Trawick-Smith 1994, p. v). Indeed,

the critical issue of whether interaction with the computer will be meaningful and lead to learning is not which input device or program is used but how teachers ask questions, give encouragement, provide assistance, challenge children's thinking, and learn from their discoveries.

The goal of this discussion is to describe the creation of a classroom environment in which teachers and children view the computer as a remarkable plaything they can enjoy together. In such a classroom, teachers and children will gain self-esteem while learning to command this powerful tool. Together they can become confident and use the microcomputer to do increasingly complex things.

Implementing computer use in the classroom

All materials can be well used or misused. No material is magical. To ensure that computer use supports a developmentally appropriate program and facilitates the development of the whole child, we suggest that certain attitudes and assumptions about computers need to permeate the program.

1. Computer use is a social activity.

2. Computer use is a child-initiated and child-directed activity.

3. Computer software allows children to explore, experiment, and problem solve.

4. Computers offer new learning opportunities when unexpected things happen.

5. Computers are one of many materials in a developmentally appropriate classroom.

These assumptions and attitudes can provide a firm foundation for the design and implementation of the computer program. We will examine how each of them affects the classroom environment and teacher–child interactions.

Assumption #1: Computer use is a social activity.

Adults usually work at their computers independently, but most young children approach computer use as a social activity. They often will work together and share ideas. One of the easiest ways to communicate the joint nature of computer use is through the arrangement of the computer area. Placing two chairs in front of the computer tells children that it is to be used with a classmate. By locating two computers near each other, teachers can facilitate sharing of discoveries and ideas among the children. If the computer area is centrally located, other children are more likely to stop, watch, comment, and add to the social interaction that is occurring around the computer.

Teachers' interactions with children can reinforce the message of joint use that the environment sends to children. When teachers talk to the whole group gathered at the computer, not just the children currently controlling the keyboard or mouse, they communicate to the children that all of them are involved. Encouraging users to explain what they are doing when classmates wander over to watch will help the watchers quickly become part of the working group around the computer. It will also clarify the thinking of the child giving the explanation and promote peer teaching.

It is easy to assume that more is better. It might follow that if children benefit from using one or two classroom computers, then adding a third computer will increase potential growth. In fact, if too many computers are available, children are more likely to engage in solitary use rather than negotiating turns and compromises with other children. The ideal number of computers per class depends on each individual group of children.

When children work together, language is essential. Children must communicate their ideas to each other. If the children envision different outcomes, they must use their most persuasive language to convince the other children that their way is best. Because the computer has only one input device, communication between users is essential. It is interesting to listen to children designing a face when using *Facemaker*. One child might suggest one set of ears; the other may turn them down because they are "old people's ears"; another might propose the green ears "cause they are scary and we want our face to be scary, RIGHT??" These children are using sophisticated language techniques to sway people toward their point of view.

Open-ended software that provides many options from which to select is particularly good for group use. Children have to agree on the options that are to be selected and why certain selections are best. Difficulties with turn taking can prevent the social use of computers. Some software lends itself easily to sharing. When children use *Millie's Math House*, they can select shapes to construct a mouse house. Children can work together to create the house, taking turns selecting the shapes, or they may each take turns creating the entire house. Action is segmented in a way that makes defining the length of turns easy. Other software, such as drawing programs, do not provide obvious segments by which to define turns, and children may need more help in negotiating turns. A wise teacher will help children define methods for determining when to pass on control of the input device. When first introducing computers to the classroom, teachers may wish to select more "shareable" software to ensure that children's joint use begins with positive social interactions.

It is important for teachers to carefully observe the computer play in their classroom, assessing factors that encourage or discourage social use. Unexpected events may significantly affect the nature of computer use. Many teachers find that they want the children to become familiar with the process of creating with a program before introducing the printer. In one classroom of 4-year-olds, the children regularly played on the computers with friends, exploring many options, but when printers were added to the classroom, joint use decreased significantly. Observation showed that children became possessive of what they created once a permanent product was possible. Even pointing out that a copy could be printed for each user did not ease the problem greatly.

By using a switch box to connect two computers to a printer, children have more opportunity to print, which may make sharing easier. Duplicate pictures can be printed and placed in a book for the class library, thus focusing attention on shared learning. Parents often enjoy helping to create a library book related to a theme. In an open environment, none of us is too old to play!

Assumption #2: Computer use is a child-initiated and child-directed activity.

Independent use of computers by children depends on the presence of wisely selected software (see Haugland & Shade, chapter 5). In reviewing software, it is important to keep in mind the children's past experience with computers. Programs that may be too difficult for novice users may be independently used by chil-

dren who have had more experience with computers. Children's file management programs like *KidDesk* allow teachers to set up a unique selection of software for each child, thus avoiding the use of programs that would cause frustration for a particular child.

Software often has many different parts. Getting acquainted with all the potential uses of one piece of software can be overwhelming. When introducing new pieces of software, teachers should show children the minimal number of commands that make use possible. This focus makes the new program simple to use and leaves many wonderful things for children to discover on their own. For example, when using *Color Me,* a drawing program with a menu of options, the teacher might introduce only drawing with the mouse and perhaps how to use the menu to change colors. The children will soon discover the "fill" feature and develop an understanding of enclosed spaces based on successful and unsuccessful efforts to fill (with color or patterns) a shape they have drawn. Often discovery of the "erase" feature leads to delightful interactions. One 3-year-old filled the screen with green, then changed the cursor to white and began moving it back and forth across the screen announcing, "I'm cutting the grass like Dad does."

One way to communicate to children that they are able to use the computer independently is to be sure that there are times when a teacher is not in the computer area. If children are left to make their own decisions and solve their own problems, they will see the computer as something that they can control. They will also call on each other for help. The addition of voice to most early childhood software allows children much greater autonomy. In fact, young children often hold conversations with the voice and delight in declaring that they know something before the computer tells them the information. In *Electronic Easel*, children select primary colors to place in paint cans. The voice narrates, "You chose red," then "You chose yellow"; the child often interjects "And I made orange!" before the computer voice can complete its narration, "You made orange."

Assumption #3: Computer software allows children to explore, experiment, and problem solve.

It is important to select software that children can explore in their own way and control without worrying about making a mistake. Computer programs that respond purposefully to children's exploration encourage further investigation. These software programs enhance children's learning much more than do programs that accept only a very limited number of possibilities or that, at the other extreme, give random visual response to any input. A growing number of programs offer both a divergent (explore and discover) mode and a convergent (find the answer) mode.

For young children, the computer is most appropriate as an open-ended material whose value is in the use, not in the end product. When children want to know what a certain key or command will do, they are much bolder about trying it than are their teachers. The rate and order of discovery of the *Color Me* menu, mentioned previously, varies with the child. Some children are intrigued by changing the width of a line; others, by filling enclosed spaces or using the eraser. Some discover early on that they can also type letters and words on their pictures. Teachers who enthusiastically celebrate children's risk taking will find that children sharing of their discoveries with teachers and peers becomes the norm.

While using the computer, children often create and solve their own problems. Mark was using *Bald-Headed Chicken,* and he accidentally selected a sun from the menu. "I don't want that," he said in disgust. Beau suggested dropping the sun off the screen. Sara's solution was to cover up the sun with some clouds. Jamie dealt with it by integrating the sun into the story: he made a sun family to go with the chicken family. Susie used the same scenario to create a joke: one chicken with 8 suns and a caption that read, "Why did the

Figure 1. *When several children were playing with the* **Bald-Headed Chicken** *program and accidentally selected a sun, Susie added seven more suns to create this joke. (D.C. Heath & Co.)*

chicken get so hot?" (see figure 1). These children were stretching themselves intellectually to arrive at goals they set for themselves.

Programs with features that empower teachers to make choices and set levels are often mastered by the children, as well. Children watch the teacher key in the password and set the level. When the teacher is gone, children delight in retyping the password, resetting the level, and waiting to "surprise the teacher." The key to promoting active learning is encouraging the children to experiment and not responding negatively when their experimentation exceeds our expectations, for instance, when it gives them access to the teacher menu!

Assumption #4: When unexpected things happen, computer interaction offers new learning opportunities.

Dealing with glitches or "bugs" is part of the process of using computers or any new or complex material. Children learn how to work with the computer by watching how the teacher responds when a problem arises. Children enjoy helping the teacher think through what might be wrong. They can help by checking to see if the disk is in right, whether the switches are turned on, whether the wires are plugged in, and so forth. Children learn quickly which things to check. This kind of activity makes them feel as though they are really in control of the computer. One 4-year-old reported that she had "fixed Daddy's computer for him! He didn't know the mouse wasn't plugged in, but I saw it, so I told him how to fix it!" she explained.

An inadequacy in the software can lead children to search for solutions. A 5-year-old dictated a letter to the designer of a drawing program when he discovered that even though the instruction card said that one could fill with white, the program did not allow it. In his kindergarten class he had seen programmers demonstrate how to change what a program does. From his experience he had learned that people design and can redesign a program. It is often easier to convince children to write requesting changes than to convince teachers that requests may make a difference.

Assumption #5: The computer is one of many materials in a developmentally appropriate classroom.

It is important to convey to children and parents that computers are not something special or unique; they are another tool that we can use as we choose. This concept can be communicated to the children in a number of ways. Placing the computers in the classroom, rather than in a lab, enables the children to use or not use them as they wish. It also promotes spontaneous involvement with the computer. For example, children may decide to use *Bailey's Book House* or *Magic Slate* to create invitations for a special party, real or imaginary.

By using a file management program that displays a number of programs, children can select the program they want, whether they can read or not, by clicking on a picture or *icon*. By our emphasizing the process rather than the product, children do not feel pressured to perform at the computer any more than at other centers. Teachers who are comfortable with microcomputers do not regard them as a special material but rather as providing one of the activities that make a classroom a good place for children to be, a place to grow and develop understanding of themselves and their world.

The development of the whole child

How do computers fit into the curriculum of the early childhood program? According to Bredekamp, "developmentally appropriate curriculum provides for all areas of a child's development: physical, emotional, social and cognitive through an integrated approach" (1987, p. 3). Teachers provide materials and activities that foster development in many different areas. Materials such as blocks are valued because they can be used to support physical, cognitive, and socioemotional growth. Computer play is another activity that can support many different areas of development.

Facilitating language development

Computer use can increase language fluency by providing wonderfully exciting topics that children want to discuss with teachers and peers. Language is elicited during dramatic play, by working with peers, through creating pictures, when dictating stories, and while using programs that talk.

As teachers, we know that dramatic play generates language. Children tend to use rich language to develop and sustain their imaginary play (Davidson n.d.). The computer offers another forum for dramatic play. The *Explore-a-Story* series allows children to invent and develop a pretend story using animated characters as the actors in the story. Children tend to narrate what they are doing as they move characters around on the screen. As Darshan moves the chicken in *Bald-Headed Chicken*, he says, "Now the chicken is going to the pond. It's thirsty, so it stops to drink."

Although pretend play can happen with any software, programs with moveable figures around which children can cre-ate their own stories lend themselves particularly well to computer dramatic play. Teachers can encourage story development by asking questions that will spark imaginative play: What is happening? Where is the chicken going? Why does he look sad? If the program has a print option, then printing various parts of the pretend-play episode may spark retelling of the story to the teacher or to peers.

Children also talk as they create with art materials. The story may be based on representational drawings, or it may accompany what appears to be abstract art. As Orion blobs bits of green all over the page, he explains, "It is raining all over the town, and the animals, and the robbers." He then begins covering up the page with black paint. "Now it is night, and the robbers can't see the treasure." Similar narration of artistic creation can be heard as children make pictures on the computer with graphics programs. If two children are working together, often a joint story will develop, with each child expanding on the ideas of the others. When teachers ask children to "tell me about your picture," children will realize that their stories and ideas are valued. Writing down words to go with the story will enable the child to hear the story again and again.

Children enjoy seeing their words captured in print. A word processing program is an ideal tool for doing this. It allows teachers to record the child's story at a conversational pace and to record longer stories than would be possible if the teacher were taking the dictation longhand. Computers can easily make multiple copies, so when two children create a story together, each child can have a copy. The teacher can also keep a copy for a class storybook. These books are read often and spur the other children to become authors so that they can have a story in the class book. Talking word processors, such as *Kid Works 2*, allow children to create stories with pictures, see the pictures turned into words, and hear the words read. Young children can listen to pictures verbally labeled, while more sophisticated users can see how their pictures turn into words and use these words to create stories.

Many of the newer programs talk, and some even record speech. In *Mickey's ABC's*, children press a letter, the computer says the letter and a word starting with the letter, then Mickey's actions and comments incorporate the word. For example, if a child types *L*, the computer will say *"L, as in light,"* while Mickey turns the light off in the room and says, "Dark, Huh?" Programs such as this allow children to hear labels for a wide variety of objects. They usually elicit language from the children, as well. *Just Grandma and Me* will recite words or whole sentences in English, Spanish, and Japanese. The potential for use in a bilingual classroom is endless!

When selecting software to encourage language, teachers should look for (1) programs that will elicit lots of excitement and the language that goes with it; (2) software that is open ended, allowing children to decide together what will happen; and (3) software that generates pretend play. Computer play encourages longer, more complex utterances, leading to the development of more fluent language.

Fostering physical development

Working on the computer stretches children's eye–hand coordination in a number of ways. When using the keyboard, children must be precise; hitting the wrong key may get unintended results. Also, it is important to hit the key quickly and then release it. A prolonged push may produce a string of the same letter, or it may make the computer rush through a menu or program too quickly. Small movements of mouse and joystick create large movements on the screen. It takes practice to know which hand motions will get the cursor to move to the desired place. The desire to control the computer motivates more careful hand motions.

Children can get frustrated when errors in precision create unexpected and unwanted results. Teachers can help children to deal with the frustration that such errors can cause.

1. Treat the problems matter-of-factly: "Sometimes computers don't do what we want them to. Let's see if we can find out how to fix the mistake."

2. Carefully sequence the software used in the classroom. When the mouse is first introduced, use software that allows more freedom of movement. Games that require precision, such as *Peanuts Maze Marathon,* should not be introduced until children have become comfortable controlling the mouse. Also, consider the size of menu items. If a child is still awkwardly manipulating the mouse, then it will be hard to position the cursor in small boxes on a menu.

Supporting socioemotional development

Our first assumption was that computer use is a social activity. When children use the computer together, they have to negotiate turns and resolve differences of opinion regarding the direction the game should take. As anywhere in the classroom, this negotiation process does not always proceed smoothly. Teachers can guide children toward finding solutions to problems that arise.

Peer teaching at the computer is common, with one child sharing his or her discoveries with another. Peer teaching requires children to build new social skills. With help from a teacher, children can learn the difference between *doing* a program for a child who is unsure and *explaining* the program. This is not an easy distinction. Teachers will need to consistently model and define useful helping methods.

Assumption #2 is that children initiate and di-rect their own computer use. By allowing children to use an "adult" machine, we help them to feel powerful, adding to their self-esteem. Children learn that they can create on the computer: they can create pictures, stories, and imaginary worlds. Creating is an extremely personal process. It is an expression of who the creator is. Such self-expression validates the importance of each child as an individual.

Fostering cognitive development

The early childhood classroom fosters children's cognitive growth. Often cognitive growth is seen narrowly, in terms of mastering specific skills—counting, identifying shapes and colors, matching and sorting objects. These skills are certainly a part of cognitive growth, but only a small part. Cognitive development is much broader than this. It involves making sense out of the world, exploring objects and materials to understand their properties, discovering the interaction between things, seeing the predictability of cause-and-effect relationships, generating and solving problems, and drawing conclusions—whether correctly or incorrectly—about how things happen and why.

Our third assumption was that children explore and experiment with computers, in other words, they investigate the properties of this material. First, children can explore the properties of the computer itself. What can it do? What parts

Peer teaching at the computer is common, with one child sharing his or her discoveries with another.

does it need to do this? Children are fascinated by the wires that connect the parts. Teachers can encourage this interest by using correct terms for the hardware and by facilitating discussion of what the various parts do and how the information gets from one part of the machine to another.

Children also investigate the properties of individual programs. When using a word processing program to type random letters, Darshan was amazed at how the writing scrolled up when he had reached the bottom of the screen. He typed quickly to get it to happen again. He searched for ways to get to the bottom faster, like using the TAB or the RETURN key. Children often will systematically test each key to see what, if anything, it will make the computer do. They discover that when they use different software, the keys do different things, and that each software package has its own limits. *Magic Crayon* will not allow children to move the cursor off the screen, but in *Where Did My Toothbrush Go?*, not only can children move the cursor off the screen, they can move objects off the screen and retrieve them, as well.

Teachers can foster cognitive development by creating an atmosphere that supports independent exploration. A wise teacher will ask children how they made the computer do something, rather than being the authority who tells the children how the computer works. Some of the teaching suggestions made during the discussion of assumption #2, child-initiated use of the computer, will also facilitate cognitive development. Selecting software that is open ended and allowing children to discover the options of new software on their own will provide them opportunities for exploration and problem solving.

Supporting the development of skills

Part of the learning or curriculum in the early childhood program involves practicing and mastering a wide variety of skills, such as hanging a coat on a hook, pouring from a pitcher, recognizing one's name in writing, and making a baster suck in water at the water table. Sometimes the skills will be teacher set. A teacher in a class of 4-year-olds might provide many opportunities for children to see and respond to their names in writing. Often the children will strive to master skills that they have chosen as goals. When peg boards are placed out in the classroom, some children will decide to sort the pegs so that each row is a different color. This is not a

goal that a teacher sets for the children but one that they have set for themselves.

Teachers can plan computer activities to support the development of skills. If name recognition is a goal that the teacher has set, then programs that integrate the child's name will support this goal. *KidDesk* displays the child's name on a pictured desk. In order to get to her desk, a child must first click on a picture symbol that has her name under it. Software that asks a child to type his name to begin the program, such as *Magic Crayon* and *Easy Street*, will make him pay careful attention to the letters in his name and the order of those letters. Keeping a basket with the children's names near the computer will provide a guide for those children who can recognize their names but do not know the letters well enough to produce their names in writing or typing. Many drawing programs include typing options. Children can be encouraged to add their name to the picture before printing. When teachers take dictation on a word processing program, children can enter their name as the author.

Often children will spontaneously use the computer or computer-related activities to practice skills being developed elsewhere in the classroom. A kindergarten class was developing pattern-making skills. The teacher provided a piece of software to practice patterns—*The Pond*, which entails moving a frog across the pond by hopping from lily pad to lily pad, following a repetitive pattern of turns and hops. The children, who were excited about pattern creation, spontaneously incorporated patterns into many other programs, as well. Christine made patterns in a word processing program by typing repetitive letter sequences. In classes using *Logo*, the children can enter a sequence, then have the computer repeat it endlessly, making an infinitely repeating pattern.

When using *Facemaker*, Lily programmed the face to move in a repetitive pattern: smile, wink, smile, wink, smile, wink. An off-computer version of *Facemaker* was available to help children learn the letters needed to move the facial features (Davidson 1990). Picture cards each display a letter that moves the *Facemaker* face and a face picture showing what action the letter creates. The children used the cards to plan a program for the face. The children then become the computer monitor—they are the face, making the various expressions in the program. When the class was studying patterns, children often built their program in patterns.

At times children use the computer to practice skills that are personally meaningful to them. When Kyle discovered the relationship between uppercase and lowercase letters, he often used the computer and the typewriter to print pairs of upper- and lowercase letters. Other children "count" on the computer by typing the numbers in order. Dan was frustrated when he typed the numbers because they all ran together, turning 1 2 (one, two) into 12 (twelve). He asked the teacher how to make a space, then typed the letters again with a space in between.

Enhancing thematic units by involving the computer

Thematic units are often used as a focus for the learning and development that occurs in the classroom. Teachers select a theme of interest to the children, then offer the children choices of many activities, stories, songs, and materials that relate to the theme. If the unit is "The Farm," the class may take a field trip to a farm. During the trip and when they return, the teachers talk with the children about what

Figure 2. *Using the Farm program, children can add animals and people to the scene, as Joshua did. The illustrated stories were collected in a class farm book.*

interested them. A web can serve as a pictorial representation of children's interests (Katz & Chard 1989). Teachers who are careful listeners will often be surprised at the depth of knowledge and breadth of interest that young children display (see figure 2 for a web of ideas of 4- and 5-year-olds at a Connecticut child care center, based on their comments about a trip to the farm).

Many activities are introduced by the teachers, such as opportunities for children to pretend to be farmers caring for animals in the dramatic play area and in piles of hay in the yard, to measure and pour grain in the sensory table, and to hear a farm story told to them from a bulletin board with moveable pieces and retell it later. Often children's excitement about the theme causes them to design their own activities and projects. Ben, who loves bulletin-board stories, likes to create his own version of the teacher's bulletin board at the free-art table. Other children may build fences and pens with blocks and create a huge cardboard barn. If they are fortunate enough to have computer-controlled robots, the children can create an active farmyard with the robots as animals. "Roamers" (Valiant Technology LTD, Elmhurst, IL) are new robots that receive commands from the children and, with hand-decorated covers, can be made to look like animals. In creating their farmyard, the children will be exploring directions and distance and preparing themselves for further adventures using the *Logo* language (see Wright, chapter 1; Clements, chapter 3).

The computer provides opportunities for both planned and spontaneous theme-related activities. Software can be selected that complements the unit. During a farm unit, *Sleep Brown Cow* enables children to create stories using a variety of farm animals. Using *Farm*, children can add animals and people to the scene (see figure 3). Farm stories for a class

Children enjoy manipulating computer-controlled robots, called "Roamers."

farm book can be written to accompany the computer pictures. *Rosie the Counting Rabbit* and *The Bald-Headed Chicken* depict eggs that hatch. *Mickey's ABC's* and *Farm* provide farm animal sounds to go with animated pictures. *Farm* also provides multicultural farm workers, who can be programmed by the children to speak in their own native languages. Even the sounds of the animals can be changed to match animal sounds from different countries (see *Cock-A-Doodle-Doo! What Does It Sound Like To You?* for an example of differences in how animals sound to people all over the world).

Unfortunately, due to the expense and the relatively limited number of good software packages available for young children, it is difficult to find software that directly relates to each chosen theme. Even though the software might not support a specific theme, teachers and children can adapt it to complement the unit. After a trip to the airport, teachers can use a word processor to record thank-you messages that the children dictate or to create signs for the airport being built in the block corner. Kindergartners and first and second graders can use *KidPix* to stamp airplane images on the runway they create. Children who are accustomed to having the computer as a tool in their classroom use it spontaneously to complement what they are doing. Banners and signs (*Print Shop*) are second nature to young computer experts. (For additional examples of integrating the computer into thematic units, see Appendix A.)

The computer does not have to be used to support every theme in the classroom. Teachers who plan with themes know that some themes do not lend themselves to support in certain interest areas; for example, an exploration of texture may not lend itself to computer play. But with other themes and interests, there are many ways to integrate computers. A class interest in books was a natural theme for computer support. The children dictated stories on the computer, created pictures for their stories, and used a computerized copy machine to enlarge and then copy their work. They bound the books and sold them in the dramatic play bookstore. For each theme, the computer should play an integral part only if its application is authentic.

As we grow in our expertise with multimedia applications, we will find ourselves scanning our own photos into the computer and creating our own slide shows and clip art for constructing pictures. We can even capture video clips and intersperse them with the written words and/or voices of the children. If these ideas seem hopelessly complicated, cheer up! Help is available from competent high school students! The possibilities are constantly unfolding as we explore appropriate uses of this powerful medium.

Conclusion

Teachers are being helped (and/or hindered) by a new trend in software publication. Teacher editions provide extensive options intended to help integrate the computer into the curriculum—lesson plans, activities, even workbook pages now accompany software. As with any material, we must assess the value of these additional options. Are they process- or product-oriented? Will using them promote problem solving and creativity or result in redundant review of what occurred dynamically on the screen? The fact that almost all drawing programs provide coloring book pages to be filled in should raise our awareness that we need to monitor the kinds of activities available on computers in light of guidelines for developmentally appropriate practice.

Just as children observe each other and get new ideas that they try to expand upon, so teachers can share with each other what is meaningful to their children when using a particular program. There are an increasing number of educators and parents sharing ideas and asking questions about computer usage online, using communication systems such

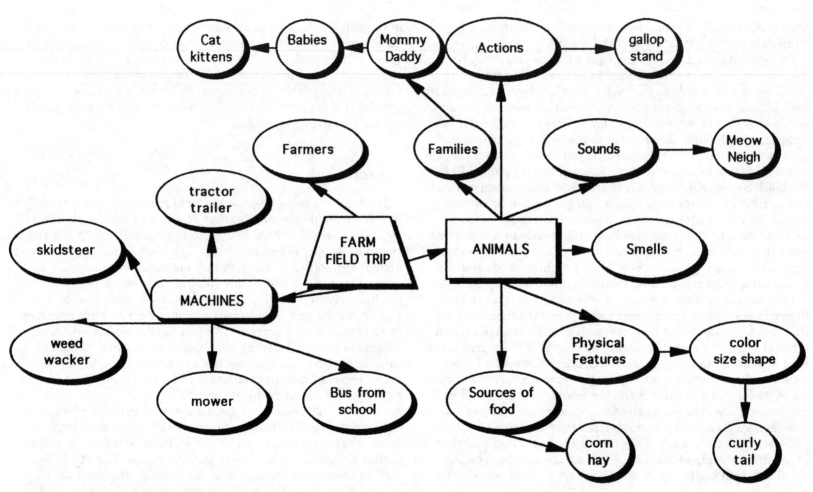

Figure 3. *Here is a web of ideas that one group of 4- and 5-year-old children generated in talking about a trip to a farm.*

as America Tomorrow Health and Education Network Services (ATHENS), Early Childhood Education Network (ECE-NET) on Internet, and other telecommunications packages. (For further information on how to access information and participate in bulletin boards, see Appendix B).

Teachers and parents are the strongest advocates for children. Whether computer technology invades or enhances our children's lives is a critical issue. Teachers, parents, researchers, and software publishers need to collaborate as we seek to discover together the full potential of this powerful new tool and its role in our children's development. As an African proverb declares, "It takes a village to raise a child." It will take all of us working together to guide the role of technology in early childhood education.

References

Bredekamp, S., ed. 1987. *Developmentally appropriate practice in early childhood programs serving children from birth through age 8.* Exp. ed. Washington, DC: NAEYC.

Clements, D.H. 1987. Computers and young children: A review of the research. *Young Children* 43 (1): 34–44.

Davidson, J. 1990. *Children and computers together in the early childhood classroom.* New York: Delmar.

Davidson, J. n.d.. *Dramatic play and emergent literacy: Natural partners.* New York: Delmar. In press.

Haugland, S.W. 1992. The effect of computer software on preschool children's developmental gains. *Journal of Computing in Childhood Education* 3: 15–30.

Katz, L.G., & S.C. Chard. 1989. *Engaging children's minds: The project approach.* Norwood, NJ: Ablex.

Often children's excitement about a theme or project leads them to design their own activities at the computer.

Trawick-Smith, J. 1994. *Interactions in the classroom: Facilitating play in the early years.* New York: Merrill.

Wright, J.L. 1985. Informatics in the education of young children. In *Informatics and teacher training.* North Holland, Netherlands: Elsevier.

Wright, J.L., & A. Samaras. 1986. Play worlds and microworlds. In *Young children and the microcomputer,* eds. P. Campbell & G. Fein. Englewood Cliffs, NJ: Prentice Hall.

Charles Hohmann

Staff Development Practices for Integrating Technology in Early Childhood Education Programs

T his chapter focuses on the chief means by which the benefits of technology for early childhood education can be realized—through the professional development of early childhood educators in the theory and practical methods that integrate technology with good early childhood educational practice. A strong case has been made in this book and elsewhere for the value of integrating technology in early childhood educational practice. Young children's appropriate use of computer hardware and software is safe and supports their learning and development.

Staff development in the context of the technology revolution

How did computers first appear in classrooms, and what role, if any, did staff development play in this? Nearly all of the first educational uses of computers were experimental. Teachers and other people who knew about computers for one reason or another brought them into schools for children to use. They developed their own programs or used programming languages such as BASIC or *Logo* for computer experiences. Staff development for computer use was nonexistent, but the need for teacher education and support was recognized, and support services began to be organized. In Minnesota, for example, support services for computer use in education took shape, as the Minnesota Educational Computer Consortium (MECC) was first organized in 1973. MECC was an association of colleges, schools, and state officials whose specific aim was to support all phases of implementing educational computer use. By the late 1970s and early 1980s, computer interest groups were springing up in schools and communities across the country.

Access to computer equipment remains an enduring issue in implementing technology use in educational settings. Acquisition was, at first, a grass roots effort, and in many cases it still is, with parents collecting soup can labels to trade in for school computers. But in public schools and Head Start programs, acquisition of computer equipment has become a centralized process for the most part. Schools began to invest heavily in computer equipment. Some schools also invested in staff development programs to support teacher use of computers and software. One of the services of MECC, for example, was to support schools' efforts to acquire computers and educational software.

Foundations for staff development patterns

Behavioristic views on the one hand and cognitive-developmental views on the other are the major philosophic and practical foundations for both child and adult learning. The behavioristic tradition views the products of learning (knowledge and skills) as externally defined, to be imparted to the learner primarily through language. In the cognitive-developmental view, the products of learning are defined within goal-oriented interaction between the learner and the elements of his or her experience.

While a behavioristic foundation is not often directly credited for prevailing practice in staff development, behaviorism is certainly consistent with much of it (Jones 1986). Content and learning activities are defined by leaders (called "trainers"). The flow of information is primarily from leader to participant, often in the form of a lecture or presentation. Even rewards are arranged contingently to reinforce learning through grades, credits, and feedback for "correct" responses to queries from the leader. The process itself is often referred to as *training*—a term with deep roots in the behavioristic tradition.

In contrast to staff development practices reflecting behavioristic views, those conceived along cognitive-developmental lines are characterized by active involvement of the learner, input from both teacher and learner in learning activities, and variation in learner outcomes that reflect the interests and experience of the individual. We are convinced that the cognitive-developmental view of adult learning is more effective and more in keeping with adult learning styles. It is also in step with the orientation to child learning on which our educational programs are based. Staff development practices with a cognitive-developmental orientation may therefore illustrate the same teaching/learning style that we would have adults use with the children they teach. Staff development practices described in this chapter emphasize active workshop involvement, application to practical situations, and individual feedback based on the learner's interests and level of progress.

The need for staff development to achieve technology integration

Integrating computer technology with educational practice has not been an assured outcome of simply placing computer equipment in educational settings. The computer's rapid penetration of the business and consumer markets has made it very popular among educators. Program administrators and classroom teachers eager to exploit computers for education and to associate their craft with the latest technologies have spent considerable sums on various technologies. However, these investments have not always been matched with the support and staff development programs needed to ensure effective utilization of the technology. Without such support, technology will likely fail to deliver on its promise of improving young children's learning.

Technology is not unique in its creating a need for staff development. The same need is found with most innovations in educational methods and materials. Educational innovations nearly always require significant support in the form of staff development to be effectively implemented in educational settings. Technology, too, requires this form of support.

Several rather visible cases have recognized and addressed the need for staff development to support the implementation of computer technology in educational settings. The Minnesota Educational Computer Consortium, mentioned earlier, was a large-scale effort of support for educational technology that had significant influence throughout the state and in the region. The Washington, D.C., school district invested heavily in educational computer technology in the early 1980s. Since 1983 the district has spent nearly $2 million a year on staff development in technology to ensure that staff have access to programs that will help them learn how to use technology in their teaching (Buchsbaum 1992). Although the Washington, D.C., expenditures for staff development in technology are quite large, even on a per capita basis, they have met only part of the need for effective technology integration in the schools.

Characteristics of effective staff development programs

Given the need for staff development to support integration of technology in early childhood educational practice, what characteristics of staff development programs are essential? Based on her analysis of the staff development literature and the findings of her own recent research, Epstein (1993) identifies critical elements of effective staff development for early childhood educators.

Practical experience. Epstein's first conclusion is that staff development instruction must be interwoven with practical experience and hands-on application to be effective. She notes that in many staff development models, theory comes first and practice comes only after theoretical work is completed. Just the opposite is needed—practical experience must support each part of the staff development program. When learning to integrate technology, this practical experience may take the form of hands-on experience with computers and other equipment, such as printers, modems, and CD-ROMs. It may also take the form of planning and trying out specific computer activities with children or with other adults. Practical application may also include selecting and analyzing specific software activities to determine related curriculum areas and support activities.

For staff development in technology to be effective, teachers must have lots of hands-on experience at the computer.

Workshops. Epstein notes that while workshops are common in staff development programs, to produce meaningful improvements in practice they must include active participation, opportunities for sharing among colleagues, and follow-up sessions, as teachers attempt to implement the ideas. Only then do workshops become an effective staff development tool. Epstein also notes that inservice programs are more effective when the individuals involved can observe programs that demonstrate high-quality practices.

In a technology context, these workshop guidelines mean that group sessions should provide generous opportunities for active involvement, such as games and simulations, off-computer activities, as well as hands-on work with equipment and software. Participants can share with one another in discussion sessions based on such topics as, "How I used a software activity with my children." The recommendation that workshops provide follow-up sessions means, in a sense, that two short workshops are better than one long one or, in general, that multiple sessions with opportunities for application and try-outs in practical contexts are likely to produce lasting results.

Models and mentors. Seeing is believing, and this saying is certainly applicable when learning about technology. Observing appropriate use of computers, for example, in the context of operating classrooms or care centers can improve the chances for successful implementation elsewhere. Observations of model classrooms that demonstrate effective practice communicate on many levels. On one level, such observations can help to dispel the feeling that "All this is very nice, but it won't work with real children." By showing real children and adults working comfortably with technology, model classrooms can also provide observers with information about techniques that may otherwise be overlooked. Seeing how pieces of colored tape are used to highlight special keys on the keyboard or observing displays of children's computer work may solve a problem that an observer has encountered in his or her own setting.

Supervisory follow-up. To implement and sustain the lessons learned in inservice workshops, Epstein notes that practitioners need ongoing, one-to-one contact with a supervisor or lead teacher. The lessons of workshops and other staff development activities must be applied and evaluated in classroom settings. This field-based consultation allows teachers and child care staff to think analytically about their work and to "generate theory out of practice" (Epstein 1993, p. 9).

An effective method for this form of support is a cycle of observation, feedback, and discussions with teachers in the context of their own classrooms. Such direct follow-up gets to the heart of implementing new materials and practices—providing feedback on the effects of staff development in actual practice and giving supervisors an opportunity to provide support and to solve problems on a one-to-one basis.

The implications of these key recommendations for staff development are several, the most resounding being that whatever takes place—whether through inservice workshops, individual study, or lecture and demonstration—must be quickly and thoroughly tied to practical application. Thus, learning about technology must be linked with curriculum and classroom management to be effectively integrated. Another implication from Epstein's research is that staff development take place over an extended period of time. One-day or one-time workshops are not effective. They require built-in opportunities to apply what is learned, as well as follow-up application in real-world settings. With these implications in mind, we move next to the content issues that shape staff development programs whose aim is integrating technology.

Some goals for staff development in technology

Reducing technophobia. Much of the general public has come to live relatively comfortably with a variety of technologically advanced devices: automobiles, VCRs, cassette tape recorders, telephone answering machines, microwave ovens, and even fax machines. While this is a considerable achievement that has required learning and experience, the technical details of all these devices are largely hidden behind user-friendly interfaces consisting of a few pedals or buttons. We are, however, still in the era when using computers is perceived by many who have had little or no experience with them as a task requiring complex technical skills. As desktop and hand-held computing devices become everyday tools, many more people will have had experience with them, and the perception of computers as technically demanding will likely diminish.

Still, for many teachers, anxiety about the perceived technical demands of using computers is a real barrier to greater use of technology. Zammit (1992) found such lack of confidence regarding computer use to be one of the most important factors hindering noncomputer-using teachers' use of computer technology in their teaching. One quickly senses such anxiety and deference to "experts" among teachers with limited computer experience.

Diminishing teachers' fear that they lack the skills to successfully use computer technology is one of the basic goals for staff development in this area. A variety of successful computer experiences over an extended period of time can do a lot to overcome technophobia. Achieving confidence in working with computer technology does not occur overnight. In addition to learning basic skills for using computer equipment, it involves learning to cope with the typical problems that arise in everyday computer use—floppy disks are damaged or erased; hard disks become inoperable; computers, although undamaged, behave abnormally for unknown reasons and must be restarted. Events like these are unnerving at first but with time are accepted as normal and manageable.

Although lack of confidence is a major factor inhibiting teacher use of technology, acquiring technical skills should not become a major focus of staff development activities, nor should it be the first topic undertaken. Rather, teachers should be involved in extended, successful, curriculum-oriented experiences with technology. A working knowledge of basic technical skills accrues quite naturally, especially if care has been taken to embed these skills in staff development activities. In this manner, technical skills can be introduced at the point at which they are needed, assuring, also, that they will be quickly put to practical use. For example, experiences with DOS-based computers will readily acquaint the user with the handling of floppy disks and with basic DOS commands, such as the CTRL+ALT+DEL key combination for restarting the computer. Macintosh users quickly become familiar with the Finder's pull-down menus and the EJECT button for removing floppy disks.

Staff development programs, however, must give some attention to providing such technical knowledge because lack of it appears to create a confidence ceiling that blocks users from making further progress.

Creating a simultaneous focus on technology and curriculum. To work well in an educational setting, computer technology—both hardware and software—must be designed or adapted to fit the educational needs. This necessity is most obvious with software. Software designed for inventory control, of course, will be of little use as an aid to teaching in a preschool or kindergarten classroom. Even a word processing program designed for middle-school students will most likely be of limited use to younger children. Likewise, computer hardware must be adapted to the needs of the children, the teacher, and the classroom space in which they are housed. To be effective with young children, computer equipment should have color displays and easy input devices, such as mouse-controlled pointers, to facilitate children's use.

Instructional practice frequently must be altered to make the best use of computer technology. Even if computers are relegated to a computer lab (and we believe that locating computers in early childhood classrooms is the most effective arrangement for young children), teachers must arrange schedules to allow the children and themselves access to the computer. To capitalize on computer learning resources, teachers need to make linkages between work that is done on the computer and work that is done in off-computer activities. Integrating computer technology frequently requires that children work semi-autonomously in small groups because it is unlikely—and even undesirable—that the classroom has enough computers for every child or even every pair of children. The opportunities for exploration, creative problem solving, and self-guided instruction that are unique to the computer call for new styles of learning and thus demand curriculum innovation along with the integration of technology. Effectively integrating technology in an educational program requires a focus on curriculum and technology simultaneously. Staff development toward integration of technology is therefore as much a curriculum development/curriculum learning process as it is one of learning to use technology.

A dual focus on curriculum and technology is best achieved when staff development has a focus on a well-defined curriculum framework that is consistent with and supportive of the technology to be used. This vision of staff development programs militates against one-shot inservice activities and against training that deals primarily with technology—either hardware or software—without a curriculum base. It is supportive of staff development programs in which implementation of technology and of curriculum changes are aligned with one another and occur at the same time.

Time frames for staff development

Staff development scenarios, although they can vary widely, typically include one or more of the following: individually guided study, curriculum development, observation and feedback, and inservice workshops (Sparks & Loucks-Horsley 1990). The first two scenarios may be quite individualistic and may take place with or without a leader. An individual or group of individuals may be assigned the task or simply decide to pursue an interest in technology. They may have been exposed to computers at home or in another work environment. They gain experience with the computer, examine software, and decide to bring computers into their centers or classrooms and begin using them with the children. They may design curriculum activities around computer topics or use computer activities to support other areas of the curriculum. Staff development of this kind may take place as independent study and/or curriculum development under the guidance of a college professor or mentor teacher or may simply be undertaken on one's own.

Observation and feedback is the third type of staff development scenario and involves observation of the teacher's work under day-to-day conditions, followed by feedback and discussion. In this type of staff development—often performed with the assistance of a supervisor, lead teacher, or consultant—the staff developer observes the individual's teaching style and activities and recommends improvements based on mutually determined goals or criteria. While this type of staff development can be the most successful in terms of producing change in teaching behavior (because it is focused on an individual teacher and closely linked with day-to-day practice), it is usually linked with some other form of staff development, such as inservice workshops or a course of study.

Inservice workshops are a fourth scenario for staff development. Workshops may involve small or large groups of staff and one or more instructors. They may last an hour or less or may extend to a week or more, depending on the workshop goals and the participants' needs. Implicit in the workshop concept is the expectation that workshop learning will provide more active involvement, more application and practice, more hands-on experience, and more peer interaction than would a lecture or a demonstration; indeed, the most effective workshops include liberal amounts of these elements. Unfortunately, many

To sustain lessons learned in inservice workshops, staff need ongoing, one-to-one contact with a supervisor, consultant, or lead teacher.

workshops fail to include these elements due to inadequate or poor design, and the workshops are consequently less effective than they could be.

Workshops can be an effective component of staff development for technology integration. Because staff must leave their classroom duties to participate in workshops, new materials and concepts may be introduced away from immediate day-to-day concerns. Technology workshops allow staff to explore computers and computer-based learning activities and to participate in sharing and discussion with peers. Because they are removed from day-to-day classroom situations, however, work-

shop activities are best accompanied by one-on-one observations and feedback activities that can effectively support transfer and implementation of workshop content.

On the short end of the time scale for staff development are one-day inservice workshops, either at the agency or school site or at a training center, such as a college campus or a school service center (e.g., intermediate school district regional training center). Such venues provide as much as five hours of contact with the instructor but typically afford little opportunity for outside work, such as projects or assignments, and may provide limited opportunities for practice and hands-on experience.

Inservice workshops seldom last more than a day or two, but staff development courses set up outside the time when classes are in session can last longer. Summer training workshops (when children are not in attendance) may last from a few days to two weeks. Training sessions of this length can provide from 30 to 60 hours of contact time with the instructor and a certain amount of outside work, such as assignments, application projects, reading, and practice.

Other formats for staff development include evening classes that meet two to three hours a week over a semester of 10 to 16 weeks (for a total of 30 to 40 hours). These, too, provide opportunity for outside work, such as projects and reading. Staff development activities involving individual study or curriculum development groups can stretch out for months or longer and consume many hours of time.

Staff development that employs all of the staff development activities described appears to be most effective. In-depth research on staff development in technology is still not available; however, research findings about key strategies or effective models of staff development are relevant to the technology area. Perhaps the most carefully researched is the Training of

Teacher Trainer (ToTT) model developed by High/Scope Foundation (the programs studied in Epstein's work [1993]), which provides two levels of staff development. For the teacher trainers, the course is arranged as a series of seven, week-long workshops spread over a semester or more. Such a program of staff development requires an interruption of regular work activities because it occupies the staff member full time for a week at a time. These individuals have 150 or more hours of contact time, as well as extensive opportunities for outside reading, application projects, and practice in day-to-day settings.

At a second level of staff development, each of the ToTT participants provides staff development services for one or more target classrooms. For the staff in the target classrooms, the trainers provided, on the average, (a) one large-group presentation, (b) monthly hands-on workshops for small groups of staff, (c) monthly classroom visits to conduct observation and feedback, and (d) three informal classroom visits each month to monitor implementation. These ToTT programs, carried out with more than 1000 participants over five years, have resulted in significant measurable improvement in early childhood educational practice in the target classrooms assisted by these trainers (Epstein 1993, p. xviii).

Workplace factors affecting staff development outcomes

School or agency policy toward inservice training, as well as the effectiveness of administrative leadership, determine the options available for staff development. Administrative support for ongoing staff development and curriculum implementation are key to achieving signifi-
cant change and improvement. Support is manifest by making necessary resources, such as facilities and program supplies, directly available to teachers (Greenman 1984). Administrators also evidence their commitment to staff development in the content of their contacts with staff members. For example, program improvement is more likely if administrators devote more time during staff meetings to program development issues than to managerial ones (Moore & Smith 1987). In short, administrators' verbal commitments to program implementation must be backed up with provision of the necessary time and resources.

Parents and the community are also factors in technology implementation. Often parents are supporters of technology, believing that the addition of technology is in keeping with the overall trend toward technology in society and that it will help their children succeed. But because effective integration of technology most often requires changes in the curriculum and the organization of learning experiences, teachers should keep parents involved in and aware of the changes taking place as technology is integrated.

Content of staff development for technology integration

Because time for staff development is almost always limited, determining what is comprised by effective and useful content for teachers integrating technology in educational programs for pre-K and early elementary children is necessary to establish staff development priorities. Further, we will want to consider how the components of staff development for integrating technology fit together to make a coherent and effective whole.

Giving a rationale for integrating technology. Any staff development effort toward integrating technology must keep in mind its raison d'etre—helping children learn—and be mindful of the limits of technology—what it can and cannot do for young children's learning. Every vision for the role of technology must find its ultimate rationale in improving the teaching and the learning of young children. The rationale for technology also must show that it is not harmful for children and that it is consistent with what are known to be effective child development principles.

There is considerable evidence that technology can deliver significant benefits for young children's learning. Some of it is reviewed in other portions of this volume. Additional evidence can be found in other excellent reviews of the subject, such as those of Clements (1993), Hohmann (1990), and Davidson (1989).

Only a small amount of time need be devoted to developing a rationale for integrating technology. Handouts and reference citations are often sufficient. A role for technology is more readily accepted by teachers of young children and their parents today than it was just a few years ago. Being familiar with evidence of technology's effect on young children is nevertheless useful for teachers to support their own thinking and to provide them with tools for justifying their efforts to parents and other community members.

Hardware. Those who work with technology must be able to operate it successfully and care for its basic needs; however, some caution is in order on this subject. Computer hardware is magnificently complex machinery. But, like an automobile, it can be used to facilitate a rewarding journey with limited knowledge of its inner workings. With an automobile,

it is important to change the oil regularly, to recognize warning signs of possible malfunction, and to know the vehicle's safe operational limits for turning, stopping, and carrying loads. Similarly, for computer technology, learning to connect and disconnect parts (keyboard, mouse, monitor, printer, etc.) is useful because staff may be called upon to set up the equipment upon arrival, to move the equipment, or to pack it away during vacation periods. In addition, knowing how to turn a computer system off and on, load programs, start up applications, and resolve minor difficulties such as locating lost files is essential.

One cannot know too much about hardware, but learning about hardware must compete with other demands on the limited time available for staff development activities. Also, much specific knowledge about hardware is best learned when a clear reason exists for knowing it; for example, teachers rapidly learn to use keys or mouse commands to restart the computer rather than turning the power off and then back on. It is best to keep hardware tips and information to a minimum and to introduce them in the context of the higher order concern—using technology effectively to support children's learning.

Software. Virtually everyone who uses computer technology with young children uses commercial software. A great deal of this software is available, and at least some is of good quality (see, for example, reviews in Haugland & Shade 1991; Buckleitner 1993). The alternative of creating one's own software is sufficiently time consuming and technically demanding as to make this alternative unrealistic for most people. Selecting, mastering, and applying published software is therefore a central component of learning to use technology. A considerable portion of staff development related to technology is necessarily devoted to learning about educational software.

Learning about software has several aspects. Frequently one must learn some technical facet of the software—how to start it, how to set the teacher options to suit the children who will use it, how to save and/or print products created as children use the software. There is also the software interface to master—the keys or buttons that make the program work—which often varies from one program to another.

Teachers are understandably anxious to review the conceptual and skills content of the software—spatial concepts, sequencing, comparisons, or music, for example. In staff development sessions, it is important to sustain this activity until teachers achieve a familiarity with all aspects of the software. It is also helpful to focus effort on materials and activities needed to introduce the software to children and on how to support children's independent use of the programs. Other topics for staff development include developing off-computer activities to extend those done on the computer and reviewing the curriculum framework that connects computer activities to the rest of the curriculum.

Curriculum. At least part of what is referred to under learning about software relates to the curriculum issues that are necessarily part of staff development for integrating technology. One of these curriculum topics is arranging computers for children's easy access. Because locating computers in the classroom is recommended for preschool and early elementary programs, computers will typically be placed in a classroom learning center. Of particular importance is allocating and managing time for children to use the computers, a topic for inservice workshops that has visible consequences when applied in classroom settings. Teachers must maximize children's access to the technology as well as integrate it with other aspects of classroom operation. For computers to be effectively used, teachers must learn techniques that allow children to use technology rather independently because providing immediate adult supervision of children's computer activities is impractical (or too limiting). For this purpose, a system of small groups and/or self-selection provides an effective mechanism (see, for example, Hohmann & Buckleitner 1992).

Additional curriculum topics related to integrating technology involve instructional pacing and assessment of computer learning. Good computer learning materials allow children to move at individual rates and along individualistic pathways through possible learning materials. Effectively using this potential of computer-based materials often requires staff development on realignment of learning goals and on assessing individual child learning.

Outcomes from staff development programs

In few cases have studies of staff development programs been able to link the whole chain of effects—goals of the program, effect on staff, effect on practice, and outcomes for children. In a recently completed study, Epstein (1993) demonstrates that in a well-designed and well-executed staff development program, beneficial effects at each link in the chain can be achieved and documented. She cautions, however, that to achieve these effects, the staff development program needs the solid backing of program administrators, must contain effective learning components, and must be carried out over an extended period of time.

Observing for themselves the appropriate use of computers with children, teachers stand a better chance of successfully integrating computers into their classrooms.

References

Buchsbaum, H. 1992. Portrait of a staff development program. *Electronic Learning* 11 (7): 18–23, 26–27.

Buckleitner, W. 1993. *Buyer's guide to early childhood software.* Ypsilanti, MI: High/Scope Press.

Clements, D. 1993. Young children and computers: Crossroads and directions from research. *Young Children* 48 (2): 56–63.

Davidson, J.I. 1989. *Children & computers together in the early childhood classroom.* New York: Delmar.

Epstein, A. 1993. *Training for quality.* Ypsilanti, MI: High/Scope Press.

Greenman, J.T. 1984. Program development and models of consultation. In *Making day care better: Training, evaluation, and the process of change,* eds. J. Greenman & R. Fuque. New York: Teachers College Press.

Haugland, S.W., & D. Shade. 1991. *Developmental evaluation of software for young children.* New York: Delmar.

Hohmann, C. 1990. *Young children and computers.* Ypsilanti, MI: High/Scope Press.

Hohmann, C., & W. Buckleitner. 1992. *High/Scope K-3 curriculum series: Learning environment.* Ypsilanti, MI: High/Scope Press.

Jones, E. 1986. Perspectives on teacher education: Some relations between theory and practice. In *Current topics in early childhood education,* ed. L.G. Katz. Norwood, NJ: Ablex.

Moore, E., & T. Smith. 1987. *The High/Scope training program one year on.* Oxford: Department of Social and Administrative Studies, Oxford University.

Sparks, D., & S. Loucks-Horsley. 1990. Models of staff development. In *Handbook of research on teacher education,* ed. R.W. Houston. New York: Macmillan.

Zammit, S.A. 1992. Factors facilitating or hindering the use of computers in schools. *Educational Research* 34 (1): 57–66.

**Michael M. Behrmann and
Elizabeth A. Lahm**

Computer Applications in Early Childhood Special Education

arly childhood special education (ECSE) professionals recognize that young children with special needs often do not learn efficiently. Their delays or disabilities frequently inhibit their interactions with the physical and social environment. "Failing to address these performance deficits assigns such children to less normative, less useful, and more dependent means of learning" (Wolery, Strain, & Bailey 1991). Many researchers suggest technology as one means of addressing these needs (Behrmann 1984; Behrmann & Lahm 1985; Clements 1987).

This chapter provides an overview of technology's role in early childhood special education, identifies features of the technologies that are important for young children, and sug-

gests some specific strategies for integrating technology into the early childhood curriculum.

Assistive technology and its legislative support

Technology is no longer only a desirable addition to teaching and access to learning; federal law now mandates that it be incorporated in educational programs for children with disabilities when appropriate. The Education of the Handicapped Act Amendments of 1986 (P.L. 99-457) contained new provisions regarding the use of technology and mandated the design and adaptation of technology for use in teaching children with disabilities. Thus it is necessary to begin looking toward ways to incorporate these technologies into the best-practice approaches of early childhood special education.

The Technology-Related Assistance for Individuals with Disabilities Act of 1988 (P.L. 100-407) developed a set of definitions that have now become common ground for most federal, state, and local institutions. The Tech Act divided assistive technology into two categories—assistive technology devices and assistive technology services—and states, "The term *assistive technology device* means any item, piece of equipment, or product system whether acquired commercially off the shelf, modified, or customized, that is used to increase, maintain, or improve functional capabilities of individuals with disabilities."

Assistive technology devices can be further divided into the two categories of high technology and low technology. Many low-tech devices can be purchased at a hardware store, selected from a catalog, or fabricated using tools and materials that can be found in many well-equipped home workshops (Franklin 1992). On the other hand, high-tech devices frequently incorporate some type of computer chip, such as the "talking clock," a computer, or an augmentative communication device. While some high-tech devices may be quite costly, many, such as the hand-held calculator, have become commonplace (Franklin 1992) and inexpensive. Table 1 shows examples of devices that fall into each of these categories that might be useful in early childhood special education.

Assistive technology also includes instructional or tool software used by children with disabilities in the learning process. For example, talking word processors can be an assistive technology device for children learning written language.

Table 1. Examples of Assistive Technologies in Early Childhood Education

Low Tech	High Tech
Simple switches	Voice-recognition devices
Head pointers	Augmentative communication devices (e.g., *Liberator*)
Battery-operated toys	
Picture boards	Alternative keyboards (e.g., *PowerPad, Intellikeys*)
Scooter	Speech synthesizers
Taped stories	Electric wheelchair
	Talking books

Word-prediction software can assist children with word-recall difficulty, as well as children with the physical inability to make keystrokes efficiently on the keyboard. Additionally, the editing, spelling, macros, and other features may provide assistance to children who are having difficulty learning to write. Some instructional software gives children with cognitive impairments or language delays the opportunity to practice basic skills, such as those necessary for social interactions. These examples are but a few from a multitude of instructional applications of assistive technology for children with disabilities that enable children to increase, maintain, or improve their functional capabilities in learning environments; thus these devices meet the definition of assistive technology.

The term *assistive technology services* means any service that directly assists an individual with a disability in the selection, acquisition, or use of assistive technology (AT) devices. Such services include the following:

1. evaluating the needs of an individual in the individual's customary environment;

2. purchasing, leasing, or otherwise providing for the acquisition of AT devices by individuals with disabilities;

3. selecting, designing, fitting, customizing, adapting, applying, maintaining, repairing, or replacing assistive technology devices;

4. coordinating and using other therapies, interventions, or services with assistive technology devices, such as those associated with existing education and rehabilitation plans and programs;

5. training or providing technical assistance for an individual with disabilities or, where appropriate, the family; and

6. training or providing technical assistance for professionals, employers, or other individuals who provide service to, employ, or are involved in the major life functions of individuals with disabilities (Franklin 1992).

Educational staff must identify and assess assistive technology needs and develop Individualized Educational Program (IEP) goals and objectives relating to assistive technology. Schools and other education providers must provide appropriate devices and, probably most importantly, training and support to teachers and related-services personnel in the use and maintenance of these devices.

Access modes

Recent emerging applications of technology provide a variety of new ways for children to activate toys or computers other than simply using the now relatively common assistive technology approach of a hand-activated switch. For example, voice activation of devices is now possible and is even incorporated into the standard operating system of newer computers. Children can also use a touch-sensitive monitor, such as the Touch Window, to directly interact with a picture or cursor; this action is cognitively less demanding than using a mouse or a switch controlling a scanning cursor. An extended keyboard, such as Intellikeys or a PowerPad, enables children to activate the software, thus keeping them away from the distractions of the central processing unit (CPU) or keyboard and keeping them in proximity to peers who may be sitting in a small group on the floor. Highly sensitive pressure switches that require a minimal amount of strength are also now on the market (Wilds 1989), as are eye-gaze control devices that enable children to only look at the monitor to activate the software. These technologies allow computer access to children with even the most severe physical impairments.

Assistive technology and the IEP/IFSP process

The Individuals with Disabilities Education Act (IDEA; P.L. 101-476), passed in 1990, extends and expands the protections of prior legislation for people with disabilities. This legislation protects the rights of more children with disabilities, recognizes greater variability among people with disabilities, and emphasizes the child, not his or her disability. The IDEA provides that if a child with a disability requires assistive technology devices or services, or both, in order to receive a free appropriate public education, the public agency will ensure that the assistive technology devices or services

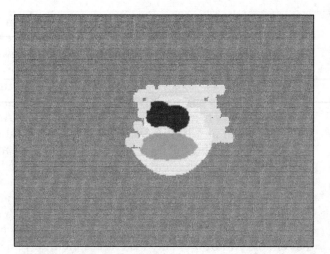 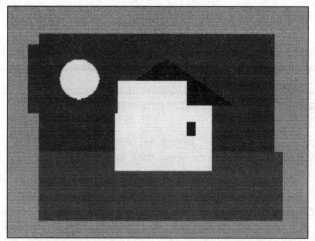

"Miss Piggy with Hair" (left) was created by means of a voice-operated drawing program (Talk and Draw, Macro International, Inc.) by an 8-year-old girl with cerebral palsy that affects her speech and other motor skills. "House" (right) was drawn by an 11-year-old boy with a learning disability.

are made available to that child as special education, related services, or supplementary aids and services that enable a child with a disability to be educated in regular classes. Determinations of whether a child with a disability requires assistive technology devices or services under this program must be made on an individual basis through applicable Individualized Education Program (IEP) and placement procedures. *Assistive technology* in this legislation includes instructional technologies that provide individuals with disabilities with access to instruction and knowledge. The IDEA also provided funding for research and training on assistive technology, confirming the commitment to assistive technology that had been initiated by previous administrative and congressional policies.

As a result of the IDEA legislation, technology is no longer only a desirable addition to instruction and access to learning; federal law mandates that it be incorporated into educational programs for children with disabilities when appropriate. This mandate highlights the need to incorporate assistive technologies into the best-practices approaches of early childhood special education.

With the recent advances in technology, and with the support of federal legislation for its use, many young children with disabilities can now have access to or have enhanced learning environments. To make the potential a reality, service providers must understand technology's role in learning and play and how to maximize the potential.

Integrating technology into the play and learning of young children with disabilities

The work of young children is play. Children expend tremendous energy having fun—exploring their new and exciting world. Young children with disabilities often exhibit the same play behaviors as their nondisabled peers; however, some do not play at all. Consequently, these children may have reduced interactions with their physical and social environments and, as a result, have less information about themselves and their world.

Present-day and emerging technologies may help address learning deficits and provide new opportunities to use environmental interactions to improve learning. For example, a child who is physically unable to speak can use a communication (voice-output) device to interact with others. Instead of using noncompliant behaviors to gain attention or to be negative, the nonspeaking child can progress through the "terrible twos" using the computer or other communication device to digitally say "No! No! No!" or, on a more positive note, to participate in group activities by having the device "sing" the refrain from "Wheels on the Bus" along with other children. Another child, with physical mobility impairments, could use switches to activate battery-operated toys that are in his play area, thus providing this child access to the play and instructional milieu as he learns to control and interact with the environment.

Not until the turn of the century was play recognized as an important component in the development of young children. Some of the early classic theories provided a rationale for play through the perspective of their theory: for example, "play gives the active child an acceptable outlet" is from the surplus energy theory, and "they learn through their play"

comes from the practice theory (Almy et al. 1984). More recent psychodynamic theories express play as a means for children to "work out emotional conflicts." Piaget (1962) introduced the idea that play is important in cognitive development and develops in stages. Other theorists describe play as important in evolution and development, as a personality trait, and as performance (Almy et al. 1984). Today, play is seen as one of the most important aspects of special education, both as a teaching context and as an end in itself (Cook, Tessier, & Klein 1992).

In general, play in the early childhood curriculum is described as a time when children can follow their own inclinations without being asked to follow a structure or routine imposed by the teacher. Some characteristics of play for which computers and other technologies may be particularly effective include intrinsic motivation, attention to means rather than ends, freedom from external rules or limitations on practice, and active engagement (Almy et al. 1984). Both low- and high-end technologies can also be used to provide access to symbolic and game playing. For example, the same simple switches can be used by two or more children with physical limitations to play a passing game, such as "Hot Potato," each child taking his turn at passing the object to the next person by pressing his switch at the appropriate time. The multitude of computer-based games also become available to these children through the use of adaptive access technology.

Young children generally engage in three forms of play: sensorimotor, symbolic, and game play (Nuba-Scheffler, Sheiman, & Watkins 1986). The level of social and cognitive complexity of play increases with the age of the child, shifting from predominantly sensorimotor play in infancy to predominantly game play in the primary grades. Sensorimotor play is characterized as functional, with motor actions dominant. In this arena, battery-operated toys controlled by switches are often used to establish understanding of cause-and-effect—for example, when the switch is pressed, the toy firefighter will climb the ladder. In the early stages, technology can play a major role in allowing access to play, providing the kinds of cognitive and language development opportunities that children without disabilities have.

Exploration and practice are also necessary to master an activity (Cook, Tessier, & Klein 1992). Software that encourages choice making allows children to move from the cause-and-effect learning of pressing a switch to using the switch to select from an array of possible responses as the child moves a cursor from option to option on the computer monitor. This type of cause-and-effect interaction may be important later as the child is introduced to instructional software or assistive technology. Computers are also nonjudgmental and infinitely patient, allowing children to explore or practice at their own pace, never tiring of repeating the same activity or story.

Symbolic or pretend play allows children to relinquish reality and use their imagination to alter the roles and objects in the play situation. One object is used to represent another in dramatic and constructive play. Software that allows children to select images, construct a picture, and then develop a story supports development of symbolic play. Other software allows a child to choose different endings to stories or to change the order of a story, providing children with the ability to develop different perceptions of the world.

Game play is characterized by the engagement of two or more individuals with a common theme. A switch-activated "spinner" can give a child with a physical disability access to board games that young children enjoy. Simple software games

that introduce children to turn taking and cooperative play are precursors for learning that lead to higher-level game playing, such as that found in multiplayer Sega or Nintendo games.

Play environments and technology in early childhood special education classrooms

Strategies for teaching young children are as diverse as the theoretical bases from which they originate. Four major approaches to special education have developed over the course of time: behavioral, maturational, psychodynamic, and transactional. Each represents a different perspective on teaching; the roles of the teacher, child, and environment in the classroom; and the role of play in the curriculum. As with any intervention approach, the development and use of technology within the ECSE classroom reflects these theories as well.

Benefits of technology from the behavioral perspective

The focus of the behavioral perspective is the shaping of a child's behavior and learning through reinforcements provided in the environment (Hodapp, Burack, & Zigler 1990). The teacher is directly responsible for structuring well-defined, sequenced activities, providing direct instruction using contingent reinforcements to help control and shape behavior. The environment is structured and controlled by the teacher; events are sequenced within the environment and presented to the child in an ordered fashion. Free play is not readily incorporated into the curriculum.

The behaviorist perspective is perhaps the one most often associated with technology. Early instructional software programs typically incorporated many behavioral components. They tended to provide direct and hierarchical instruction and required performance or mastery criteria to be displayed before the learner moved to the next level of instruction. Such software programs often used the principles of positive reinforcement, with speech, sounds, or pictures used as a reward after a correct response. Some software offered teachers options to set parameters such as mastery criteria or a reinforcement schedule. Even the reinforcements could be changed to avoid satiation. Today, many software programs continue to incorporate drill-and-practice components to build children's fluency in the rate and accuracy of skills but are not limited to this approach. These programs frequently collect and graph performance data on specific components, providing quantitative information for the teacher on skill acquisition.

Benefits of technology from the maturational perspective

The maturational perspective emphasizes the ways in which development is determined by genetic factors and governed by internal forces and physical maturation (Peterson 1987). Proponents of this perspective stress that a child is not ready for new learning until the nervous system is ready, and that every stage is a degree of maturity. In addition, researchers who view development from the maturational perspective point out that the sequence of human growth is similar across individuals (Gesell et al. 1940). The teacher's role within this perspective is to enlist the child's interest and provide a nur-

turing and stimulating environment within which children's development can take its course. The child learns through self-chosen activities, but his or her ultimate potential is determined by genetic factors. Although the child's behavior is largely determined by biological forces, the environment can play an important role in influencing, supporting, and modify-

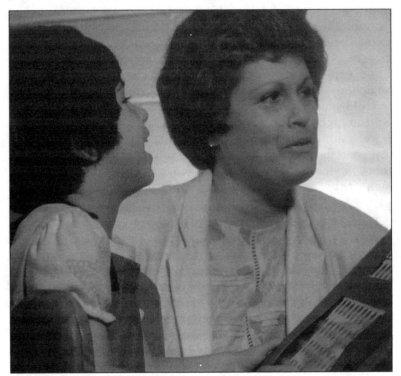

Through various assistive technology devices, children whose disabilities would prevent their using a mouse or keyboard are able to use the computer successfully.

ing behavior (Gesell et al. 1940). The teacher structures the curriculum and the play environment so that materials appropriate to the next emerging stage of development are available.

Technology is compatible with this perspective as well. Children can control age-appropriate, battery-operated toys, using switches to activate them. Additionally, many new toys on the market have microswitches and sensors built in; for example, when a page of a book is turned, a digitized voice reads the next page, or when a ball is touched, it begins to vibrate. Some toys can also be activated by movement or sound. Thus, exploration and manipulation of the environment can be achieved with low-cost technology through offering options to children with various physical and cognitive disabilities. On the high-tech end, simple robots can be controlled using *Logo,* a simple programming language that even young children can use. A child with a motor impairment can use the robot to vicariously explore and move through the environment, thus learning about space and time.

Benefits of technology from the psychodynamic perspective

The psychodynamic perspective places a high priority on the child's emotional growth and stability, self-expression, feelings of self-worth, and self-image (Peterson 1987). Emotional growth helps to define and organize the child's experiences and therefore plays a large role in development. Greenspan and Greenspan (1985) identify six major aspects of emotional growth: organizing sensations, expressing love, developing intentional communication, organizing a sense of self, creating emotional ideas, and emotional thinking. The teacher's role is to support and follow a child's lead in order to allow her the feeling of acceptance and importance, increasing her feelings of self-worth. The child develops through a mastery of her innate impulses. As the child develops, she begins to master these innate impulses and to grow emotionally. The environment plays an important role, too, as it affects the experiences that a child has. The environment should be supportive of conflict-free learning to nurture the child's feelings of self. Play is seen as therapeutic, as an opportunity to role play in a positive, protected environment.

Within this psychodynamic perspective, technology can provide children opportunities to interact with peers, using such items as a voice-output device to communicate or an expanded keyboard to participate in group activities on the computer. It can also provide opportunities for solitary imaginary play. An assistive technology user sometimes gets an added benefit: the fact that other children see the computer or device as desirable. Their envious reactions and interest may increase the self-esteem of the child with a disability as much as the ability to participate increases his self-esteem. Additionally, software designed to enhance group interaction, including turn taking and cooperative play, can provide easy access to the technology for children with disabilities as well as for those without disabilities.

Benefits of technology from the transactional perspective

The transactional perspective has gained more popularity over the past 10 years, especially after NAEYC's guidelines for developmentally appropriate practice (Bredekamp 1987) were published. The transactional approach is based on the premise that children in the preoperational years (roughly between the ages of 2 and 7) learn best as self-guided learners interacting with their environment. From *within* the transactional perspective, the teacher plays the role of guide. By providing a rich variety of activities and giving a child ample time to explore within his environment, the teacher sets the stage for learning. Instruction is more or less indirect, as the teacher focuses on a child's interactions and guides him through self-selected activities. The role of the child, from a transactional perspective, is that of a self-guided learner. He learns by interacting with and manipulating the environment, initiating and making choices. Discovery and exploration are key to the child's learning as he moves within the environment, which has been designed by the teacher. The environment should respond to the child's interests and ability levels. He should have choices and opportunities for manipulation, exploration, discovery, and problem solving, and the environment should encourage interactions.

Recent developments of multimedia software stored on CD-ROM can have a substantial effect within the transactional perspective. Music, sounds, speech, pictures, video, text, and graphics can be used to develop and enhance computer-based learning activities that accommodate different learning styles, strengths, and weaknesses. Multimedia software enhances a child's ability to explore the learning environment. The child can select options, or "learning pathways," by using a mouse to click on a button. These buttons then access graphic images, pictures, or text, allowing the child to explore in an intuitive and natural way. For example, the child may use a mouse to select a picture of a bird in an apple tree, then a voice labels the bird, and the bird flies away. Clicking on the apple causes the apple to fall and a voice to say "apple." The learning environment can be expanded by clicking on a door, which results in entering a house that then can be explored

room by room. Thus the child can control what, when, and how she investigates the computer-generated environment.

Software features important to the young learner

Teaching young children with disabilities is a complex endeavor. Not only must the teacher know each individual's abilities and goals, she must match her teaching approach to the individual child's needs and select materials to encourage individual development. These components must then be incorporated into a learning environment that will meet the needs of multiple learners with diverse abilities. Technology, as a relatively new teaching medium, must be utilized based on the features and applications of use that it brings to the teaching environment so that it, too, can be matched to each learner's needs.

Ongoing research efforts have focused on identifying elements of software and assistive technology that meet the needs of young children with special needs. Recent research has identified 62 software features that early childhood and special education experts consider important (Lahm, Behrmann, & Thorp 1993). Some of these features were noted as disability specific and some as common sense. Others did not list a rationale for their use. Four categories of features (defined in table 2) were selected for further study of their effect on young children's engagement in a computer activity: type of reinforcer (sound, voice, animation); type of picture (line drawing, representational, photographic); type of interaction (watching, doing, using, constructing, creating); and type of interface (keyboard, touch screen, touch tablet, mouse, switch).

Selecting software for young learners with special needs

As a teacher considers the use of technology in the classroom, specific child goals determine the selection of software. In addition to content areas, the goals may also suggest the instructional approach that should be taken and, consequently, the type of software to use. The theoretical perspectives discussed earlier in this chapter suggest the interaction of philosophical perspectives with instructional factors and instructional domains. These implications for software selection will be discussed for the behavioral and transactional approaches only, as they appear to be the most prevalent ones in the ECSE classroom.

Educators in the behaviorist and transactional traditions tend to have different priorities and educational uses for technology. Computer-supported instruction in a classroom with a behaviorist orientation tends to include software designed for teacher control, most often through direct instruction. These programs generally focus on a specific skill and present activities in a sequenced manner with scheduled reinforcements. In many cases the teacher is able to set up and define the number of trials offered and the type or schedule of reinforcement to be given, thereby creating the learning environment she considers to be appropriate for the child. Most of the software programs are also set up to be used with only one child so that the teacher may give direct, individual instruction. Behaviorists are very tuned in to results and will modify learning conditions, the schedule of reinforcement, and so on to determine what works for the learner.

Software programs that take the behaviorist approach commonly focus on a specific skill, such as cause-and-effect

Type of Program Responses	
Animation: *Lifelike motion*—animation representing movements you would expect in real life (e.g., in smoothness, rate, and action); or *mechanical motion*—animation representing movement, however, lacking in realistic quality (e.g., choppy, slow, anatomically incorrect)	
Auditory: *Prompts*—the user is prompted for the correct response with computer-generated sound or music cues, not voice (e.g., beeps); or *feedback*— computer-generated sound or music feedback, not voice, provided immediately following an entry (i.e., the child knows that the computer received the entry)	
Voice: *Digitized voice*—real-life voice quality in either a child's or an adult's voice, male or female; or *synthesized voice*—robotic voice quality in either a child's or an adult's voice, male or female	

Table 2. **Definitions of Software Features**

Type of Picture	Type of Interaction	Type of Interface
Abstract symbols: Text or graphics represent objects or concepts (e.g., words, icons).	**Watching/Finding:** The child attends to the program, which provides frequent demonstrations through the use of graphics, and may or may not be directed to "find" something, but no interaction is required.	**Keyboard:** The child uses the standard keyboard to activate the program.
Line drawings: Graphics resemble objects but use lines with only limited detail (e.g., Rebus symbols).	**Doing:** The child performs a requested operation that requires a one-step action on the program (e.g., clicking on the door for it to open).	**Touch screen:** The child touches the monitor screen to activate the program (e.g., TouchWindow).
Representational pictures: Good graphic images have fairly significant detail, with shading to represent dimension (e.g., Peabody picture cards or Mayer Johnson pictures).	**Using:** The child uses a computer-generated object to perform a task—a two-step action (e.g., uses a mouse to drag, child image through a door).	**Touch tablet:** The child touches a pressure-sensitive surface that is divided into several active areas (e.g., PowerPad, Intellikeys).
Photographic pictures: High-quality images reflect reality (e.g., CD-ROM photographs).	**Constructing:** The child manipulates the program to produce a specified object or picture using simpler computer-generated objects—a multiple-step action that is closed-ended (e.g., using the mouse to help a child image to bring his toys into his room).	**Switch:** The child uses an on/off switch to activate the program, which frequently requires the child to visually scan to make a selection.
	Creating: The child manipulates the program to produce an object, build a character, or create a scene of choice—a multiple-step action that is open-ended (e.g., the child uses computer graphics to create independently).	**Mouse:** The child uses a mouse or other video pointing device to indicate an item on the screen and presses a button to activate the program.

or object discrimination, and are designed to develop fluency or to remediate through a drill-and-practice format. The child is expected to follow the instructional sequence, "watching" and "doing" as directed. Correct answers lead to the next programmed activity; wrong answers require that the child keep trying or repeat an easier level of the skill. The software controls how the activity is presented to the child.

Software incorporating a transactional approach to instruction typically involve the child in activities that require "using," "constructing," and "creating" skills; for example, the child may use a tool to create a picture or construct a house. Often these programs incorporate familiar scenes, such as a house, a farm, or a zoo, to set up an appropriate, open-ended learning environment for the child. The child directs his own learning through exploration and through trial-and-error. Reinforcements often are natural consequences, such as a "creaky sound" as a consequence for opening a closed door or placement of the selected object or figure at the cursor location.

Few teachers follow one type of instructional approach to the exclusion of the others; this is also true in computer-supplemented teaching. The teacher, in selecting software to support an instructional goal for a child, must first decide on the most effective means of teaching and then choose software that matches it. For example, a teacher working with a child on cause-and-effect may use a variety of software to enhance the teaching of this understanding. If the child requires direct instruction, as in the behaviorist perspective, the teacher may choose software that uses a drill-and-practice approach because it introduces a specific concept in a sequenced manner (e.g., *Creature Antics*). In another situation, the child may learn best through discovery. The teacher may thus choose a program that introduces cause-and-effect in a broader way, such as through an open-ended exploratory program (e.g., *A Silly Noisy House*). The ultimate goal of teaching cause-and-effect is the same, yet depending on the teacher's philosophical perspective and the child's needs, the software used to supplement the lessons may differ greatly. For some children, a combination of approaches may work best.

Integrating technology into the classroom

Preschool classrooms are designed to enhance the learning and development of young children in a number of functional areas, such as independence, communication, literacy, cognition, and social skills. Activities are designed to provide opportunities for experiencing new concepts and skills and practicing previously learned ones, allowing the children to move toward their individual goals. One common approach is to use the functional skill areas as the framework for planning.

Another common approach is to use a theme as the context for activities. For example, for a period of time, animals might be the theme used as a context in which the teachers plan group and individual play activities, fine and gross motor activities, as well as literacy activities. What follows is an example of how technology might be integrated into many of these classroom activities—integrated so that the technology is not the focus but rather one medium for learning.

The wide range of software that is related to animals and designed for young children provides the teacher with the flexibility of focusing the theme in several different ways, for example, by animal habitat—home, zoo, or farm, or by category of animal—mammal, reptile, or bird. Some programs teach children information about how various animals look, and other programs use animal characters to teach other concepts, such as numbers. Still others tell animal stories or present animal pictures to be colored. This range of programs is also available for other unit areas, such as body parts, nursery rhymes, school, family, community helpers, foods, transportation, and seasons. Often these programs can be combined with other materials, such as puppets, books (in some cases there may be a book and a computer story that are identical), and toys.

Child choice periods

Most early childhood programs include periods in the day, ranging from brief to lengthy, when children are free to engage in play activities of their choosing. Such times provide opportunities for choice making, self-direction, and social interactions with peers. Assistive technology devices such as the WOLF (voice-output device) or PowerPad (alternative computer input device) can be programmed with the day's play options. Nonverbal children can indicate their choices by pressing the desired picture, which will make the computer say, "I want to play blocks." Devices such as these also help children visualize and limit the scope of choices, thus facilitating choice making. Because of the pairing of a graphic representation with a linguistic expression, these devices reinforce this linkage; they may also pair a written word with a picture and/or a spoken word and thus help the child make these connections.

Activities that are described in the planned activity or storytime sections may also be used as learning center activities, and many of them can be used by several children to-

gether. Some software programs actively invite group participation. For instance, several software programs introduce children to game playing through turn taking. One of these is *Rockets to the Moon*, in which each child uses a marker to advance around the game board.

Each day the computer can be set up as a choice option, with a program focusing on similar functional skill areas. If the teacher is using a theme unit approach, these programs would also be related thematically. For example, a variety of programs featuring animals are available: *Talking Animals*; interactive fiction/adventure games like *Katie's Farm*; learning games, including those with a cause-and-effect focus such as *Run Rabbit Run, Big/Little I or II,* and *The Three Little Pigs*. These programs represent a variety of ability levels, use different input devices, and can be used alone or with a friend. They can be used for functional skill development for cause-and-effect, choice making, scanning, visual tracking, concept development, and story sequencing. Carefully chosen programs can meet the needs of the functional and the thematic approach.

Morning circle

Circle time is often used to present a number of concepts and skills to the children. Common activities include sharing names and looking to see which children are there and who is missing (fostering children's learning and recognizing written and spoken names); discussing days of the week, seasons, and holidays; sharing objects brought from home (possibly related to the thematic unit); and listening to information the teacher needs to share about events to take place during the day or week. Participation in these activities can be enhanced by a talking PowerPad with potential responses pictured on it, giving the nonverbal child the opportunity to participate by "speaking" his name at the appropriate time.

Circle time might also provide an opportunity to introduce a new theme-related or skill-focused computer program that will be available later during center time. The children might sing a class song with the assistance of the computer to get everyone participating for the day. For example, "If You're Happy and You Know It" or "Wheels on the Bus" are computer-generated songs frequently used in preschool settings. These programs use the PowerPad to present pictorial representations of each verse. The children can press their verse of choice. The class may also choose a special theme-linked song, such as "Old McDonald's Farm." On some days the computer may be used to assist with the singing, while on other days an adapted Tape-A-Mike might be used to capture the children's independent or group performance. With these uses technology can bring new meaning to participating in the language-intensive activities of circle time.

Direct instruction

Realizing that all children need some direct instruction to efficiently achieve new skills, teachers generally devote some time during the preschool day to structured, planned activities. Teachers use these activities to specifically address deficit skills or to guide children into new areas of knowledge and skill development. Some children need to have more practice than do other children to gain the skill. A switch with a battery-operated toy for learning cause-and-effect offers a child the opportunity to become a more proficient switch user. This proficiency in switch use may be important for later access with a communication device. Toy animals that have

been adapted for switch activation are ideal for this structured learning time because they do not require one-to-one teacher–child interaction. If the child is more cognitively advanced, the toy could be used as a "cursor" that must advance to a specific target to get a reward.

For other children in the classroom, this time might be used for specific vocabulary-building activities. *First Words* is a computer program that teaches receptive language, with words thematically organized. The program collects performance data that assists the teacher in monitoring a child's progress toward a specific learning goal. Other programs for directed language instruction might include *Sticky Bear Opposites, Bear Jam Body Parts,* and the interactive *Hide N Seek With Fluffy.*

This instruction may also focus on developing early number concepts for some children. Programs that use animals for number skill development include *Number Farm, Rosie the Counting Rabbit, Playroom,* and *Millie's Math House.*

Snack

Snack time, like circle time, is a natural for focusing on language, communication, and choice-making skills. The teacher can program a WOLF or Cheap Talk, two inexpensive synthesized voice-output augmentative communication devices, with the names of the specific snacks that are offered. Children can use these augmentative communication devices to request their choice of snacks, to pair communication symbols or pictures with the tangible item, or to practice turn taking. The device may also provide a way for a child to give simple "yes" and "no" responses so that he may respond to table talk during snack, and a way to requesting "more" when he desires additional food.

Storytime

Technology can address numerous literacy skills. Some software programs have a drill-and-practice format, such as those incorporated in the planned activities. Others are similar to the "reading aloud" activity that most teachers perform daily. Programs such as *The Adventures of Jimmy Jumper* and *Just Grandma and Me* provide digital narration of stories but also give the child control over the pace of the story. In most cases the child can control the number of times a page can be repeated, allowing her to independently engage in the activity and even have the story repeated over and over as many times as she desires. Teachers and parents often tire of this repetition, but a computer has infinite patience. This activity can also benefit the child who typically is a passive learner during storytime, possibly due to a physical disability; with this program he can act as the page turner.

The teacher may choose to read the traditional printed book to the whole class and use technology later to supplement that activity. The children can participate in the story by commenting on the pictures and sharing their thoughts. As an extension of the activity, children may re-read the story on the computer or even, with some software, rearrange the ending of the story in different ways. Two examples of such programs with an animal theme are *Explore-a-Story: The Three Little Pigs* and *The Ugly Duckling*. Other software, such as *Kid Pix,* allows children to create their own animal stories using tools to free draw or stamp pictures of animals on a page and then verbally record their story about the picture using the microphone feature. These stories can be printed out and used to decorate the room or to send home to share with parents. Other software, such as the *Pelican Big Book* series, allows children to generate their own stories and then print out, in color, books as big as posters that can be used for storytime.

* * *

The discussion of integrating technology throughout the day illustrates the use of technology to assist with functional skill development and its presentation using a thematic framework if desired. Objectives for the children can be addressed through a variety of on- and off-computer tasks. The computer is simply one of the materials through which children learn. The computer and appropriate software can assist teachers in providing young children with multimodal learning opportunities to meet their needs. Technology can also provide access to learning materials for some children who cannot access standard print or who are unable to manipulate materials by hand.

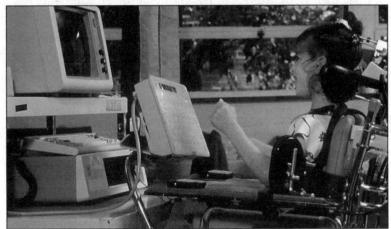

Teachers must consider individual needs and capacities in selecting both software and hardware to suit each child.

Conclusions

Technology has become an important and powerful tool for young children and for teachers in early childhood during the past decade. As tools for children, hardware and software now can provide easy-to-use access to the learning environment. For children with special needs, assistive technology provides access to the classroom environment through low-tech adaptations as well as through high-tech computer- and microprocessor-based applications. The computer enables virtually any child to access software designed to enhance learning by providing access through adaptive input devices, by outputting in a form that young children can understand, and by presenting information through software programs that help children to direct their own learning and to learn at their own pace. Additionally, young children can be introduced to tool applications, such as keyboarding and word processing. These applications represent assistive technology for everyone who has to communicate in writing.

References

Almy, M., P. Monighan, B. Scales, & J. Van Hoorn. 1984. Recent research on play: The teacher's perspective. In *Current topics in early childhood education*, Volume V, ed. L.G. Katz. Norwood, NJ: Ablex.

Behrmann, M.M. 1984. *Handbook of microcomputers in special education*. San Diego: College-Hill Press.

Behrmann, M.M., & E.A. Lahm. 1985. *A hierarchical framework for teaching young multiply handicapped children to use the computer as a tool*. Paper presented at the Council for Exceptional Children Conference, April, in Anaheim, CA.

Bredekamp, S., ed. 1987. *Developmentally appropriate practice in early childhood programs serving children from birth through age 8*. Exp. ed. Washington, DC: NAEYC.

Clements, D.H. 1987. Research in review. Computers and young children: A review of research. *Young Children* 43 (1): 34–44.

Cook, R.E., A. Tessier, & M.D. Klein. 1992. *Adapting early childhood curricula for children with special needs*. New York: Macmillan.

Franklin, K. 1992. Supported employment and assistive technology = a powerful partnership. In *Rehabilitation counselor's desktop guide to supported employment*, eds. S.L. Griffin & W.G. Revell. Richmond, VA: Virginia Commonwealth University, Rehabilitation Research and Training Center on Supported Employment.

Gesell, A., H.M. Halverson, H. Thompson, F.L. Ilg, B.M. Castner, L.B. Ames, & C.S Amatruda. 1940. *The first five years of life: The preschool years*. New York: Harper & Row.

Greenspan, S., & N.T. Greenspan. 1985. *First feelings*. New York: Viking Penguin.

Hodapp, R.M., J.A. Burack, & E. Zigler. 1990. The developmental perspective in the field of mental retardation. In *Issues in the developmental approach to mental retardation*, eds. R.M. Hodapp, J.A. Burack, & E. Zigler. New York: Cambridge University Press.

Lahm, E., M. Behrmann, & E. Thorp. 1993. *Features that work for teachers: Software features in early childhood special education*. Technical report, Center for Human Disabilities, George Mason University, Fairfax, VA.

Nuba-Scheffler, H., D.L. Sheiman, & K.P. Watkins. 1986. *Infancy: A guide to research and resources*. New York: Teachers College Press.

Peterson, N.L. 1987. *Early intervention for handicapped and at-risk children*. Denver: Love.

Piaget, J. 1962. *Play, dreams and imitation in childhood*. Translated by G. Gattegno & F.M. Hodgsom. New York: Norton.

Technology-Related Assistance for Individuals with Disabilities Act of 1988. U.S. Public Law 100-407, sec. 3, p. 102, stat. 1046–47, 19 August 1988.

Wilds, M. 1989. Effective use of technology with young children. *NICHY News Digest* 13: 6–7.

Wolery, M., P. Strain, & D. Bailey. 1991. In *Reaching potentials: Appropriate curriculum and assessment for young children*, Vol. 1, eds. S. Bredekamp & T. Rosegrant, 92–111. Washington, DC: NAEYC.

Patricia A. Ainsa, Daniel Murphy,
Suzanne Thouvenelle, and June L. Wright

Family Involvement:
Family Choices at Home and School

As educators, many of us have been involved in exploring the computer's role in the classroom and child care center; we have spent less time focusing on children's experiences with technology in the home and how these experiences mesh with the ones they have in early childhood programs. Yet electronic media in the home are a key aspect of our children's changing world, as reports from the United States, Australia, and Japan confirm (Times Mirror Center for The People and The Press 1994; Downes n.d.).

Television, a powerful communication tool, was "an unmitigated disaster by overuse in the home . . . a disaster by default in the classroom," as Ohles (1985, p. 51) reminds us in his article, "The Microcomputer: Don't Love it to Death." Now television has been joined by videotapes, computers, electronic games, and music videos in claiming the leisure time of our families. The challenge of ensuring that microcomputers and video games have positive rather than negative effects in children's lives is closely akin to the challenge we have faced for years with respect to television. With all media we confront similar issues of social responsibility, including concerns about the depiction of violence and gender or ethnic stereotypes (Levin & Carlsson-Paige 1994). The underlying question is, What are the core values, knowledge, and skills that we believe children need, and how can we help *all* children to develop them? (Fatouros, Downes, & Blackwell 1994).

Growing up surrounded by a combination of print, images, and sound, children today have been described as "two channel learners": they learn at school, but they also get a lot of their information and attitudes outside of school through various entertainment-oriented media (White 1987, p. 55).

Computers in the home and community

According to a recent survey by the Times Mirror Center for the People & The Press (1994), nearly one-third of U.S. households report owning a personal computer. Not surprisingly, ownership is highly related to socioeconomic status and educational level. Only 11% of households with income less than $20,000 have personal computers; another 11% of homes in which the respondent has not completed high school have computers. By contrast, 56% of homes with a family income of more than $50,000 have computers. Overall, homes with children are more likely to have computers than those without children (39% versus 25%), but among the least affluent households (with incomes less than $20,000), the presence of children makes no difference in computer ownership. Many households that do not have computers, however, have video games. In addition to the video game units found in one of every three U.S. homes, millions of portable units, such as Gameboy, have been sold (Silvern 1992).

In addition to using computers and video game units at home, families may explore the computer and other technological wonders in public places such as museums. At the Capital Children's Museum in Washington, D.C., families can enjoy paint/draw programs, estimation games, and *Logo;* Boston's Computer Museum displays the history of computing and an extensive array of computer activities, including a life-size computer for children to command and observe; and Philadelphia's Science Museum features an extensive array of virtual reality experiences for children and adults. Just as we encourage families to share fine works of art with their children, we should encourage them to take advantage of such public media displays, which typically incorporate state-of-the-art technology and often include explanations of the learning potential of new media forms.

Another resource for families is computer clubs, a variety of which have come into existence in recent years. Although some clubs are targeted to adults, some are designed particularly for children. A club may offer options to the family, such as subscribing to a software magazine or even receiving a compact disc sampler that provides samples of programs. Using the latter, family members may preview the newest programs together, select the software they want, and purchase by phone the password that makes the selected program immediately operational. Software may also be previewed by modem or at local computer stores.

Concerns and resources

As computer access and available software increase dramatically, parents have issues to consider that did not arise until recent years.

To encourage children to work together with siblings or playmates, parents can select software that offers opportunities for cooperation and interaction.

Work or play?

At the most basic level, parents face the question of the role that computers should play in the lives of their children. Some parents believe that children should be using the computer primarily to promote learning. Others are comfortable seeing their children use the computer primarily for entertainment, yet they also may fear that the children will become too engrossed in games of skill and adventure at the expense of other activities.

Research confirms that children who can control their own computer use tend to see their activities at the computer as play. By contrast, children who are told what to do on the computer see the experience as work (King 1986; Baird &

Silvern 1990; Hanor n.d.). However, the distinction between work and play disappears when appropriate, engaging software is available and children's selections are intrinsically motivated. Electronic games may appear to be "just fun," but embedded in that fun children can discover new tools for problem solving and a sense of ownership of their own learning (Baird & Silvern 1990).

Software selection

How do parents know what programs are good for their children? The new words *edutainment* and *infotainment*—and the marketing hype that goes with them—may confuse even the most technically savvy among us. Moreover, as publishers race to the marketplace to be ready for the skyrocketing home market that is anticipated, they are allocating less time to having educators pilot software development. As a result, those who are knowledgeable about children's development and the potentials of computer technology need to play a larger role in evaluating published software and in helping parents learn what to look for in choosing programs for the home. Fortunately, some software publishers are taking their responsibility to educate parents quite seriously and are including carefully written guidebooks for parents with their products.

As adults we sometimes look for intellectual growth in narrow terms, and in so doing we may overlook the potential for creative designing and imaginative portrayal inherent in this new tool. It is wise to look for software that allows children to save, reuse, and change their creations and that lets children grow by providing layers of complexity and greater fluidity in organizing and presenting their ideas (Kafai & Soloway

1994; Hanor n.d.). Parents who select software that is open-ended and who seek a balance between different genres—art, music, storytelling, writing, and problem-solving environments; and encyclopedias, atlases, and dictionaries—will find that children are skilled at selecting what they find challenging, educational, and fun.

As teachers and parents, our challenge is to recognize that various forms of technology will continue to play a key role in children's lives. To give up on trying to understand and participate in the expanding world of technology is to relinquish valuable opportunities for shared experiences. By becoming partners with our children in that learning environment, we can both learn and guide, ensuring that commercial producers do not entirely determine what happens in the world of technology. (For a complete discussion of how to select software, see Haugland & Shade, chapter 5. The Resources section at the end of the book cites several comprehensive guides that review a variety of software and help parents grapple with key issues [e.g., Raskin & Ellison 1992; Salpeter 1992].)

Social relationships

Parents often express concern about the computer's influence on children's social development; they fear that children become isolated when absorbed in computer games. In fact, a high level of social interaction and cooperative learning takes place at the computer (Natashi & Clements 1993; Strommen 1993). Computers promote social behaviors when children share their knowledge with peers and parents as they progress from novice to expert (Levin 1981). The teacher/learner roles at school and in the family may be reversed as children teach their parents about the computer (Ferrari et al. 1985).

Parents using a writing program with their children are amazed at the storytelling ability the children show.

To encourage children to work together with siblings or playmates, parents can select software that offers opportunities for cooperation and interaction, such as programs that allow each child to play a specific role. In an adventure game like *Mixed Up Mother Goose,* children naturally take on their own varying roles. One becomes the keyboard whiz who skillfully guides the character around town, another becomes the map reader, and a third remembers where the lost items were seen (perhaps making note of this information in writing).

Another child who remembers all the Mother Goose rhymes recites them to recall which character lost which item. Sometimes adult mediation is needed to help children realize their different strengths and contributions to the team, but with their strong motivation to solve the adventure, children can often identify their own roles (Levin 1981).

Some satisfying group experiences for school-age children are producing club newsletters, complete with pictures and professional-looking text, and creating flashy banners and cards for special events. These productions can be family creations for special friends or grandparents. Writing together at the computer, each member of the family can contribute, and everyone can make editing suggestions when the message is reread. Because changes are so easy to make, writing at the computer gives adults and children a sense of flexibility that tends to promote greater fluency. In one study, parents who used a nature/writing program with their children expressed amazement at their children's storytelling ability; they were also surprised that so much high-quality, interactive software for children exists (Wright, Seppy, & Yenkin 1992). A single opportunity to interact together may spark a continuing family project.

Teaching techniques

Parents, many of whom did not grow up with computers, find themselves with many decisions to make and little background knowledge to call upon. Eager for their children to succeed, parents sometimes become impatient with the time that young children need to acquire basic computer skills at their own pace. Teachers and parent educators need to help parents understand that children differ in their reactions to various programs, as well as to the devices available for controlling the cursor. One child may do best with the mouse, for instance, while another prefers the keyboard. Such preferences apparently do not depend on age; a 3-year-old may choose the keyboard while a 5-year-old opts for the mouse. Many teachers report that it is best to let children find their own way to control the mouse or other devices; adult assistance seems to confuse them.

Children also benefit from controlling their choice of program through a menu. Sometimes the child may choose to work in a new program, and at other times she may return to old favorites, just as children return to favorite and familiar toys or books. With these options, the child can gradually master programs to the point at which she can enjoy their full potential and use them most creatively.

The home–school connection

Researchers suggest that the way to ensure meaningful use of the computer in the home is to bridge the gap between home and school. In a study by Hess (in Deringer 1986), children in three kindergarten classes had access to computers at home and at school. When the school provided guidance, parents were very involved with their children's computer use at home until each child gained competence, at which point parental participation dropped off. Parents enthusiastically supported the project and noted with delight that children's TV viewing declined as they became involved with computers.

Family workshops stimulate parent involvement with children's computer use at home as well as parent support for the microcomputer's role in the classroom. Such workshops, offered during the day and evening to accommodate nonworking and working parents, may include presentation of the educational philosophy, demonstration of hardware and software, hands-on experience of the same kind the children experience, videotapes demonstrating children's learning styles, questionnaires to gain information regarding parents' attitudes and knowledge about microcomputers, and description of the parent volunteer program (as well as invitation to participate).

Family members may volunteer to help with computer learning in their child's classroom on a weekly basis or for a particular project, for instance, to serve as editor of a book that the children write. Parent volunteers display growth in their understanding of the developmentally appropriate uses of the computer when they begin to critique the strengths and weaknesses of the software and comment on the children's different learning styles. Volunteers tend to be enthusiastic about participating, as was this father:

I told my boss that I take off Thursday mornings to help the children use the computers. It's the way I can see how they learn and how my daughter's learning is different from others—it's the most fun I have all week!

(Father of a 4-year-old girl, Center for Young Children, College Park, MD)

Parent volunteers may request to take the computers home on weekends to become more familiar with the programs with which they are working in the classroom. In this way parents discover more complex levels of the programs, which they then feel secure in introducing in the classroom because they are comfortable with their new role as "experts" on a program of their choice.

Getting parents involved: Case studies

Four case studies of projects may extend our understanding of the ways in which parents and other family members may be involved in supporting technology in early childhood programs. Three of the four case studies were conducted with low-income families. Although a greater proportion of low-income families than middle-income families have no home computer, many families of ample income do not have computers (Times Mirror Center for The People and The Press 1994). Middle-class parents, too, may lack experience in using computers. Despite differences between low- and middle-income "computerless" families, successful efforts to involve low-income families in their children's computer learning may have implications for working with relatively "low-tech" families of all income levels. In each of these case studies, technology has been an effective catalyst to stimulate family involvement in young children's learning. These projects describe home–school–community interactions that employ the computer as a tool with which families explore and enjoy together.

Case study 1: A multigenerational classroom experience

Experiences with family members in a low-income, limited-English–proficient (Spanish-speaking) population have extended our knowledge of involving parents and grandparents as technology advocates. For 12 years in El Paso, Texas, hands-on learning opportunities with computers have been offered to children, parents, and grandparents (Ainsa 1989, 1992). Staff experiences have confirmed the importance of including the older generations of a family in children's learning, as

Parent volunteers report that they learn a lot about children's thinking and learning as they help them to use computers.

riencing. Stationed at different computers displaying various software packages, the children demonstrated their new computer expertise for family members. Computer-generated certificates were distributed to parents and grandparents who participated in the session.

A second level of involvement was attained by family members *receiving in-depth training,* provided through the school or through Head Start. With such training, family members became familiar with methods for supporting children's learning and extending writing and reading activities at home. The activities in the training were designed to connect children's classroom computer experiences with home experiences, thus promoting development of literacy skills. Parents and grandparents were given instructions and materials in their primary language and encouraged to work with children at home.

Some parents and grandparents expressed interest in *becoming more computer literate.* Teachers developed a series of eight workshops to train family members to become computer users. Participating parents and grandparents were able to get university credit for this training and could directly access university computer labs.

Certain parents and grandparents showed a very high, sustained level of interest in working with computers and young children; in fact, their enthusiasm and commitment led to their *serving as classroom volunteers* or even as paid aides. They directly assisted children in using computers and helped parents and grandparents who were computer novices. They evaluated the parent training initiative, as well as the software and computer curriculum experiences in each classroom. Some family members moved from the volunteer role to paid employment as classroom or computer lab aides.

Finally, some individuals reached a level of interest *combining*

noted by other parent educators (e.g., Seefeldt et al. 1990). In the El Paso project, parents and grandparents showed varying levels of technological interest and involvement; five such levels were identified.

Many family members had a level of interest that may be characterized as *seeking basic information.* Project staff found that this level of interest could be satisfied through an open house that offered family members a chance to preview software in the same classroom setting that children were expe-

technology advocacy and volunteerism. Some parents and grandparents, seeing firsthand the tremendous benefits to children from technology, volunteered their time and energies to extend the opportunities to children and families who did not yet have access to computers. These parents and grandparents worked hand-in-hand with educators to raise the awareness of local businesses, state legislators, and funders. They generated plans and strategies to ensure a place for technology in educational and child care settings. Recognizing the importance of hands-on computer training and support for family members like themselves, as well as for teachers, they worked hard to advocate for such training.

Case study 2: Working with teenage parents

In 1990, Milwaukee's Social Development Commission Head Start Program sponsored a summer (10-week) computer-assisted learning program for 17 Head Start teen parents, who were between the ages of 18 and 24. The program offered hands-on training; individualized peer-facilitated learning in basic writing, reading, and math skills; word processing; touch typing; and exploration of career options. In addition, parents worked with their children using developmentally appropriate software.

Staff emphasized the importance of using the principles of adult learning to create an empowering learning environment. Vital in this context was recognizing that young parents, especially those in difficult life circumstances, need opportunities to feel in control of their learning and outcomes. To be effective as the primary educators of their children, young people need to experience success in their own learning. Supporting parents in their role as the child's primary

educator had the additional payoff of strengthening parents' commitment to pursuing educational and career goals of their own. Finally, the adolescent parents' self-esteem—and thus the effectiveness of such a program—was increased by promoting friendship and support among the parents, as well as between parents and Head Start staff.

At a more specific level, several elements seem to be particularly important in designing and implementing an effective program for teen parents:

- Identify staff who can work well with young parents, getting to know them and fostering rapport.

- Establish a minimum number of sessions that participants must commit to attending, a clear method for monitoring their progress, and on-site child care for their children.

- Identify peer facilitators with leadership ability and interest in technology to serve as coaches and to work individually with participants when they encounter difficulty.

- Provide sufficient hardware and software to permit pairs to work at each computer. Because printouts are very important to participants who have not had routine access to computers, a printer should be available for each pair of computers.

- Conduct a weekly debriefing to give participants, peer facilitators, and staff members the opportunity to discuss progress, frustrations, and the joys of accomplishment. Participants and staff in the Milwaukee project found that such meetings kept communication open and the learning atmosphere positive.

With greater confidence as a result of their successful participation in the summer project, eight parents resumed their high school education, pursued a program at a technical college, or attended a local university. Six participating parents were enlisted in Social Development Commission apprenticeships that included word processing, bookkeeping, reception, and parent support group facilitation. To increase long-term impact, the coordinator arranged for the software and support materials and processes (e.g., Individualized Learning Plans [ILPs], and orientation notes) to be integrated into a community center computer laboratory that offered instruction in basic skills, General Educational Development (GED) preparation, and school readiness.

Case study 3: A new approach to literacy

By and large, all parents want their children to be successful in school and in life, and they will do almost anything to help their children have better lives. However, parents who have had negative school experiences themselves have greater difficulty interacting with the school as agents in their child's education. Many feel that they are watching their children experience the same negative consequences that they had in school. Parents with limited literacy are often particularly anxious about contacts with teachers and school staff. Low parental literacy also affects children directly by limiting their access to books and to hearing books read aloud; they are at serious risk of becoming nonreading adults. Early intervention programs, such as Head Start and Even Start, can help to break the intergenerational cycle of illiteracy.

The pilot phase of the Head Start/IBM Partnership Project, begun in 1987, focused on introducing classroom computer software to children, but the benefits to parents who served as classroom volunteers soon became clear. These parents' initial goal was to learn more about the computer and to become comfortable helping their children in the classroom. The

Eager for children to succeed in the age of technology, parents at all income levels are enthusiastic about computers in the classroom; many parents spend time enjoying the home computer with their children as well.

parents used the children's software (*KIDWARE2+*), which provides voiced instructions (in any language), eliminating the need to read text on the screen. This feature allows parents with varying literacy skills to use the software independently, thus enhancing their self-confidence, interest, and motivation.

This classroom experience stimulated some parents' desire for more focused literacy and job-training software applications to help them improve their own skills. Consequently, they were offered introductory hands-on computer training, including word processing—on an IBM word processing program with voiced instructions to teach simple word processing skills (*Primary Editor*

Plus)—the following letter poignantly expresses what one mother wanted to tell her children about her initial experience at the computer.

```
dear children, I am learning to work an IBM computer. I
am trying very, very hard to learn the most possible. It
can be very helpful to everyone in the family. I am ask-
ing you to bear with me because it is a great experience
for everyone to learn. I Love You Very Much. Wish Your
Mother luck kids. With Love, A Head Start Mother,
Deridder, LA
```

(January 1989)

In response to parents' request for help to improve their keyboarding, the project offered introductory touch typing. As a direct result of the experiences provided by volunteering in the Head Start classes and using computers for their own skill building, several parents were hired in positions that required knowledge of technology.

Project participants saw helping families to establish economic self-sufficiency a valuable aspect of having computers in Head Start programs. Parents also were enthusiastic about their children having opportunities to use computers. Because the computers were used in an integrated fashion within the Head Start program, children and parents had opportunities to share the equipment and experience a sense of self-esteem and motivation to learn.

Case study 4: Parents as software evaluators

With the growing number of programs available for young children, teachers are unable to explore all of the options. One component of a university lab school effort to stimulate parent interest in the computer's role in the classroom was the "Computer Weekend," named by one of the parents (Wright & Church 1986). A group of parents, who were serving as classroom computer assistants, volunteered to try out programs in their homes, observing their children's responses and completing a checklist of criteria for developmentally appropriate software. Parent feedback was useful not only to the programs but also to increase teachers' awareness of what criteria were important to the parents. Moreover, this project validated the parents as important partners in shaping their children's educational plan.

Not only mothers and fathers, but grandparents, senior citizen volunteers, and high school volunteers became involved in this project. What began as a parent education effort became a home–school–community connection. The key to its success was letting the parents become initiators.

Conclusion

In these case studies we see numerous strategies that can be used to link young children's classroom computer experiences with the home. Discovering the family members' concerns and interests is a crucial first step. All parents can learn to foster children's learning and computer literacy. Only through literacy can today's children become fully participating members of the new information age, the 21st-century society.

Because many parents see technology use as a key life skill, they believe—and desperately hope—that simply having access to and experience with computers will make their children's economic future better than their own circumstances. Although this perception may not be totally accurate, it reflects parents' commitment to their children's education and future. Moreover, parents' strong belief in the value of technology suggests that computers may be a good point-of-entry for involving parents in their children's education and—for parents whose own literacy and job options are limited—perhaps helping them to acquire new skills.

Evidence that many parents at all income levels see technological competence as essential to their children's future can be seen in parent groups' hard work to help schools and child care programs acquire computers. A more difficult challenge, but a critical one, is enabling parents to understand how computers may be used to the children's best advantage—and how they, as parents, can help. In this arena, as in other aspects of young children's care and education, we must build a strong partnership between the home and the early childhood program. Such a partnership will help early childhood educators to ensure that what they do is culturally relevant, equitable, and effective for all children.

References

Ainsa, T. 1989. Improving family literacy through technology in early childhood. *Journal of Reading Improvement* 26 (3): 266–69.

Ainsa, T. 1992. Empowering classroom teachers via early childhood computer education. *Computing in Childhood Education* 3 (1): 3–14.

Baird, W.E., & S.B. Silvern. 1990. Electronic games: Children controlling the cognitive environment. *Early Child Development and Care* 61: 43–49.

Deringer, D.K. 1986. Computers for education in the home: Can schools tap their potential? *Education & Computing* 2: 13–18.

Downes, T. n.d. Children and electronic media in the home. In *Exploring a new partnership: Children, teachers and technology,* eds. D. Benzie & J. Wright. North Holland, Netherlands: Elsevier.

Fatouros, C., T. Downes, & S. Blackwell. 1994. *In control: Young children learning with computers.* Wentworth Falls, NSW Australia: Social Science Press.

Ferreri, M., D. Klinsing, C. Paris, S. Morris, & A.P. Eyman. 1985. Home computers: Implications for children and families. In *Personal computers and the family,* ed. M.B. Sussman, 41–57. New York: Haywood Press.

Hanor, J. n.d. Using an aesthetics lens to investigate young children's experiences with educational technology. In *Exploring a new partnership: Children, teachers and technology,* eds. D. Benzie & J. Wright. North Holland, Netherlands: Elsevier.

Kafai, Y., & E. Solomon. 1994. Computational gifts for the Barney generation. *Communications of the ACM* 37 (9): 19–22.

King, N.R. 1986. Play and the culture of childhood. In *The young child at play,* eds. G. Fein & M. Rivkin. Washington, DC: NAEYC.

Levin, J.A. 1981. *Computers in non-school settings: Implications for education.* ERIC, ED 243 409.

Levin, D.E., & N. Carlsson-Paige. 1994. Developmentally appropriate television: Putting children first. *Young Children* 49 (5): 38–44.

Nastasi, B.K., & D.H. Clements. 1993. Motivational and social outcomes of cooperative computer education environments. *Journal of Computing in Childhood Education* 4 (1): 15–44.

Ohles, J.F. 1985. The microcomputer: Don't love it to death. *Technological Horizons in Education* 13 (1): 49–53.

Raskin, R., & C. Ellison. 1992. *Parents, kids, and computers: An activity guide for family fun and learning.* New York: Random House.

Salpeter, J. 1992. *Kids & computers: A parent's handbook.* Carmel, IN: SAMS, Prentice Hall.

Seefeldt, C., B. Warman, R. Jantz, & A. Galper. 1990. *Young and old together.* Washington, DC: NAEYC.

Silvern, S.B. 1992. Are video games zapping your child's mind? A guide to the proper care and feeding of the video-game child. *Prevention* 44 (8): 57–58, 121–25.

Strommen, E.F. 1993. "Does yours eat leaves?" Cooperative learning in an educational software task. *Journal of Computing in Childhood Education* 4 (1): 45–56.

Times Mirror Center for The People and The Press. 1994. *Technology in the American household.* Washington, DC: Author.

White, M.A. 1987. Imagery as the new language of the information age. Paper presented at the Eighth National Educational Computing Conference (NECC), June, Philadelphia, PA.

Wright, J.L., & M.J. Church. 1986. The evolution of an effective home-school microcomputer connection. *Education and Computing* 2: 67–74.

Wright, J.L., J. Seppy, & L. Yenkin. 1992. The use of digitized images in developing software for young children. *Journal of Computing in Childhood Education* 3 (3–4): 259–81.

The Challenge for
Early Childhood Educators

**Gwendolyn G. Morgan and
Daniel D. Shade**

Moving Early Childhood
Education into the 21st Century

The computer is not the first form of technology to make its presence felt in early childhood education. For example, our profession accepts technology in the form of audio cassettes, records, and printed books, and these materials add to the range of activities that children experience. In the case of books, for instance, although many teachers of young children have almost abandoned telling stories, they need not do so; the same classroom certainly can have both books and storytelling. Likewise, it is possible to have many learning technologies in the same classroom with other active play materials and equipment, such as blocks, finger paint, and play dough. None of these materials are mutually exclusive.

One could loosely apply the term *learning technology* to any material used in an educational setting. Dockterman (1991) recounts the history behind the chalkboard as the educational technology that replaced individual slates used by children a century ago. Likewise, paper and pencil, crayons and finger paint, blocks and other manipulatives are all educational technologies. However, most educators commonly refer only to those items that plug in as educational technologies, and many argue that anything that plugs in cannot be educational. Addressing this concern is the primary focus of this chapter.

Plug-in technologies in early childhood

Many plug-in technologies are used and valued in early childhood programs. Children can actively use record players, tape recorders, cameras, and video recorders to create, to frame, to play forward and play back. Children have been listening to and identifying farm sounds on tape recordings for at least the past 25 years. Before the advent of published books on tape, teachers were making their own by recording onto a blank tape their reading of classroom favorites so that nonreading children could enjoy the story over and over. Special education teachers, among others, use a tape recorder with young children to record their voices, giving them the experience of immediately hearing themselves on the machine.

Polaroid made cameras accessible to young children. In learning to frame and capture what they were seeing, children gained power and control over their environment. Recently young children have begun using videotape to record their field trips and explorations on the playground. Most 5-year-olds think that a bug is something to stomp on, but recorded through the lens of a camera—whether stop-action or video—bugs become something special. The camera almost seems to elicit from children the desire for more intricate exploration. Or perhaps, in some artistic sense, the children are transported through the camera lens and become one with the world they are observing. Children can turn on and off this tunnel vision as interesting things occur to be recorded.

During a summer camp run by one of the authors, the master teacher inspired the children to use a video camera to make commercials for the restaurant that was set up in the dramatic play area. Krigbaum (1994) tells about young Arapahoe and Shoshone children and their teachers who videotaped their gummy-worm fishing trip. They then inserted the video footage into a computer application called *Kid Pix*, which allowed them to make a book about their trip that included the video footage. As we can see by these examples, plug-in technology is just another powerful educational tool. With appropriate teacher guidance, these tools can be highly interactive, can be controlled by children, and can empower children to do many exciting, playful things.

Challenges in using computers with young children

One could safely say that no new educational technology ever introduced was free of challenge. Certainly storytelling teachers were at first resistant to using children's picture books. Teachers who were accustomed to each child having his or her own slate were resistant to using the chalkboard, especially because classrooms at the turn of the century were multi-age and quite large (Dockterman 1991). Teachers who feel comfortable presenting their lessons in one established way may resist new methodologies. As we wander through our respective campuses, we wonder at the slowness with which dry-erase boards are replacing dusty, dirty chalkboards. But replacement is inevitable. Electric typewriters replaced manual typewriters, single-purpose word processing machines replaced electric typewriters, personal computers replaced word processors, and desktop publishing software replaced simple word processing packages. On the other hand, some things never change. The pencil and crayon have survived the progression of the educational technologies just described. In the same way, we are confident that even as our world becomes ever more technical, many of the traditional activities and materials of early childhood education will stay with us. It would not surprise us to find them becoming all the more important as we make an effort to offer a balanced education to young children.

Wartella and Reeves (1983) noted that as new educational technologies replace older ones, the new seem to follow the same functions as the old for some time. For example, the first application of the personal computer in education was little more than an electronic workbook or ditto page. From a different perspective, we notice that some people never take full advantage of the potential of a word processing program because they cannot stop thinking of their computer as a typewriter.

Davidson (1989) noted that a similar process occurs when introducing computers and many other materials used in the early childhood classroom. First, the teacher may have to spend some time becoming familiar with the material herself. Second, she may need to introduce and explain the material to the children. And third, it may take some time for children to become independent users.

The remainder of this chapter presents a brief overview of the special challenges that have faced the appropriate use of personal computers with young children since approximately 1982. First we deal with the challenges that have been successfully overcome, then we move on to challenges for which a resolution is in process, and finally we take a look at the challenges that remain. Although the objectives are obvious, the strategies for successful resolution depend on all teams working together.

Challenges overcome

Many of the challenges to computer use in early childhood education have involved theoretical misunderstandings and other misconceptions about computer use. In this section we will take a look at some of these misunderstandings and the ways in which they have been addressed.

Misconstruing Piaget

Some early childhood educators have interpreted Piaget's theory, including his description of the *preoperational* and *concrete operations* stages, as implying that all children younger than age 7 develop cognitively only by manipulating materials with their hands—and thus should not be using computers in educational settings. Although Piaget did assert that young children construct much of their knowledge through active manipulation of the environment, this interpretation of his theory is too narrowly literal in two major respects.

First, the meaning of active construction and concrete operations may be taken verbatim. As Clements, Nastasi, and Swaminathan (1993) noted, "what is *concrete* to the child may have more to do with what is meaningful and manipulable than with its physical nature" (p. 56). For instance, the graphic representations of pigs and chickens on a computer-generated farm may be as real, or *concrete*, to the child as are the plastic pigs and chickens in the block area, at least when the child can move these images around by using the mouse.

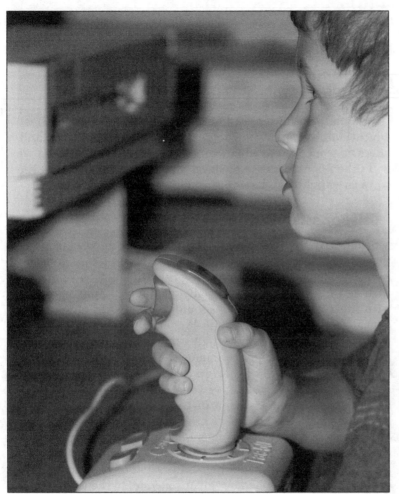

Although young children can learn to use the keyboard to interact with the computer, many find it easier to operate the newer, user-friendly devices, such as the mouse, joystick, trackball, and touchscreen.

Second, descriptions of cognitive stages by Piaget and others represent milestones along the developmental pathway rather than stereotypic depictions of what can invariably be expected of children at a given age. Moreover, Piaget never implies that the child makes an instantaneous leap from one stage to the next; cognitive development occurs incrementally as children explore and interact with the world around them (Vygotsky 1978; Piaget 1983).

Research on what children can do cognitively at various ages has shown that in certain respects they are more capable than we once thought. For instance, they have some understanding of conservation (e.g., the amount of juice in a tall glass does not change when poured into a short, fat glass) and under some circumstances are able to take the perspective of another person.

Selling kids short

Davidson (1989) illustrated how gross misconceptions of young children using computers might come about. According to her, early childhood educators make second-hand judgments based upon their own limited experience with computers. If an adult computer novice has "used a computer to search for data or tried to master the many procedures of a desktop publishing program, the thought of children using computers may be mind boggling" (Davidson 1989, p. 13). Yet in today's world, where children operate microwave ovens, videotape players, and video game machines, only a hermit would question a young child's ability to learn how to use a personal computer.

In the early 1980s, when young children's competency with computers was first documented, computers had self-starting programs, which required the children to insert one or more disks into the disk drive (e.g., Apple II, Atari 800); tape drives; and non–self-starting software (e.g., Commodore 64, IBM PC Jr.) that often required using a complex command language in order to load and run a computer program. And the children who performed these seemingly miraculous feats were mostly nonreaders (Shade et al. 1986; Shade & Watson 1987; Brinkley & Watson 1988; Clements & Nastasi 1992; Clements, Nastasi, & Swaminathan 1993). Now that hard disk drives have become the norm in computer configurations and users no longer need to change disks, using the computer is far easier for children. Further, most new software for young children is operated by pointing the cursor at a small picture (icon) and clicking the mouse.

Computers have become more accessible to the young child, as color monitors and graphics have improved and as short-term and long-term file storage has increased. Software interfaces have been developed—such as Apple's *At Ease*, Berkeley Systems' *Launch Pad*, and Edmark's *KidDesk*—that function as a liaison between child and hard disk drive and simplify personal computer operation for nonreading children by providing picture or icon menus and speech synthesis. And no list of hardware and software developments that have benefited young children would be complete without mentioning how circumvention of the keyboard was first made possible by the joystick and later improved by the mouse and the trackball.

Little doubt remains that young children can learn to operate microcomputer hardware and software. Numerous studies (Muller & Perlmutter 1984; Klinzing 1985; Borgh & Dickson 1986; Lipinski et al. 1986; Shade et al. 1986; Shade & Watson 1987; Brinkley & Watson 1988) dating back to the early 1980s revealed that young children can learn to independently turn computers on and off, remove and replace diskettes properly, follow instructions from picture menus, talk meaningfully about their computer activity, work successfully in dyads, help one another, take turns, and share the computer. Hence, after children's initial exposure to the computer, a teacher can treat the computer center more or less like other centers in the room, which children explore at times of their own choosing and at their own pace.

Video game mentality

Another early challenge to the use of computers with young children centered on the assumption that computers socially isolate children, not only displacing other important learning activities but turning the children into automatons. Perhaps many of the people who made these predictions had only seen children playing early video games, like "Space Invaders," the novelty of which made them very hypnotic. Critics of preschool computer use often misinterpreted Papert's (1980) early efforts to motivate educators and teachers to take the initiative and use the "holding power" of the computer to children's advantage as just another fanatical claim that the computer would solve all of our educational problems. What we believe Papert meant was that the power of video games could be used to draw children into rich learning environments. During the same time that comments such as these appeared in the literature, a comprehensive study (Lipinski et al. 1986) investigated the effects of microcomputers on the social behaviors and free-play choices of two groups of children, one group from a full-day program and the other from a half-day program. Results indicated that children were rarely observed alone at the computer; in fact, social behavior was just as likely to occur around the computer as in the other

play areas. As for displacement of other activities, the computer initially was sometimes observed to draw children away from traditional activities, such as fingerpainting and block building, presumably because of its novelty. However, within two weeks children's participation in most activities had returned to baseline levels. Other early studies (Clements & Nastasi 1985; Borgh & Dickson 1986) support these findings. In a more recent study, Haugland (1992) discovered that preschool and kindergarten children average about 14 minutes at the computer during a one-hour free-choice time.

Drill-and-practice drones?

Another early vision of young children using computers portrayed children sitting for lengthy periods responding to drill-and-practice programs like robots. This notion came from claims that the only two computer activities available to young children were programming and programmed learning (Elkind 1987a). It is true that most of the software available to young children in the early to late 1980s was of the drill-and-practice variety. Recent calculations (Shade & Haugland 1993) have shown that although 75 to 80% of software on the market is still drill oriented, the other 20 to 25% encompasses some excellent open-ended, discovery-oriented programs (see later chapters).

Materials for "miseducation"?

Although the microcomputer has its own unique characteristics and potentials, in one sense it is like other materials in early childhood education: it may be used appropriately or inappropriately. Recently Haugland and Shade (1990) presented a developmental approach to selecting software, demonstrating that the software *and* the teacher (Clements 1987) determine how computers will function in the early classroom. Why should we single out this technology as potentially harmful when audiotapes, picture books, and even crayons can be implements of "miseducation" (Elkind 1987b)? Nothing inherent in the computer forces children to grow up too fast too soon. Like other materials, computers are neither panacea nor pernicious (Clements 1987). When used appropriately, with discovery software and teacher guidance, computers can give children a far more active role than does television (Hyson 1985). The computer is a less static medium than the picture book (Piestrup, as cited in Gordon & Browne 1985) and as open-ended as crayons (Watson, Nida, & Shade 1986). As a symbolic machine the computer offers experiences that have much in common with other representational modes, such as communicating with gestures, speaking, pretend play, counting, tapping a rhythm, singing, or making a picture or a clay object (Sheingold 1986, p. 27). Further, as Sheingold suggested, computers are part of our everyday world, and as such they should be included in the early childhood classroom as objects to explore, manipulate, and understand, as are typewriters, tape recorders, and record players.

Current challenges, possible solutions

Personal and professional bias

Using computers with young children remains a controversial issue. Each year, when we present at NAEYC's Annual Conference, we still encounter people who misconstrue Piaget, sell kids short, equate all software with video games, fear that the computer is unsafe or too fragile, believe all computer software to be drill-and-practice, and generally believe that the computer contributes to the miseducation of young children. The challenges that lie ahead call for solutions. We must move onward.

Few practitioners have had the opportunity to observe appropriate use of computers in early childhood settings, thus they may assume that the inappropriate use they have observed is the necessary norm. Inappropriate practices of computer technology abound. Microcomputers can be used exclusively for drill-and-practice. They can be used in isolated computer labs rather than socially, in the classroom. Computers can be set up in ways that frustrate children by making them compete for too-short periods of use. They can even be brought in from outside on a fee-paying basis by specialists who know little of child development and do not care about all children having access. Computers can be used to play on parents' anxiety about their children's school success and induce them to buy drill-and-practice software that advertisements claim will improve their child's intelligence.

The directors and teachers in high-quality early education programs will reject such practices and may associate them with microcomputer use in general. When this leads to rejection of the technology as a whole, many rich learning opportunities are lost. The early childhood educational community needs to see that computers can be used in developmentally appropriate ways. Beyond books like this one that seek to communicate the value of developmentally appropriate integration of computers into early childhood programs, teachers need training programs in appropriate use of computers with young children.

When we set up a computer program for young learners, two considerations are important. The first is Dr. Robert Lawler's question (personal communication, January–April

1983): What can the child gain from this experience that can be acquired in no other way? If we can not answer this question, then a computer is not the material we need. The second consideration is noted by the National Association for the Education of Young Children: "Enjoying the curriculum is an important but insufficient criterion for curriculum selection" (NAEYC 1991, p. 31). Children may appear to enjoy their computer experience in all of the applications previously listed as inappropriate, but in the simplest of terms, that does not mean it is good for them.

Teachers' discomfort with computers

Another challenge to the appropriate use of computers with young children is the discomfort that some practitioners feel as a result of their own lack of skill in using the equipment. Even early childhood programs that have microcomputers initially underutilize them; teachers who feel incompetent and unskilled do not use them at all. Training teachers in the use of computer equipment helps enormously. In our experience, teachers will not fare well with computers in the classroom until they have gained a level of comfort based on competence. Becoming capable of doing simple things, such as setting up a computer and loading fonts into a printer, goes a long way toward reaching this comfort zone. Therefore, any program that purports to train preservice or inservice teachers must include training in basic functional use of computers as well as in developmentally appropriate application. In our opinion, 50% of the training time should be hands-on exploration of equipment and software; based upon course evaluations, anything less appears to be inadequate.

A word here about the computer learning curve seems appropriate. Some skills have steep learning curves (intense but over quickly) and others have gradual learning curves (not intense nor over quickly). Learning to ride a bike typically has a steep learning curve. If you are placed on the seat of a bike, told to hold onto the handle bars, and given a shove downhill, you will learn to ride the bike, perhaps after a few falls, within a short time. On the other hand, learning to play a musical instrument has a gradual learning curve. One starts with learning how to hold the instrument, then to play a few notes; gradually, over several years, one becomes proficient (with the exception of prodigies like Mozart and Beethoven, whose learning curves were much steeper!). Adults who are learning to use computers have an initially steep learning curve, in which they spend intense periods of time—from 5 to 15 hours—getting familiar with the hardware and software. From this initial period, the learner gains a good working knowledge of the equipment and software with which she is working and, to some extent, would be able to transfer this knowledge to her learning of other equipment and other software programs. After a few more hours, she may even begin to help others solve their computer problems. In essence, first-time computer users can expect to invest a lot of time at the beginning but can expect to see payback in a very short time, including more professional-looking work and more work accomplished. The same is true when introducing the computer to children in an early childhood classroom. Initially the teacher needs to remain close to the computer or check in with the children frequently. But we have observed that it does not take children long—given how self-motivated they are to use computers—to become independent users, and this frees the teacher to pursue other classroom responsibilities.

Teachers' need for conceptual foundation

Along with lots of hands-on exploration of hardware and software to give users familiarity, comfort, and competence, teacher training must give participants something equally important: a strong conceptual foundation for using computers in the early childhood program. Such a theoretical base will not only help ensure that teachers appropriately integrate computers into the curriculum but will also give them solid justification for their educational practices when critics accuse them of being faddish or, worse yet, "high tech."

Teachers' philosophical resistance to using the computer can be an even greater obstacle than their discomfort and unfamiliarity with computer hardware. This resistance will not be overcome by training from computer specialists; early childhood specialists must be the teacher educators. Faced with the unknown and with no impetus to explore it, the professional may avoid using a computer, on the ethical principle, "First do no harm." Teachers' resistance to using computers with young children based on theoretical misgivings and their reluctance based on discomfort with the technology are two different things; each needs to be addressed in an adequate teacher preparation program. Recently the National Council for Accreditation of Teacher Education (NCATE 1992) decided that professional studies should include "knowledge about . . . the impact of technology and societal changes on schools" and "knowledge about and appropriate skills in . . . instructional technology" (pp. 49–50).

Good teachers of young children are astute observers of what children do and how they learn. As with other materials, observing children's use of computers will give the teacher many clues to each child's process of constructing knowledge.

A teacher must be able to read those clues to teach effectively. If teachers are unable to make the connection between the child development theory they have learned and their culture's evolving tools, then teacher education should be examined.

There is much in accepted theory and research about human development that is applicable to the use of microcomputers, as the various chapters of this volume describe. A recent study (Morgan et al. 1993) revealed that most center-based early childhood staff and family child care providers are not required to have much training for their work. In most early childhood settings, teachers with four-year degrees in early childhood education or child development are the role models for their field. If these college-trained individuals, as a group, are more rigid and biased against computer use than are practitioners with less education, then the responsibility rests with the colleges and universities to make certain that early childhood educators embark on their careers prepared, with appropriate skills and attitudes about computers and other technologies used in early childhood education.

Lack of access to appropriate software

Although the availability of open-ended, discovery-oriented software for young children is increasing almost exponentially, teachers do not always have access to these programs. Sometimes teachers do not get to choose the software because someone else in the school or center, perhaps the "computer teacher" or principal, has purchasing authority. Often, even when teachers are allowed to spend a limited amount of budgeted dollars on software for their class, they are given catalogs that contain only drill software or catalogs from only one company, which may not provide developmentally appropriate software. Most of the time teachers have no control over what software is purchased because an integrated learning system (a complete curriculum package) on math or reading has been purchased for the entire school, district, or system. Yet we know from research that teachers who use the computer in their programs teach more effectively when they choose their own software and integrate it across their curriculum (Clements & Nastasi 1992). At present the commercial marketing and distribution of software favor large purchases, and this presents a problem similar to that with textbook distribution, which also frequently does not allow for individual teacher choice.

Even if 25% of the software now on the market is developmentally appropriate (Shade & Haugland 1993), the other 75% is still a serious problem. Teachers would not be using children's books as an important part of the curriculum if all or most of the books available were inappropriate or of poor quality. Most practitioners have seen some examples of software that have only a novelty interest for children or that are little more than electronic workbooks. Many teachers simply are not aware of the increase in the number of high-quality software programs geared to the way young children use play materials, but these teachers are concerned and continue to search for appropriate software (Haugland & Shade 1994).

The computer as panacea

In this country we often look at our great technical achievements as proof that what we are doing is worthwhile. For example, the expense of space exploration is often justified by the spin-off technological wonders that we use everyday. But there is more to quality of life—and more to good early childhood edu-cation—than technology. As we have emphasized, the computer should be seen as an augmentation or extension of the classroom curriculum. We fear that large, integrated learning systems are being touted as the entire curriculum. We fear that software and hardware manufacturers are sending a message that their "solution" packages are the answer to every district, school, and teacher problem. Most of all, we fear that many teachers and administrators are listening to these advertising messages. It depends on us, the consumers of educational products, to act on behalf of the children by not purchasing inappropriate software products.

Long-term challenges: Obvious objectives but no immediate strategy

Early childhood educators have come a long way in our struggle to overcome the barriers to developmentally appropriate computer use with children, but we cannot yet claim complete success. Three obstacles remain to be overcome if computers and all of the engaging, playful activities they bring with them are to be made available to children for significant lengths of time.

Expense

The high cost of computer equipment has been and continues to be a major challenge to the use of computers in school districts and small early childhood programs. Even large child care centers tend to have smaller budgets than small schools. A center's biggest equipment-budget items—the slide, the swing set, and the climbing apparatus—are less expensive than microcomputers. Currently, computers powerful enough for the classroom or office (Macintosh and IBM-compatible platforms) are running in the $1,500 to $2,000 retail range, and the average price of an early childhood software program is $35 (Buckleitner 1994). A center trying to balance a tight budget might wisely choose to spend its money on a wide variety of other equipment and supplies first and buy the computer later. (See Appendix C for some helpful hints on what to buy.)

Computer labs

Schools have chosen to set up separate computer labs, which are less expensive than placing computers in every classroom. There may be reasons other than expense, however. For instance, Papert sees the labs as a result of school efforts to make computers "a subject all their own," something he labeled the "immune response" (1993). We believe that computer labs have also been a response to parental demand, which in turn is fueled by advertisement pressure. Administrators realized that they could stretch their budget by putting 15 or 20 computers in a room under the direction of a "computer teacher," rather than putting 2 or 3 computers in each classroom, and consequently training only one teacher (the computer lab also placated parents who thought their children disadvantaged without a computer). The problem is just the opposite for small child care centers. Rather than having to worry about saving thousands of dollars, the center director must weigh her or his priorities to decide if purchasing a computer is warranted, given other center needs, and if so, where the $2,000 is going to come from.

The most serious outcome of the computer lab is the resulting isolation of the computers. In essence, computer labs move com-

Setting up a "computer lab" may be less expensive than placing a computer in each classroom, but it reduces the possibilities for integrating the computer into the curriculum.

puters from integration across the curriculum to location across the hall. In a lab setting, children's exposure to computers and opportunities for collaboration are limited and yield questionable long-term gain. According to Papert (1993), our schools currently have a million computers and 50 million students; thus, "A million computers divided among fifty million students gives each child one-fiftieth of a computer. I do not think that the significant benefits that computers have brought to me would have accrued from a fiftieth of a machine" (p. 37). Any adult who tries to share a home computer with a spouse and/or children would probably agree with Papert's assessment.

Rapid changes in technology

An exciting but frustrating challenge to the use of computers with young children is shopping and comparing prices to your needs so that you buy a computer that you can afford and that will last for a while. Computer technology changes rapidly. A year ago, a "fast" computer had an operating speed of 33 MHz (one megahertz equals one million cycles per second, so 33 MHz is 33 million cycles per second). Now, with the latest kind of computer chips, operating speed has reached 80 MHz. Also in the past year, CD-ROM technology has begun to dominate the software market. With constant advances in computer technology, how much is enough for the early childhood classroom? If we equate a top-of-the-line computer to a high-performance sports car, do young children need such a high-performance car, or is an ordinary compact car good enough? This question cannot be easily answered. Given the majority of software available on the market today,

the basic computer might be barely adequate, yet the more powerful one would be more than they need. We've heard it argued, and we agree, that young children require powerful machines because they are nonreaders and must have *very* user-friendly software with features such as speech synthesis. Looking at the newest software coming out for children, a computer somewhere between the basic and more powerful models seems appropriate. (Please refer to Appendix C for suggestions on how to choose a computer that will suit your needs as long as possible.)

Conclusions

Challenges to the use of computers in early educational settings are as old as the personal computer itself. Many of the early challenges have been addressed and put to rest by informed education professionals, but we still face many obstacles. Meeting these challenges will require a creative coalition of dedicated software and hardware vendors, educators, and early childhood practitioners to cut paths through the jungle of media hype to produce the kind of hardware and software that young children can "play" with to develop a love for learning (Papert 1993).

Software vendors will have to be willing to forgo the large-scale sales that result from sales of integrated learning systems and must develop high-quality software that can be used across the curriculum rather than being *the* curriculum. Although computer prices have been falling steadily for the past few years, overcoming the price barrier will require hardware vendors to develop a powerful educational computer package for less than $1,000 that includes a monitor, a keyboard, speech and sound production, a printer, and a mouse or trackball. Making it possible for computers to fulfill their role in early education settings will require funding high enough to allow school districts to adequately train teachers in the appropriate use of technology across the curriculum. And finally, those educators and practitioners who were early advocates of computing in early childhood and have been working toward reform will need to rededicate themselves to continue to combat advertisement hype, parent pressure, and government lethargy.

Efforts in this direction have already begun, with the formation of the Technology and Young Children Caucus (TYCC) in 1992. TYCC meets annually at the NAEYC national conference and for the past three years has co-sponsored a preconference session with the NAEYC Technology Panel and the High/Scope Foundation. In these sessions teachers, directors, and educators from all levels have cooperated with hardware and software vendors to bring NAEYC conference participants an opportunity to observe and interact with appropriate technology for young children, as well as to give conference participants an opportunity to hear the latest innovations in computer theory, research, and practice.

The following questions arise from previous discussions. Some have already been raised and are put forth again for the sake of review. Others were implicit in the discussions. These seem to be the seminal questions around which the computer debate will revolve for the next decade.

• Are we teaching child development theory too narrowly so that students are unable to apply theory to new developments—such as computers—in their world?

• How can we address the bias of highly educated professionals who are resistant to new modalities?

• Does computer use promote any kinds of learning and development that are different from those acquired through other educational strategies?

• How can teachers use computers to accommodate differences in individual learning styles and cultural background?

• Should teacher education programs be preparing all teachers to know when and how to use computers (and of course when not to) in their classrooms, and if so, how?

• Should college accreditation standards and teacher education guidelines require technological knowledge and expertise?

• In what ways could designers of software for young children make more extensive use of early childhood professionals' child development knowledge and expertise, including the principles of developmentally appropriate practice?

• How do teachers get information about software, and how can they control what is purchased? What criteria can they use in selecting the software they want to use?

• What kind of software distribution system would empower teachers to make important decisions for their classrooms?

Answers to these questions and others yet to emerge will move early childhood education into the 21st century—not by replacing traditional early childhood activities and materials but by opening the door to worlds of discovery as we learn to use computers and computer software in a developmentally appropriate manner.

References

Borgh, K., & W.P. Dickson. 1986. Two preschoolers sharing one microcomputer: Creating prosocial behavior with hardware and software. In *Young children and microcomputers,* eds. P.F. Campbell & G.G. Fein, 37–44. Englewood Cliffs, NJ: Prentice Hall.

Brinkley, V.M., & J.A. Watson. 1988. Effects of microworld training experience on sorting tasks by young children. *Journal of Educational Technology Systems* 16, 349–64.

Buckleitner, W. Ed. 1994. *Children's Software Revue* (Newsletter) 2 (4). (Available from Mr. Warren Buckleitner, 520 North Adams St., Ypsilanti, MI 48197-2843.)

Clements, D.H. 1987. Computers and young children: A review of the research. *Young Children* 43 (1): 34–44.

Clements, D.H., & B.K. Nastasi. 1985. Effects of computer environments on social-emotional development: Logo and computer-assisted instruction. *Computers in the Schools* 2 (2–3): 11–31.

Clements, D.H., & B.K. Nastasi. 1992. Computers and early childhood education. In *Advances in school psychology: Preschool and early childhood treatment directions,* M. Gettinger, S.N. Elliott, & T.R. Kratochwill, 187–246. Hillsdale, NJ: Lawrence Erlbaum.

Clements, D.H., B.K. Nastasi, & S. Swaminathan. 1993. Young children and computers: Crossroads and directions from research. *Young Children* 48 (2): 56–64.

Davidson, J.I. 1989. *Children and computers together in the early childhood classroom.* Albany, NY: Delmar.

Dockterman, D.A. 1991. *Great teaching in the one computer classroom.* Watertown, MA: Tom Snyder Productions.

Elkind, D. 1987a. The child, yesterday, today, and tomorrow. *Young Children* 42 (3): 6–11.

Elkind, D. 1987b. *Miseducation: Preschoolers at risk.* New York: Knopf.

Haugland, S.W. 1992. The effect of computer software on preschool children's developmental gains. *Journal of Computing in Childhood Education* 3 (1): 15–30.

Haugland, S.W., & D.D. Shade. 1990. *Developmental evaluations of software for young children.* New York: Delmar.

Haugland, S.W., & D.D. Shade. 1994. Early childhood computer software. *Journal of Computing in Childhood Education* 5 (1): 83–92.

Hyson, M.C. 1985. Emotions and the microcomputer: An exploratory study of young children's responses. *Computers in Human Behavior* 1: 143–52.

Klinzing, D.G. 1985. *A study of the behavior of children in a preschool equipped with computers.* Paper presented at the meeting of the American Educational Research Association, April, Chicago, IL.

Krigbaum, M. 1994. *The adventure begins* [Videotape]. Cupertino, CA: Apple. [Available from NAEYC]

Lipinski, J.M., R.E. Nida, D.D. Shade, & J.A. Watson. 1986. The effect of microcomputers on young children: An examination of free-play choices, sex differences, and social interactions. *Journal of Educational Computing Research* 2 (2): 147–68.

Morgan, G., S. Azer, J. Costley, A. Genser, & I. Goodman. 1993. *Making a career of it.* Unpublished manuscript, Center for Career Development in Early Care and Education, Wheelock College, Boston, MA.

Muller, A.A., & M. Perlmutter. 1984. *Preschool children's problem-solving interactions at computers and jigsaw puzzles.* Paper presented at the annual meeting of the American Psychological Association, August, Toronto, Canada.

National Association for the Education of Young Children. 1991. Guidelines for appropriate curriculum content and assessment in programs serving children ages 3 through 8. *Young Children* 46 (3): 21–38.

National Council for Accreditation of Teacher Education. 1992. Standards, procedures, and policies for the accreditation of professional education units. Washington, DC: Author.

Papert, S. 1980. *Mindstorms: Children, computers and powerful ideas.* New York: Basic.

Papert, S. 1993. *The children's machine: Rethinking school in the age of the computer.* New York: Basic.

Piaget, J. 1970. Piaget's theory. In *Carmichael's manual of child psychology,* Vol. 1, ed. P.H. Mussen, 703–32. New York: Wiley.

Piestrup, A.M. 1985. In *Beginnings and beyond: Foundations in early childhood education,* eds. A.M. Gordon & K.W. Browne, 399–402. New York: Delmar.

Shade, D.D., & S.W. Haugland. 1993. *1993 Developmental software awards.* Paper presented at the annual conference of the National Association for the Education of Young Children, November, Anaheim, CA.

Shade, D.D., & J.A. Watson. 1987. Microworlds, mother teaching behavior and concept formation in the very young child. *Early Child Development and Care* 28: 97–114.

Shade, D.D., R.E. Nida, J.M. Lipinski, & J.A. Watson. 1986. Microcomputers and preschoolers: Working together in a classroom setting. *Computers in the Schools* 3 (2): 53–61.

Sheingold, K. 1986. The microcomputer as a symbolic medium. In *Young children and microcomputers*, eds. P.F. Campbell & G.G. Fein, 25–34. Englewood Cliffs, NJ: Prentice Hall.

Vygotsky, L.S. 1978. *Mind in society: The development of higher psychological processes.* Cambridge, MA: Harvard University Press.

Wartella, E., & B. Reeves. 1983. Recurring issues in research on children and media. *Educational Technology* (June): 5–9.

Watson, J.A., R.E. Nida, & D.D. Shade. 1986. Educational issues concerning young children and microcomputers: Lego with Logo? *Early Child Development and Care* 23: 299–316.

Suzanne Thouvenelle, Mario Borunda, and Ceasar McDowell

Replicating Inequities: Are We Doing It Again?

Despite the relative newness of personal computer technology, its importance in children's lives is apparent. The disturbing patterns of inequity that are already emerging beg the attention of early childhood educators and call for their active response.

This chapter explores three topics in the context of technology as an educational innovation: (1) the increasing importance of technology in early childhood education; (2) the inequities in children's access to technology in education as a function of gender, cultural and linguistic background, and abilities; and (3) strategies that concerned early childhood professionals can adopt to promote equal access for all young children.

Within this framework we revisit past inequities that have accompanied educational innovations. We explore how an innovation in education reflects the social, cultural, and educational beliefs of the time during which it is constructed. We urge educators not to repeat the mistakes of the past. Finally, we offer possible strategies for meeting the challenges inherent in introducing equality of access to educational innovation.

Technology is becoming increasingly important for early childhood education

Any discussion about technology and early childhood education must examine this fundamental question: Is technology an essential part of preparing young children for their participation in the global community of the 21st century? Today's schools have a growing list of important concerns that educators must incorporate into their daily routines. Some of these concerns border on the mundane, and some are central to the daily survival of the children. With increasing issues of health care, violence, substance abuse, family instability, and illiteracy, why should we concern ourselves with equity issues as they relate to technology in schools, in general, and in the early childhood classroom, in particular?

For the past century, education in the United States was thought to be "the great equalizer." Educators who feel this responsibility must play a leadership role in providing equal access to the newest tool of the 20th century. At the heart of citizenship is the ability to be a contributing member of society. This requirement is one of the reasons that reading and writing are always considered important aspects of one's ability to gain full citizenship. These basic skills are required for an individual to become economically self-sufficient, hence a contributor to society rather than a burden.

With the advent of the silicon chip, another challenge to full citizen participation in society has emerged: technological illiteracy. Unlike reading, technological literacy has yet to be defined, but the definition is emerging as the technology steadily redefines the ways in which we interact with others and gain our knowledge of the global world community. Technological proficiency is the new skill required of today's young children, who will be our 21st-century workers. We as early childhood educators must be concerned with the technological preparation of young children.

Ten years ago the height of our understanding of and involvement with technology in schools was limited to Sesame Street and The Electric Company, or to the highly specialized use of mainframe computers for a limited number of "gifted and talented" high school students who were interested in programming. Today the diffusion of technology has shifted the landscape of technological experiences of children. Our chief concerns are expanding from how many hours children spend watching TV to include time spent with *video games*, video recorders, Multi-User Digital Displays (MUDDs), and electronic bulletin boards.

We have come to realize in the past 10 or so years that the experiences of children growing up today are significantly different from the experiences that adults had as children. Accordingly, we need to realize that in order to create meaningful learning environments for children from diverse communities, we must incorporate their experiences. We must offer learners relevant experiences, not isolated facts and skills that have little meaning to their daily lives. Technology is clearly part of the context of children's lives, and, as such, technology has the ability to present vital representations with which children can identify.

In children's everyday environments outside the home, a computerized world is the norm. Store clerks pass merchandise over an optical bar code reader; a child's temperature is taken with a disposable electronic thermometer; the telephone is a one-stop shopping device; and parents, siblings, or friends move in and out of their daily experiences with a beeper attached to their waists. Clearly, a growing disparity exists between the technological experiences children have and those that their parents and teachers have had as children. Because we lack similar childhood experiences, we can only surmise the effect of the technology on children's sense of their world and the role that technology plays in their understandings.

Becker (1988) estimated that by the end of the 1980s there would be at least 2.4 million computers in use in schools. In actuality, at the beginning of the 1990s, approximately 3.5 million computers were installed in elementary and secondary public schools, or one computer for every 13 students (Quality Education Data, Inc. 1993). Ten years ago the ratio was one computer to every 125 students (Becker 1988). Edwards (1993) reported that in 1991 an estimated 25% of households owned computers; in addition, more than 25% of the nation's preschools offer computer activities for young children.

With more and more technology and good-quality software becoming available, the question is no longer whether children will have access to the computer but, instead, which children will have access, and how will technology enrich the learning environment for young children?

Considering the activities of third, fourth, and fifth graders now communicating with friends around the world (recently reported in *The Wall Street Journal*: Pereira 1994), it is exciting to think about how today's children will conceptualize their roles as citizens within a global community. Internet, the electronic superhighway, has quickly been adopted and adapted by some educators in the form of EDNet, Frednet, and others. Will all of these educators be fully functional users of the information superhighway, or will only some of them competently access the knowledge of the global community?

Technology, as noted above, is becoming so widespread and vital that technological knowledge in using computers is now a basic skill. Recent findings suggest, however, that access to technology in early childhood education is unequal for girls and boys, and for children of diverse backgrounds, needs, cultures, and languages. We need to think of technology as an innovation that has the potential to change how we learn, teach, and even how we organize schools. We do not want technology to support a growing gulf between schools in affluent suburbs and those in inner cities. Press (1993) observes that we are in danger of drifting into "third world" education, in which a two-tiered school system maintains the social status quo.

In exploring this topic, we must first understand that there is nothing inherent in technology that limits or makes it inaccessible to people across the age span and across developmental levels. If this is the case, then we must ask, Why is technology available differentially to girls and women, to people of color, and to the economically poor? These conditions result because of tacit policy and behavioral choices that we make; the technology itself does not limit its accessibility. As educators we can make a difference by supporting equitable access to technology for all children.

Rosemary Sutton (1991), in her seminal article, summarized gender, racial, and social inequalities. Implications drawn from a decade of research on the educational use of computers in schools conclude that computers maintain and exaggerate inequalities. The following conclusions summarize Sutton's research concerning gender, racial, and social class differences in the educational uses of computers.

• Girls used computers in and out of school less than did boys.

• African American students had less access to computers than did White students.

- The presence of computers in a school did not ensure access.

- Teachers, while concerned about equity, held attitudes that hindered access—they believed that better behaved students deserved more computer time and that the primary benefit of computers for low-achieving students was mastery of basic skills (i.e., drill-and-practice software).

- Richer schools bought more equipment and more expensive equipment.

These findings clearly point to dangerous patterns emerging that could lead to gross inequities if we do not give careful attention to how we incorporate this growing innovation into the everyday lives of all children and adults. An important part of the scenario is how to incorporate technology into the current educational curriculum.

In the next section we use a historical analogy to explore how insights into the teaching practices of math were developed and how teaching methodologies congruent with these new understandings evolved. Technology is now undergoing similar transformations. We are beginning to offer children experiences that allow them to explore and discover technology as a tool. As a tool, technology simply offers another medium through which children can construct understandings of how the world works.

A historical analogy

In considering the issues needed to thoroughly understand and implement technological literacy in schools, we can learn from the past. A look at past innovations and curricular re-forms is instructive in determining the social, professional, and educational changes necessary to prevent potential inequities from occurring. Educational and social decisions that were made (or not made) resulted in poor practices and longstanding biases. A clear example of this occurrence can be seen in the introduction and growth of mathematics in public education during the 18th and 19th centuries in the United States.

Two interesting parallels exist between the evolution of numeracy and the evolution of technology. The first parallel is that each required a major breakthrough that made access easier to wider audiences. For numeracy it was the adoption and dissemination of the decimal system of money (shortly before the American Revolution). This standardized the system and made it more accessible to all people. For technology the breakthrough has been the introduction and availability of the personal computer, which has allowed almost unlimited access to a world of information.

The second parallel is an educational one, affecting teaching practices. Initially, math was considered appropriate only for mature minds (adolescent and older). With refinements in the knowledge base and changing teaching practices, educators discovered that math could be taught to children as young as 4 or 5 years old. Similarly, during the 1960s and 1970s, technology and computers for educational uses were primarily in institutions of higher learning. Now 3- and 4-year-olds are learning to manipulate a keyboard and realize that they can control what happens on the screen.

Cline-Cohen (1982) delineated the stages of math teaching practices. Math was originally a skill only for people in certain professions. As mathematics became integral to people's lives, it became an essential element of education and was

Currently, girls use computers less than boys do, both in and out of school.

viewed as a foundation for rational thinking. As it became more common and valuable, it was expected to be taught in schools. Even then it was taught only to older boys in their teens.

Soon questions about educational practice emerged. Educators struggled with how best to teach math. More effective methods were developed, and the value of arithmetic was recognized. Not only was it useful for computation purposes but it taught "men" to think. The importance of teaching young boys about math became clear; girls were routinely excluded.

After years of refining teaching methodologies and streamlining math concepts, the conventional notion that arithmetic was a subject fit only for mature minds was completely overturned. Soon methods were being offered to teach mathematics to 4- and 5-year-olds. Underlying these revolutionary notions were previously unacknowledged concepts.

Cline-Cohen (1982) pointed out two concepts in particular. The first was that arithmetic could be done in the mind without paper and pencil, and young children could grasp these computational ideas. The second was that through inductive thinking, children could discover the basic rules of arithmetic. By working carefully selected problems, children would discover the inherent principles of mathematics. These thoughts concur with Pestalozzi's theories that children could take an active part in the learning process. At the time, these were certainly revolutionary ideas about childhood.

Cline-Cohen further observed that the evolution of numeracy also included a strong dose of gender bias. During the early 19th century, girls rarely progressed beyond the first few years of school, and arithmetic was generally taught only to older children. As arithmetic became more a part of elementary education, other prejudices came into play, particularly stereotypes about the nonmathematical feminine mind.

Arguments for teaching girls about math challenged these stereotypes and social norms. In the 18th and 19th centuries, women did not participate in business and had little to do with financial and management matters. Exposure to mathematics, therefore, was not an essential element of a girl's education. Later, when arithmetic became an established part of the school curriculum, girls were not offered math. This resulted in a disparity in skills due to less educational opportunity for girls. This disparity eventually became depicted as part of the "natural, unalterable differences between the sexes" and supported the social belief that women were "essentially intuitive, imaginative beings," not ordered and disciplined.

It took strong women with foresight to challenge the stereotypes of their day. Emma Willard and Catherine Beecher opened schools for girls that taught a full range of mathematics, from computation to geometry and trigonometry. Today the vestiges of these beliefs and patterns continue as mathematics and numeracy maintain gender-biased gatekeeping functions. In generalizing from this example of how social, cultural, and educational beliefs constructed the practices and knowledge of mathematics, we cannot but imagine what it might mean in the life of young girls to have positive early experiences with computers before society convinces them that computers are for boys.

The example of mathematics demonstrates that when an innovation is introduced to education, knowledge and practice are constructed by social, cultural, and educational beliefs. It points out the ease with which a rigid teaching sys-

Female teachers have a strong opportunity to influence how young girls view technology and its importance to their everyday lives.

experiences irrelevant to the world of knowledge and thus makes education/schooling less important to them.

The concept of the nonmathematical feminine mind was a cultural belief. At the time this cultural belief was apparently innocuous, but in retrospect its influence permeated educational curricula and promoted unintended negative consequences. Results of this cultural belief led to gender-biased teaching practices and eliminated a major opportunity for women and girls to learn math. Beyond that, this effect on teaching has seriously affected the abilities of women to equitably access opportunities for economic and social status.

Although this historical analogy highlights gender discrimination, similar beliefs and events have shaped access to education differentially across racial, cultural, and special needs groups.

Moreover, these early influences have a lifelong effect. In *Educating Americans for the 21st Century* (National Science Foundation 1983), the National Science Board Commission on Precollege Education in Mathematics, Science and Technology discusses the direct relationship between a child's early learning experiences and his or her later success in math, science, and technology.

tem can be created when intended for a particular audience (such as boys, the most capable students, or older children) while ignoring cultural, gender, race, class, and power issues that children and their families bring to educational and care settings. Removing a constituency, especially an under-represented one, from the process of creating pedagogy renders it invisible and contributes to an educational world not related to experiences. This makes minorities and their

Concerned early childhood professionals can adopt strategies to promote equal access for all young children

Concerned educators have an important role to play in promoting equality in both access to technology and the type of software produced. In this section we discuss ways in which teachers can promote the equal use of technology by all children within their own classrooms. We also suggest qualities that teachers can look for when selecting appropriate software for promoting equal access, including the unbiased representation of girls and women and of racial and cultural minorities; and support for languages in addition to English. Educators can develop a keen awareness of implicit negative messages and select software programs that actively promote empowerment on the part of all learners.

We group recommended strategies into five categories: (1) promoting gender equality, (2) promoting language equality, (3) promoting cultural equality, (4) promoting equality for children with special needs, and (5) promoting equality by helping teachers become more comfortable with technology.

Promoting gender equality

Current research on the treatment of girls in school indicates that girls are the only group in our society that begins school ahead and ends up behind. Girls start school ahead of boys in speaking, reading, and counting skills, but through school their achievement test scores show significant decline. Girls receive fewer academic contacts, less praise and constructive feedback, fewer complex and abstract questions, and less instruction in how to do things for themselves (Sadker, Sadker, & Long 1989). Stated broadly, it seems that the school environment, confounded by society's sex-role socialization of children, stretches and stresses boys while it encourages girls to let their abilities atrophy (Stanford 1992).

There are a number of ways in which educators can proactively work to promote girls' interest in computers and technology: (1) consider girls' interests and interaction styles when se-lecting and evaluating software for classroom use; (2) understand that female teachers in particular are powerful role models for young girls—teachers' use of computers as a routine tool for their own purposes can motivate and help sustain young girls' interest in accessing computers; and (3) promote equity by offering special times for "girls only" to use computers.

Carefully chosen software has no identifiable sex-related content. Although the content may have no apparent sex-related attraction, typically arcade games and some commercial software products portray aggressive settings involving weapons and missiles or other objects being propelled through space. These software programs are generally more appealing to males than to females (Clements 1991). Software reflecting this arcade-game format frequently incorporates scoring that fosters competition instead of cooperation or collaboration. Girls do not seem as interested in this competitive type of experience.

In many classrooms girls often must compete with boys for access to computers. Then, when they have the opportunity to use the computers, the choice of software available does not meet their interests or styles of interaction. Teachers can be more aware of the needs of young girls in terms of the types of interaction required by the software and the content of the selection in order to stimulate and maintain girls' interest in using computers. Research indicates that girls' interaction styles frequently are more collaborative than are boys'. They listen to one another's ideas, express agreement with other children, are willing to incorporate different ideas into a broad context, and when they begin to talk they acknowledge what others have said (Stanford 1992). These characteristics are not congruent with the competitive features that are built into many software programs that appeal to boys.

Teachers are a powerful example, especially for young children. Teachers who are comfortable using computers for their own needs and who use the computer as a tool demonstrate to young children that technology is an important and "grown-up" medium. In particular, female teachers have a strong opportunity to influence how young girls view technology and its importance in their everyday lives. Young girls receive no stronger message than when their teacher sits down at the keyboard of a computer and becomes busily engaged with a software program. This behavior powerfully conveys to young girls the appropriateness of women interacting positively with computers, that computers are useful, and that computers are a tool that deserves to be mastered by girls and women.

Establishing a time when young girls have uninhibited access to computers may be necessary. Often boys have had more experience with technology and games such as *Nintendo* or *Sega Genesis*. Generally, boys are able to readily interact with computers. Their competition to use the computer and their aggressive play frequently intimidate the less experienced and thus more reticent girls. The atmosphere that prevails at the computer center is one that prevents girls from freely approaching and exploring the possibilities of the computer. Initially, offering a rotating time for girls and then boys permits girls to explore the computer without having to directly compete with boys. Once girls have gained an idea of the opportunities that computers provide to support collaboration and creativity, they will be more likely to persevere and maintain their interest in accessing the computer as a tool for their creations. A "special time for girls" will then become unnecessary.

Often the bias in technology is so subtle that we don't notice it initially, yet this very subtlety underscores the need to carefully scrutinize the content and messages reflected in the computer presentation before we accept it for use in our classrooms. To finish this section we present an example of an incident that occurred in a preschool. One of the earliest alternative keyboards, designed to support easy access for young children, is the Muppet Learning Keys. This keyboard offers an attractive representation of colors, numbers, and letters; however, on close examination of the layout, a four-key segment labeled "HELP" raises some concern. The graphic that represents "HELP" is Miss Piggy, heavily bound and tied, lying on the railroad track with a train bearing down on her. On the other hand, the male characters on this keyboard are holding stop and go signs. They are definitely in charge and have control over situations. This juxtaposition of such portrayals of male and female representations should be cause for alarm among early childhood teachers. What messages are we communicating to young girls and boys?

In a Maryland preschool several mothers insisted that the Muppet Learning Keys be removed from the computer center. These mothers were more aware of the subtle communications embedded in the learning experience than were professional educators. The mothers were concerned that their daughters would internalize "poor me" messages from pictorial representations of sows tied to railroad tracks. Early childhood professionals must provide girls positive early experiences with computers, not perpetuate the biases that already exist in our society.

Few learning materials define sex roles by so illustrating the physical attributes of the material or activity itself. Preferences of materials and activities by boys or girls appear to be shaped by social conventions and expectations, which are transmitted by peers, parents, older siblings, teachers, television, and the mass media (Campbell & Schwartz 1986).

Promoting language equality

Today's schools face the challenges of educating a diverse linguistic population. Although 90% of educators employed in the public schools are Anglos who speak predominantly English, increasingly this does not reflect the student population they serve. Speech and the natural language processes that are a part of whole language are very important for young children. In particular, young children from non–English-speaking backgrounds have much to gain or lose depending upon their early language experiences in the classroom. A major contributor to early school failure of non–English-speaking children is their submersion into classrooms where the children's own culture and language background are neither incorporated nor valued (NAEYC & NAECS/SDE 1991).

The National Association of State Boards of Education (NASBE), in its 1994 position statement, acknowledges the importance of meeting the needs of all students in an increasingly diverse society by stating that schools must provide a strong foundation in English, as well as opportunities to acquire or maintain a second language. In the service of this challenge, NASBE specifically recommends that we

- advocate for a stronger system of English instruction for all students;

- encourage all students to be proficient in one language in addition to English, and that second-language acquisition begin at an early age;

- look at ways to provide quality programs for all children, regardless of their economic and social circumstance; and

- assume a very active role in assuring second-language acquisition within the context of deep respect for cultural heritage.

We are faced with a situation in which many young children require instruction in their native language to support their acquisition of early concepts and to affirm their cultural background. Yet in most cases, because generally teachers do not speak any language except English, we are unable to provide such native-language instruction. Non–English-speaking students do not experience the language supports they need to help them successfully acquire early concepts in their native language and transfer these to a majority-language environment (English). Computer software that provides native-language instruction, spoken out loud, can help young children from home backgrounds other than English. These children can make a successful transition from understanding basic concepts in their home language to understanding them in English. Further, teachers can feel comfortable that they are offering the native-language support that these young children need even if they do not speak the children's language.

Although the following general strategies identified by Garcia (1990) do not specifically reference the use of technology, they are equally valid—perhaps especially so—in the context of technology. By applying these strategies through technology, computers can be used to enhance many aspects of the instructional organization of classrooms and promote the success of children whose native language is not English.

- Emphasize functional communication between teacher and children and among peers.

- Organize the teaching of basic skills and academic content around thematic units.

- Organize instruction in such a way that children are required to interact with others using collaborative learning techniques.

- Help children progress systematically from writing in their native language to writing in English, allowing them to make the transition without pressure from the teacher.

- Support teachers who are highly committed to the educational successes of the children in their classrooms and who serve as child advocates.

- Encourage principals who are highly supportive of their teaching staff and who promote teacher autonomy while remaining aware of the need to conform to district policies on curriculum and academic accountability.

- Involve parents of all cultural and linguistic backgrounds in the formal parent-support activities of the schools—taking care not to isolate one group from another—thus encouraging a high level of satisfaction with and appreciation for their children's educational experiences in schools.

As an example, three of these strategies are reflected in the following anecdote of children using computers: first, functional communication is emphasized; second, teaching of basic skills and academic content is organized around thematic units; and third, instruction is organized in such a way that children are required to interact with others using collaborative learning techniques.

One day recently, two children were working together with *City*, from the *Neighborhoods* software. Alexis was at the controls (mouse and keyboard). He is a Mexican American boy who has spoken very little, if any, English this year and doesn't seem to understand much. Behind him stood B.J., a very bright child who is reading at perhaps second-grade level, a very verbal child, and a class leader. Together they were creating a mixed-up scene, with people and things where they didn't belong, and giggling at the sight of it. B.J. would say, "put the police car on top of the park bench," or "put a man inside the garbage can," or "put the slide on the sidewalk," and Alexis would do it. They were using all the prepositions we try to teach all year—top, bottom, in front of, behind, etc. This showed a clearer understanding of English than Alexis had demonstrated all year long. Alexis and B.J. had so much fun creating their picture that they forgot to "save" before they went out to the playground.

When they came back inside, the teacher asked Alexis if he could re-create the picture. This time B.J. was not there to "coach," and while Alexis re-created the city scene, he talked to himself about what he was doing. "I need a police car. I need a thing he put in his hand (briefcase). Oh, I forgot to put a tree. I need another tree—I had three trees. Oh, and I put a man over here, and a man right here, too. That's all now." This was 10 times more English than the teacher had heard from Alexis all year long.

(Joy Henderson, teacher, McKee Primary School, Bakersfield, CA)

Providing natural language experiences in a child's native language supports the development of a strong link between home and school, thus facilitating successful school experiences for young children with limited English proficiency. Instructional strategies that acknowledge, respect, and build upon the language and culture of the home serve these children well.

There is a growing array of software that supports this approach. *Children's Writing and Publishing Center* is now available in both Spanish and English versions. Other examples of software that provide versions in two or three languages include *Grandma and Me, Arthur's Teacher Troubles,*

Peter Rabbit, Cinderella, and *KIDWARE2+*. The *KidWare* set of software programs provides the opportunity for teachers to record all audio files in any language desired. Spanish, Vietnamese, and Finnish versions have already been created. In addition to English, children can record their own words in their native language, allowing a computer-generated scene to include multilingual accompaniment.

Promoting cultural equality

In addition to providing language diversity, publishers and educators must attend to how culturally and ethnically diverse individuals and symbols are portrayed in software. One of the earliest attempts to present multiracial figures appeared in *Mixed-up Mother Goose*. In this adventure activity the initial screen offers the child eight characters with different skin, hair, and eye color. The child selects a character that she wants to be, and throughout the adventure she uses the arrow keys to move her character and explore the computer environment.

In accord with our recognition of the need to provide children meaningful and relevant contexts for learning, technology offers the opportunity to tailor learning experiences for individual children. Software programs can be designed to incorporate children's native language and culture, to reflect their interests, and to target their developmental needs. For example, the software program *Neighborhoods* illustrates this flexibility, offering children a choice of a farm, city, or Alaskan village environment. Software with the background scenery of an urban setting can stimulate an inner-city child's motivation to construct her own "city" reflective of her experiences.

Sheila was 6 years old, a year older than the others, large for her age, and of a different race. The children did not want to let her play *Farm* with them. The teacher suggested the software program *City* and invited Sheila to use it. Sheila immediately identified with the environment and made a wonderful picture, explaining to the others all the objects she chose. She gained real status in the group because she could talk about something familiar to her.

(Wheelock College, Boston, MA)

Promoting equality for children with special needs

Software can offer a child the chance to focus on his or her own interests and the unique needs of other children.

Anthony, a 4-year-old, selected the red-haired boy. He almost always chooses to be this character because he has red hair. Anthony had been using "City" to set up a school playground. He put up a swingset, seesaw, and park benches, and he added children playing. From the menu, he then selected a little child in a wheelchair. He took this child to the swingset and asked, "I wonder how kids in wheelchairs swing?"

(A preschooler in Alexandria, VA)

This example illustrates the power that creating a micro-world can have in stimulating young children's sensitivity. At age 4, Anthony is becoming aware of the concept of a barrier-free environment.

Let's compare this scenario to a recently advertised attempt to make children aware of people in wheelchairs that states, "Count the little ducks swimming in the pond" (one duck swims in a wheelchair). Typically, swimming offers wheelchair-bound children an opportunity to move freely in the water. Artificial

Using the computer to provide language and literacy experiences in a child's native language helps build a strong link between home and school and enhances learning for young children with limited English facility.

Promoting equality by helping teachers

When the teacher is comfortable with technology, she can more easily offer the computer as a meaningful tool. She is more able to actively create an environment with appropriate software programs that motivate children to freely explore and learn from one another, much as they do in other social learning contexts. Only through a teacher's acceptance of technology can it be established as a tool to enhance children's learning.

Determining the quality of a computer-based experience and how it supports the curriculum is difficult for the teacher if she cannot get beyond the anxiety of accessing the keyboard. Such teachers, because of their technological inadequacy, remain distant and are reluctant to critically evaluate the content that is reflected in the software. They are unable to draw on their own expertise in evaluating general classroom materials when the medium shifts to something as unfamiliar as software.

Further, feelings of technological inadequacy seriously limit a teacher's creativity in designing connections between computer software programs and other classroom learning activities. The computer should serve as one more medium through which children explore and create understandings of their world. Computer experiences should offer support for social learning strategies inherent in young children's play. However, the teacher will have difficulty incorporating technology at this level if she is afraid that she will break the computer. When teachers are unsure of either the computer or their own technical adequacy and do not feel comfortable calling on readily available help in case of an "emergency," the computer experience is relegated to an arcade game format. In such cases

attempts to portray adaptive devices serve only to confuse children who are just becoming aware of how children with special needs function. In developing and evaluating software, it is important to portray situations realistically. When presented with authentic situations, young children like Anthony are able to respond with interest and empathy.

children are permitted to use the computer "after their work is done." This use of technology serves to place the computer at the same level of use as competitive video games and does little to support children's problem solving, higher order thinking, or collaborative interactions.

Often children are more eager to engage with technology than are their teachers. Children come to the classroom with readily available knowledge of technology's possibilities. Frequently their technical capabilities with computers outdistance the teacher's knowledge and experience. Refusing to acknowledge the children's experience in this technological arena can result in several direct problems, including a failure to enhance the role that technology can play. Other issues emerge when a teacher is unwilling to accept the paradigm shift inherent in the knowledge/power imbalance. In the case of technology, the teacher is no longer a purveyor of knowledge but a coach, who guides children as they explore and experiment with technology-based information and construct their meanings and understanding of the world. This knowledge/power imbalance in the traditional classroom can result in problems if the teacher attempts to maintain control.

Teachers need training and sufficient time to explore and use children's software. They also require software programs that allow them to understand and use the computer as a tool for their own purposes. These three prerequisites to adequate use—hands-on training, time for practice, and availability of tool-based software for teachers—can dramatically affect the ease and confidence with which early childhood educators approach computers and technology.

Frequently teachers are not provided sufficient training and support that allows them to become comfortable with computers. They do not have the time to explore the technology in the ways we are advocating they permit the children to explore it. They may experience training that focuses on how to access a particular children's software program, but they are not offered software that they could use effectively as a tool for their needs. Embracing technology as a tool for children is difficult when you, the teacher, have not experienced it as a tool for your own uses.

Offering teachers opportunities to make the transition from exploring software to using the computer as a tool will enhance their confidence and lessen the anxiety with which they approach technology. In time, their experience with computers will lessen their technological anxiety and they will begin to accept this new tool as a powerful medium for learners of a new age. With ongoing support and encouragement, perhaps teachers will navigate the information superhighway as competently as do the children they teach.

A call for equity

The mandate for today's educators is twofold: (1) to support equity of access to technology for all children—for girls and boys, and for children of diverse backgrounds, needs, cultures, and languages; and (2) to strive to integrate technology in meaningful ways across all curriculum areas for all learners. By helping children to understand the nature of technology as their tool for the future (and for the present), we will help them to successfully resolve future challenges. Meeting this mandate will ensure that all children have equivalent opportunities to become fully participating members of the global community that is rapidly emerging.

Offering children a personalized learning environment with software that can be customized in their native language demonstrates technology's flexibility. Software programmed to greet a child by name in her native language enhances her self-concept, personalizes her learning experience, and reaffirms her culture. The computer can become a powerful learning tool in the hands of competent early childhood educators who apply developmental principles to software selection and use.

Yet many teachers have not yet had the opportunity to try out computers in a hands-on way. Anxiety exists among some early childhood educators because they don't like computers, just as many teachers do not like math. Some teachers do not like reading either; they do not read in their spare time. Yet all of us would probably agree that it is every early childhood educator's duty to instill a love of stories and other language arts activities in the young children we teach. Isn't the same true for technology? To borrow from Polly Greenberg's (1993) observations regarding math, it is not a matter of whether *we* think reading, math, or computers are important but a matter of giving each child a fair start in case *she* thinks so.

The challenge for educators today is to create educational activities and environments that are attentive to the needs of different communities and the gender, race, class, and power relations associated with those communities. This means making parents and community members part of the process of generating knowledge. The future of education depends less on what technology can do than on what we do with technology. Let's be careful to get it right.

References

Becker, H.J. 1988. Using computers in instruction. *BYTE* 12 (2): 149–62.

Campbell, P.F., & S.S. Schwartz. 1986. Computers in the preschool: Children, parents and teachers. In *Young children and microcomputers,* eds. P. Campbell & G. Fein. Englewood Cliffs, NJ: Prentice Hall.

Clements, D. 1991. Current technology and the early childhood curriculum. In *Issues in early childhood curriculum,* eds. B. Spodek & O.N. Saracho. New York: Teachers College Press.

Cline-Cohen, P. 1982. *A calculating people: The spread of numeracy in early America.* Chicago: University of Chicago Press.

Edwards, C. 1993. Life-long learning. *Communications of the ACM* 36 (5): 76–78.

Garcia, E. 1990. *Education of linguistically and culturally diverse students: Effective instruction practice.* Santa Cruz, CA: National Center for Research on Cultural Diversity and Second Language Learning.

Greenberg, P. 1993. How and why to teach all aspects of preschool and kindergarten math naturally, democratically, and effectively (for teachers who don't believe in academic programs, who do believe in educational excellence, and who find math boring to the max). Part 1. *Young Children* 48 (4): 75–84.

National Association for the Education of Young Children and National Association of Early Childhood Specialists in State Departments of Education. 1991. Position statement: Guidelines for appropriate curriculum content and assessment in programs serving children ages 3 through 8. *Young Children* 46 (3): 21–38.

National Association of State Boards of Education. 1994. Bylaws and resolutions, second language acquisition. Alexandria, VA: Author.

National Science Board Commission on Precollege Education in Mathematics, Science and Technology. 1983. *Educating Americans for the 21st century.* Washington, DC: National Science Foundation.

Pereira, J. 1994. Computers, the gender divide: A tool for women, a toy for men—Video games help boys get a head start. *Wall Street Journal,* 16 March.

Press, L. 1993. Technetronic education: Answers on the cultural horizon. *Communications of the ACM* 36 (5): 17–22.

Quality Education Data, Inc. 1993. *Technology in public schools.* Denver, CO: QED.

Sadker, M., D. Sadker, & L. Long. 1989. Gender and educational equality. In *Multicultural education: Issues and perspectives,* eds. J.A. Banks & C.A. Banks. Boston: Allyn & Bacon.

Stanford, B.H. 1992. Gender equity in the classroom. In *Common bonds: Anti-bias teaching in a diverse society,* eds. D. Byrnes & G. Kiger, 87–102. Wheaton, MD: Association for Childhood Education International.

Sutton, R.E. 1991. Equity and computers in the schools: A decade of research. *Review of Educational Research* 61 (4): 475–503.

Cynthia Char and
George E. Forman

Chapter

12

Interactive Technology and the Young Child: A Look to the Future

Budding creativity, self-expression, and experimentation make early childhood an exciting time. Young children are actively exploring the world around them—objects, people, sounds, and events. Whether at the water table at school or the kitchen table at home, children are discovering and learning much about the physical and social world through play, experimentation, and interactions with other children and adults.

While early childhood is, by its very nature, an exciting time, early childhood in the 21st century is likely to prove even more exciting because of the role that electronic media could play in the young child's development. Previous chapters have described some of the roles that educational technology currently plays in early childhood education. This chapter takes a speculative look at the future. We foresee a dramatic increase in the ways that technology will positively affect children's learning while becoming increasingly integrated into the materials and social relationships of the young child's world.

We believe that as we approach the 21st century, the educational community will move beyond being merely informed consumers of the "output" of the computer industry. Using their special insights and expertise, educators will begin to assume a more proactive role in harnessing the power and capabilities of newly emerging technologies. The result will be significant advances in the use of technology to enhance young children's learning and development.

Paradoxically, the distinctive power of interactive technology will best be realized when it is more fully integrated into the child's nontechnological world. Rather than being regarded as a unique object or extraordinary machine set apart from other learning materials for young children, technology presents some intriguing possibilities and new conceptions of educational potential when it is woven into the already rich fabric of children's experiences in the world. We envision that fuller integration as taking the form of six major dimensions.

Moving beyond the computer's two-dimensional world: Links between dynamic 3-D objects, pictures, and written code

On-screen manipulatives—graphic objects resembling real and familiar objects, which children can move around the screen—are now featured in several educational software programs. They offer children opportunities to explore properties of such mathematics manipulatives as pattern blocks, base-ten blocks, and coins. The on-screen manipulatives that work most successfully are ones that take into account the inherent two-dimensionality of computers. The child is not able to reach into space or to heft the weight of the object on the screen, feel its density or temperature, or experience the force of its movement. These limitations make it difficult for the child to use his intuitive knowledge of objects to help

grasp certain abstract mathematical and scientific concepts related to the objects depicted on the screen.

One of the interesting forays beyond the flat, two-dimensional computer screen has been the "Smart Blocks" of the Massachusetts Institute of Technology (M.I.T.) Media Lab. Rather than being tethered to the computer, Smart Blocks have microprocessors in the blocks themselves in the form of little "and/or" switches. These Smart Blocks allow children to build and control "smart" Lego toys, such as battery-operated vehicles that are programmed to behave in certain ways sensitive to their environmental input. For example, a child can build a light-loving or light-averse car that seeks or avoids sources of light, or a car that responds to sound and turns on or off its motor when she claps.

If we take this smart-object approach one step further and directly link objects to communicate with a computer, additional possibilities emerge to introduce the world of making symbols to the child. Why begin the child's road to symbolization by directly teaching the symbol system? Why not take advantage of the computer as the conduit for symbolic code and use the power of the computer to automatically symbolize the performance? Imagine a toy car that (1) remembers exactly the path along which the child has rolled it, (2) can autonomously reenact that path as the child watches, (3) displays a graphic map of that movement on a small screen, and (4) allows the child to re-program the car's movement by manipulating the graphic map on the computer screen (see Forman 1988b). The graphic representation deepens the child's understanding of pattern (e.g., detour, efficient travel, intersection) as it automatically takes "graphic dictation" of the child's play with the toy. This system allows the child to alter the graphics (which might be termed *invented notation*) to

As technology moves beyond the flat, two-dimensional computer screen, children are able to manipulate blocks, robots, vehicles, and other toys with microprocessors in them (see p. 15 in chapter 1 and p. 88 in chapter 6 for descriptions of the pictured "Roamer Robots").

Interactive Technology and the Young Child: A Look to the Future—C. Char & G.E. Forman change the movement of the car robot (see Nemirovsky, n.d., for prototypes of these systems).

These types of systems are innovative in at least two ways. First, the system offers "playable replayables"—the child can see her own decisions of how to move the car played back to her. Remember, after the child plays with the car, she can push a button on the computer and, as she sits and watches, the car will replay every move that she has had the car make. Being able to observe one's decisions replayed affords greater opportunities for reflection and examination. True learning comes not in the doing of something but in the reflection on what one has done. The second innovative aspect of these systems is that the child does not have to learn a computer language to change the car's action. The computer automatically generates a string of numbers, letters, and graphics that represent the movement of the car. Then the child edits these symbols, knowing full well to what they refer because she has seen them produced. This tenet of never severing the relation between a symbol and its meaning is also found in whole language instruction (see Forman 1985, 1988a, 1993).

Thus, rather than continuing to treat the computer as necessarily an all-purpose machine, solely consisting of a screen output and standard keyboard or mouse input, there are clear advantages in offering the computer in more specialized, diverse forms that take advantage of the three-dimensionality of familiar objects. This trend is already evidenced in the growing number of specialized tools, toys, and game environments containing microchips (e.g., electronic music keyboards, driving and flight simulators using steering wheels) that take advantage of the three-dimensionality of familiar objects. An additional characteristic of three-dimensional technological playgrounds and construction sets is that they can be linked to other forms of text or graphics notations and thus offer children the opportunity to explore the physical and symbolic worlds simultaneously, such as with the replayable car with its computer screen display, or a slide that has sensors along its length that cause a matrix of lights to display an acceleration curve next to the slide as the child whizzes down its length.

The computer as crossmodal canvas

One of the virtues of computers derives from its function as a symbol machine, with which young children can represent and manipulate different symbol systems (including language, pictures, mathematics, and music) and create various symbolic products (such as stories, mathematical expressions, and songs). Much of the software designed for young children in the early 1980s (and disappointing numbers of software today) tended to break up the child's world into alphabetic pieces. The plethora of young kids' software focusing on number and letter recognition, while driven by notions of "core learning objectives" for young children, is undoubtedly reinforced by frequent reliance upon keyboard input and in the computer's early beginnings as a machine for handling digital/alphanumeric code. Although increasing numbers of software programs use graphics and sound to enhance children's understanding of the connections between letters and sounds, words and pictures, and numerals and concepts of number, the heavy emphasis continues to be on written notational systems.

Other software products link written notational systems with auditory counterparts. For example, some computer and word processor packages convert a child's inputted written text into synthesized speech. Similarly, a child using music editing software can place notes on a musical staff and have the result translated into the corresponding musical tune. In the preceding examples, the child is provided with a standard notational system and is invited to become familiar with and learn that new, formal system.

One fruitful area not yet explored lies in how computers might provide children with crossmodal canvases on which to invent and design their own notational systems and to explore links between the various modalities of sound, visual form, and kinetic experiences. For example, how might a child use color, form, and line to represent a piccolo's sprightly melody versus a steel drum band's loud, syncopated beat? Rather than simply doing "creative drawing to music," he would be inventing his own notational system, deciding which colors or types of lines to assign to different tonal qualities (e.g., instruments, volume, pitch). These sound/visual element pairings can then be reused to create other musical drawings. Thus, the child uses the computer both to generate the visual notations and to play the notations to generate the musical sounds. Via this two-way street, the child writes as a means to learn to read and reads as a means to learn to write, themes central to whole language instruction.

Creating and decoding invented notational systems could be collaborative efforts between children. A child might use a bold, thick red line in regular dashes to represent the snappy march cadence of a snare drum and a thin, snaky line to represent the tremulous musical appeal of an oboe, and present his classmate with this pictorial trace to see whether she can reconstruct the musical pattern.

Some currently available draw/paint programs designed for young children include sound effects, but these programs are already preprogrammed with associated sound effects decided upon by the software designer rather than the child. Thus, the software often act as "effects generators," with which children become more interested in "What does this button/icon do?" rather than becoming engaged in the more purposeful, intentional activity involved in deciding how various auditory elements such as musical instruments, tones, rhythms, and volume might be represented visually with different colors, boldness of line, and visual forms and patterns, and vice versa.

Such crossmodal environments might be used to enhance children's experiences not only in music and art but in language. Imagine text on a computer that makes sounds that can be modulated by adjectives. Typing *loud laugh* would cause the computer to laugh heartily; typing *soft laugh* would cause the computer to laugh more softly. Or the child may write a whole story, and the computer will scan the text and make appropriate sound effects, sometimes alerting the child to descriptors that she really did not intend to include. And think of the possibilities with mathematics. Imagine numerical patterns—for example, 8, 7, 6, 5, 6, 7, 8—that the child could represent with animated graphics on a computer. Perhaps the child would make eight stacked squares with one falling off each second until the stack was reduced to five squares and then reconstructed, square by square, to the original stack of eight. Other children would then be asked to guess what numerical patterns the authoring child had in mind. And music. Imagine the child drawing an upward slanting curve using a stylus on a graphic tablet connected to the computer. The curve is fat at the lower left and tapered as it rises to the upper right. When the child hits the *return* key, the computer would generate a tone that increases in pitch and diminishes in volume. The child would thereby learn to "read" his own symbols from left to right, bottom to top, rather than treat the symbols as pictures of static forms—that is, the meaning of the curve rests in moving the eyes across its contour rather than taking it in as a stationary whole. Therein lies the difference between notations and pictures.

Multimedia microneighborhoods

Interactive video products are now available that offer vivid collections of photos, sounds, and video clips to broaden young children's awareness of the world around them. Often striving to offer children glimpses of the novel and exotic, these disks usually provide the "world beyond" rather than the "world of" the child. Notably, these multimedia products are closed systems that could cynically be regarded as high-tech Viewmasters, with children as viewers rather than contributors.

Better yet, why not allow children to be master video storytellers or documentary producers? Putting cameras in the hands of children enables them to capture the real, immediate, and familiar world that they experience and are curious to know more about. Through the use of digital video, cameras can now be akin to electronic field boxes in which to collect a visual sample of the world, much like how a bug box and net allow one to capture insects for further examination and to share with others. Instead of simply using a camera to record the sights and sounds of a field trip, we want children to be able to create a data base of personal experiences that can be (1) revisited by browsing, via random access, any part of the experience, and (2) layered with other representations that the child makes of that experience, thereby deepening

her understanding of its pattern and its place in the greater context. These data bases can be created even by young children if we are careful to make access to the content user friendly. For example, great advances have been made in data bases that are indexed by small pictures (e.g., Kodak CD, Aldus Fetch).

Teachers of young children are fully aware of the educational value of special field trips—how a visit to a local hospital, dairy farm, or firehouse can raise more interesting questions than it answers, and how different children come away from the same experience with such varied impressions and questions.

We feel good about these special trips and consider their expense worthwhile. We feel this way because we have seen the ripple effects for weeks to come, as the children collectively revisit these experiences in their drawing, their stories, and their sociodrama. These are not generic experiences, like reading about a hospital or watching a video on how the fire department responds to a house fire. The memories are highly contextualized by the emotional reactions the children had on site, the personal questions they were able to ask the experts, and the navigation from their classroom to the site and back. They remember a hundred aspects, and each of these raises a hundred speculations about what is related to what and why. "If it took us so long to get to the fire station, how long would it take for the fire truck to get to the school?" "My fire hat kept bumping the collar on my jacket. Why does the fire hat have that funny rim sticking out the back, anyway?" Children become interested and speculate about the content specifically because they were *in* the content, they were surrounded by the content, and therein reasons to ask questions arose. Can technology preserve the belonging between children and group experience?

Imagine that a group of children make that same trip to the dairy farm, this time armed with a digital video camera. The children watch cows being milked and the hay harrowed and baled, and they take almost continuous footage while there. Returning to the classroom, the teacher and the children begin to add to and edit certain shots of the video to communicate their experience to other children. One group of children were quite taken with the hay baler but could not explain what the machine really did. By stepping through the video segment, they are able to slow down and isolate the various actions of the hay baler, and they add their comments to the action. For those processes that happened inside the machine, the children make their own inferences and represent them with drawings, which they scan into the computer. Individual children's different audio tracks accompanying the same video segment also heighten their awareness of point of view.

Another small group of children create and run two movies at once to communicate the relative rates of two events, such as milking a cow by hand and milking by machine. The digital video allows the children to reflect more closely on time-based concepts, such as process and rate of change.

Capturing this field trip on digital video does not minimize the power of the children's group experience; rather, the essence of the experience will now exist across time and space for future reflection, interpretation, and revisiting. With the marriage of computers and video, we have a new opportunity, an opportunity to build microworlds that are not foreign places but scaled-down versions of real experiences that the children have had. Rather than creating microworlds based on Mickey Mouse or Big Bird, digital video empowers the teacher to help children become the characters in the microworld. We could call these personal representations *microneighborhoods,* in which the

When children videotape their experiences on field trips—and later revisit them—they reach new levels of understanding of what they have seen.

characters have the faces of the participating children, the backdrop is their own living space, and the stories are their own.

Technology for groups: Social interaction, collaboration, and reflection

Another important dimension for future consideration is how technology might be more fully integrated in children's social world to support the social dynamics of young children's interactions—their interest in other children and in cooperative work and play. We already know that children often work in pairs or trios at the computer screen as they respond to and create with computer software. Yet technology can go even further in encouraging collaboration among children and in helping them take the social perspective of others.

Social perspective taking happens most clearly when technology is used as a production tool and a communication tool; that is, when children collectively produce projects that are made to deliver a message to others, social perspective taking happens. For example, children can collaborate to create an animated screenplay on a computer. With software of the future, each child designs an animated character with a defined manner of moving and persona (e.g., scary, kind, gullible, impulsive). The children can add their own voices to the animation using a simple audio digitizer. The project members decide how to weave these characters into a coherent screenplay and invite the other members of the class to see their play. The final production is projected on a large screen in front of the whole class (current projection systems use a panel that fits directly on top of an overhead projector). The children can even deliberately leave a character out of a scene and

have a volunteer child stand in front of the large projected animation and fill in the action with his own voice and movements.

What are the advantages of doing this activity on a computer rather than on huge murals? First, software allows children to experiment with new elements and to erase an element if, after negotiating, they agree that they do not like it. Children are more apt to collaborate when they can easily alter and undo new elements, and the computer allows them to take greater risks because the consequence does not permanently change the work of any one child yet gives them a view of what might be. Software also allows children to animate the objects and add text that is synched to these moving pictures and stories. Some research strongly suggests that multimedia story-composition tools can support interesting collaborative storytelling among children, and that these visual media can heighten, rather than diminish, children's interest in and awareness of the role of language in enhancing story meaning and genre (Char 1990a).

In a somewhat different vein, an electronic mat, working like a large touch screen resting on the floor, could support various group activities in art, movement, music, and mathematics (Char 1990b). For instance, each child could choose a color and then slide, hop, or tiptoe across the mat in her stocking feet, creating a visual trace behind her for collaborative artwork. For music, different areas of the mat—or different children—could be designated as different instruments, and children could form an orchestral ensemble by marching in place, skipping, or jumping. For mathematics, children could join hands and explore what's involved in forming various geometric shapes, such as circles, squares, and triangles. Creating such a mat takes into account the fact that young children are highly mobile individuals, comfortable with—and reveling in—the sheer joy of motion and large body movements and gestures. These examples are types of the crossmodal canvas that we described earlier.

Interactive technology might also support children's awareness of social interactions and self-reflection about social behavior. For example, Josh is a young boy who very much wants to join into the block play with Ben and Ean, who continue to rebuff him. The teacher decides to videotape the three boys building with blocks, and then shortly following the taping, she plays the tape for the boys. The teacher says to each boy, "I would like each of you to print three pictures from the videotape. Choose a picture that shows something that you either like a lot or do not like a lot. Then bring the pictures over and we will talk about them." The children are familiar with the video printer and have used it before to document their activities. The three boys view the tape, print frames from the video, and then take their video prints to the teacher. They discuss among themselves what they found interesting about those moments in time. As the discussion progresses, Ben and Ean begin to understand that they have systematically excluded Josh, even in cases where the photo indicates that he could have been a help. In this way, the media helps children take another child's perspective and become less egocentric.

Furthermore, as the children talk about their video photographs, away from their actual work with the blocks and the territorial behavior that these objects elicit, they learn more about each other's interesting ideas, including Josh's. They sequence their photos to rebuild their work session and consider constructions they did not make but can, and will, the next time with the blocks.

Integration into the life of the classroom

A visit to classrooms using computers usually reveals that the computers are located in the back of the room or tucked away in a corner. Unfortunately, a computer placed near the back of the class as a workstation, instead of near the teacher's desk or in the center of the room, runs the risk of creating a second classroom, one separate and isolated from the materials, activities, and experiences that form the educational core of the classroom. We should shift the function (and location) of a computer so that it serves more like the class blackboard, actively used by the teacher to interact with the content spontaneously, as children pose questions, and to generate what-if scenarios and simulations to check children's theories to foster class discussion. The computer can serve as the "blackboard that remembers" by creating files of everything written on the electronic blackboard, doodles and all. The type and marks can be printed on hard copy for children to refer to later. These exact printouts capture much more information than the sketchy notes common to most young children.

The computer might also serve as a huge worktable around which groups of children conduct individual or small-group projects and integrate computer work with related hands-on work and investigations. Computer-based work can provide teachers with an archive of children's work, to be included in the children's portfolios. This archive could include color drawings and samples of handwritten work that children have made with a graphics tablet connected to a computer. Teachers and children can browse through these electronic portfolios in search of new ideas for activities, as a platform for parent conferencing, or as a class presentation of the children's work. Thus, rather than being relegated to the back of the classroom, technology can be an integral part of teaching and learning—as a demonstration tool, as a flexible environment for children's independent and collaborative exploration and expression, as a recording device for hands-on investigations, and as an informal assessment tool (Char 1991). All of these uses help move the computer to the center of the room—not the front or rear—

where teachers and children work collaboratively, side by side, as co-learners.

In the future, video scanners and printers will be less expensive yet of higher quality. A child will be able to point a miniature camera at the table top, manipulate some curriculum materials—for example, Cuisenaire rods—and then review her actions later on screen. The computer will analyze these movements, using the digitized video, and ask the child to explain her intentions to the computer. We are quickly approaching the age of intelligent tutors for the young child. However, such mechanized tutors will have to be even "smarter" than current machines because the computer must be able to easily read the young child's actions.

Digital video is being used to teach science to young children. Andee Rubin at Technical Education Research Centers (TERC; see Rubin 1993) uses a camera connected to a computer to record a child running. The computer then plays back the child's run, frame by frame, with electronic dots on the screen representing the location of the child's key body parts. By watching the movement of these dots, the children can see a meaningful representation of their own acceleration and deceleration during the run. The software even allows the computer to transform these dots into more conventional time-and-motion charts, providing children a kinetic and visual memory for their run.

Integrating the different worlds of the child

The final type of integration that we propose concerns bridging the different worlds and cultures that children move in and out of: homes, schools, after-school settings, libraries, museums, and places in the community. A child's daily routine is partitioned by barriers of time and space, creating a too-often fragmented world. Rather than our treating these different places as separate boxes with impenetrable bound-

aries, how might technology help make them interrelated facets of a child's world? Networking and telecommunications offers a powerful vehicle to link parents, teachers, after-school club leaders, librarians, museum educators, and other educators and individuals in the community who have a vested interest in the well-being and development of young children. Advances in technology enable not only written text to be transmitted and received but images and sounds as well.

What advantages does communicating via computer have over the current channels of phone communication and written letters? Technology enables messages to be transmitted instantaneously while remaining wholly "resident," that is, the message will be available for either party to read when time is available, thereby avoiding the perpetual rounds of phone tag that are all too familiar to many. Networking can facilitate not only increased communication between various parties but increased collaboration and utilization of resources as well. With networked computers, children could conduct a social studies project on their neighborhood by actively involving members and resources of the community— requesting digitized photos of the neighborhood from the local historical society, obtaining maps from city hall and the town library, soliciting oral histories from parents and from elderly members in the community, and sharing their collected information with the children in another school in a nearby state. In this way, technology can offer the electronic scaffold on which to rebuild the social relationships and connections essential to forming a stronger, more cohesive community that can better support the development of each child.

Summary and conclusion

We have come a long way since the early 1980s, when microcomputers first began appearing in classrooms and homes.

Research, educational practice, and developments in the software and hardware industries have contributed significantly to our knowledge and experience of interactive technology's educational potential for young children's development. Granted, serious hurdles remain to be overcome before these visions become a reality, including the limited resources for early childhood education, the high cost of technology, and the formidable challenge of providing sufficient teacher training and support. However, if we dwell on these constraints and we don't seek ways to eliminate them, we may never grasp the full potential and value of young children's technology-based learning.

As briefly touched upon in this paper, research and design efforts capitalizing on new developments in computer hardware and software point to a number of intriguing possibilities of ways that interactive technologies can offer children a variety of powerful tools and environments—three-dimensional "playgrounds," crossmodal canvasses, multimedia "micro-neighborhoods," and technological tools for supporting and extending children's social interactions and awareness. We also argue for pushing hard on various fronts for greater integration, such as linking three-dimensional objects and computers; connecting different modalities and notation systems; merging video worlds and children's shared experiences in the immediate and familiar world; utilizing technology to support the social nature of the child; bringing technology-based learning centers into the real, physical center of learning in the classroom; and bridging the different and varied worlds of the child at home, at school, and in the community.

It is critical for us all to use our intellectual energy and creativity to push the limits of the software and hardware industries, research and development efforts, and educational practice. Only through our best collective thinking, hard work, and dedication will interactive technology offer valuable opportunities for young children's learning and development in the 21st century.

References

Char, C. 1990a. *Computer animation and interactive video: New forums for children's collaborative story composition.* Sixth Conference on Computers and Writing: Writing the Future, University of Texas at Austin and Texas Technical University, 17–20 May, Austin, TX.

Char, C. 1990b. *Interactive technology and the young child: Insights from research and design.* Report 90-2, Reports and Papers in Progress, Center for Learning, Teaching and Technology, Education Development Center, Newton, MA.

Char, C. 1991. *Computer graphic felt boards: New software approaches to children's mathematical exploration.* Report 91-1, Reports and Papers in Progress, Center for Learning, Teaching and Technology, Education Development Center, Newton, MA.

Forman, G. 1985. The value of kinetic print in computer graphics for young children. In *Children and computers: New directions for child development*, No. 28, ed. E.L. Klein. San Francisco: Jossey-Bass.

Forman, G. 1988a. The importance of automatic translation for the representational development of young children: Get a code of my act. *Genetic Epistemologist* 16 (1): 1–5.

Forman, G. 1988b. Making intuitive knowledge explicit through future technology. In *Constructivism in the computer age,* eds. G. Forman & P.B. Pufall. Hillsdale, NJ: Lawrence Erlbaum.

Forman, G. 1993. The city in the snow: Applying the multisymbolic approach in Massachusetts. In *The hundred languages of children: The Reggio Emilia approach to early childhood education,* eds. C. Edwards, L. Gandini, & G. Forman. Norwood, NJ: Ablex.

Nemirovsky, R. n.d. On ways of symbolizing: The case of Laura and the velocity sign. *The Journal of Mathematical Behavior.* In press.

Rubin, A. 1993. Video laboratories: Tools for scientific investigation. *Hands On* 16 (1): 4.

Jane Davidson*

Using Computers to Support Thematic Units

Thematic units are often used as a focus for the learning and development that occurs in the early childhood classroom. Materials and activities in many areas of the classroom, as well as group-time stories and songs, may center around the chosen theme. If the unit is about dinosaurs, for example, children may

- build caves for rubber dinosaurs in the block area;
- excavate for dinosaur bones and fossils in the sand table;
- ride tricycles in a lifesize chalk outline of a dinosaur on the playground;
- use stencils to outline and then color a variety of types of dinosaurs;
- sort dinosaur pictures by what the dinosaurs like to eat;
- write stories about dinosaurs;
- make dinosaur-shaped cookies;

- listen to dinosaur stories;
- make a classroom graph of the children's favorite dinosaurs;
- see how many people are needed to stretch the whole length of a brontosaurus;
- move like dinosaurs to a story narrated by the teacher; or
- role-play a paleontologist working in a lab where fossils are studied and dinosaur skeletons are reassembled.

The activities provide opportunities to encourage all areas of development as well as learning in the more traditional school areas—language arts, science, social science, and so forth.

During a thematic unit of study, children use blocks, sand, outside play, movement experiences, mathematics, dramatic play, books, language arts, cooking, and many other types of

Taken in part from Chapter 11 of Children & Computers Together in the Early Childhood Classroom *by Jane Davidson (1989, Delmar Publishers)*

activities to explore the subject. Teachers also can use computers to enhance units. Computers can support a unit on three levels:

1. Specific software can provide unit-related information.
2. Tool software—such as graphics or writing programs—can be used to create unit-related products.
3. Computer-related activities—those designed to support specific computer skills or concepts—can be designed to support the unit theme.

This appendix describes some of the ways that each of these levels of computer support can enhance a specific unit—in this case, dinosaurs.

Using unit-related software

The easiest way to support a unit with the computer is to supply unit-related software. This is not always possible because age-appropriate software on the topic may not exist. In the case of dinosaurs, a number of software programs are available. Some, such as *Dinosaurs,* are more closed-ended, leading children to discover through trial-and-error such information as which dinosaurs were meat eaters and which were plant eaters, and where various dinosaurs lived. New CD-ROM disks offer extensive visual and textual information about dinosaurs and their habitats. Some children are fascinated by the dinosaurs' various habitats and eating habits, while other children are not. Children should be free to use—or not use—the software as their personal interests and skills dictate (as is true for all software). For those children who enjoy mastering this information, teachers can

provide additional off-computer sorting activities. Plastic dinosaurs or pictures of dinosaurs can be sorted by type, habitat, or eating habits. Children could be encouraged to use the software as a resource for checking the accuracy of their off-computer sorting.

Other programs, such as *What Makes a Dinosaur Sore,* are more open-ended, allowing children to use the computer to move the dinosaurs and objects around as they narrate their own story. Software about dinosaurs gives children a chance to use what they know about dinosaurs as they talk together about what they are doing on the computer, but non-dinosaur software can also be used to support an interest in the subject.

Using software as a tool to support unit activities

Children often spontaneously incorporate topics they find interesting into their activities and creations. If the class is discussing dinosaurs, dinosaurs are likely to appear in children's paintings, play dough creations, dramatic play, and drawings. Graphics programs on the computer offer another medium through which children may create unit-related pictures. Children can draw dinosaurs, dinosaur habitats, dinosaur paths (which can be printed off and used for rubber dinosaurs to follow), or jumbles of dinosaur bones.

During a dinosaur unit, dinosaurs may be found in children's writing, as well. They may use a word processing program to type a list of dinosaur names, or they may narrate dinosaur stories for teachers or parent volunteers to type. The children or the teacher can suggest dinosaur-related story themes, such as "The Day the Dinosaur Came to School," or more realistic stories describing "When the Dinosaurs Lived." The class may use the word processor to type a fact sheet on dinosaurs, which can be sent home to parents or distributed to other classes.

If a computer-controlled robot is available, children can dress it up as a dinosaur by adding a construction-paper dinosaur tail and head. Large "armor" plates taped along the robot's back can turn it into a stegosaurus. The children can then direct the dinosaur-robot. They can create a dinosaur environment by using paper towel rolls decorated with paper palm leaves to represent trees. Additional dinosaurs can be created by taping pictures of dinosaurs to hollow blocks, boxes, or paper towel rolls. The children can give the dinosaur commands to make the robot say hello to or run away from the other dinosaurs and to make it bump into trees attached to paper towel rolls, toppling them over.

Using computer-related activities to support units

Independent computer use requires many skills: turning the computer on and off, selecting and loading the desired software, finding needed keys on the keyboard, manipulating the mouse, selecting the desired part of the program from the menu, following and designing multistep procedures, and decoding picture directions. Children need not have these skills before they begin using computers; skills will develop as children explore computers. Off-computer activities can support and extend these skills. The more experience children have finding keys on a keyboard, the less difficulty they will have locating desired letters. Some of the practice can be on the computer, but children can also practice by jumping from letter to letter on a floor mat designed as a large keyboard. Off-computer activities can also be designed to complement a thematic unit.

To practice using pictorial clues, children can use picture cards to remind themselves of the parts of a song. For example, the song "Old McDonald Had a Farm" can be changed to "Old McDonald Had Some Dinosaurs." The lyrics can be revised as follows:

Old McDonald had some dinosaurs, E I E I O,

And one of the dinosaurs was a tyrannosaurus, E I E I O.

With a tyrannosaurus here and a tyrannosaurus there,

Here a tyrannosaurus, there a tyrannosaurus,

Everywhere a tyrannosaurus.

Old McDonald had some dinosaurs, E I E I O.

The teacher can hold up a picture to show children that the first dinosaur is the tyrannosaurus. The second picture could be a triceratops. After singing the "everywhere" line of the triceratops verse, the children can repeat the "here, there, and everywhere" line for the tyrannosaurus, repeating lines for the earlier dinosaurs after each new dinosaur name is sung. The picture clues can be used to remind children which name to sing when.

Teachers can add additional activities that complement the themes and interests of the children. The microcomputer is a flexible tool; its use is guided by the interests of the children and the teacher. As it becomes increasingly easy to create shapes, digitize pictures, and add voice to presentations, teachers and children become increasingly in charge and empowered to represent their ideas in dynamic ways.

Bonnie Blagojević

Early Childhood Education and Computer Networking: Making Connections

With the technology available today, educators can connect with people, ideas, and information from their home or worksite in ways we could never imagine before. Exploring the possibilities is exciting. To get started, you need a computer and a way to access an information highway, or *network*. There are many ways to do this.

The Internet is a system of more than 10,000 interconnected computer networks around the world (InterNIC Information Services 1994). Direct, full access to the Internet offers a powerful way to access and exchange information with friends and colleagues locally, nationally, and internationally.

Full Internet access is often available through university systems to staff and students. Other opportunities to connect to the Internet are becoming increasingly available through *freenets* (which offer community-based access) and in certain states that have already committed to getting educators in the state online. Contact your state's department of education to see if Internet access is available at this time to educators in your area.

Dial-up access requires a computer, a telephone line, a modem (to connect the computer to the phone line), and a network to connect to. Information networks can be reached through vendors such as ATHENS (America Tomorrow Health and Education Network Services), America Online, Delphi, Prodigy, CompuServe, and others. Fees and services vary. You may want to ask, Does the network charge a flat or an hourly usage fee? Is the connection number nearest you a local or a long distance call? Do they offer Internet access? What kind of Internet capabilities do they have, just E-mail or others, too? What else is being offered for educators?

Internet discussion-group lists offer opportunities for inquiry, debate, and information exchange on just about every topic you can imagine. Currently there are three Internet lists for early childhood educators—Early Childhood Education online (ECEOL-L), Early Childhood Education Net (ECENET-L), and a new Reggio Emilia List (REGGIO-L), devoted to discussing aspects of the Reggio Emilia approach to early childhood education. Children's literature, elementary education, international project exchanges, K–12 education, special needs topics, and counseling are some of the many areas available to educators through specific Internet lists.

Discussion groups are just one aspect of what is available on the Internet. You can send electronic mail, or E-mail (messages that are free to anyone in the world who has an Internet address), read news groups, be in contact with online experts, participate in online courses, and learn to work with a variety of search tools and methods of information access and retrieval that will take you to places where you have never been before, accessing information from around the world!

ERIC/EECE Clearinghouse (1-800-583-4135) can give you sign-on information for the ECENET-L, ECEOL-L, and REGGIO-L lists, and general information related to networking and early childhood, including a list of toll-free numbers of commercial vendors, a list of freenets, and information on states that have already started connecting their educational systems statewide. Contact ERIC/EECE (E-mail address: ericeece@uxl.cso.uiuc.edu).

ERIC/EECE also operates the *PARENTS AskERIC* Internet-based question-answering service. Questions posted on child development, child care, parenting, sibling relationships, and other aspects of early education and related concerns are responded to within two working days. To use PARENTS AskERIC, send an E-mail message containing your question to askeric@ericir.syr.edu (their E-mail address). The response you receive will contain information from the ERIC data base, full text information (if available), and referrals to other information resources on and off the Internet.

ATHENS (America Tomorrow Health and Education Network Services), formerly ATLIS, is both an information service, with news and reports from many leading early childhood organizations (including NAEYC), and a communications service that connects early childhood professionals with each other. NAEYC provides news and information on current resources to ATHENS. The ATHENS bulletin board provides an open forum for discussing issues in early childhood, ranging from emerging policy at the federal, state, or local level to helpful hints on how to deal with problem situations in your center; or practical ideas for activities for young children.

Communications features let you process your mail off-line (freeing your telephone for other uses) and transfer files to other ATHENS users. Your ATHENS subscription also includes a mail address on the global Internet and allows you to send and receive Internet E-mail. The service is organized to help you manage your professional activities and personal and staff development. A subscription to ATHENS allows you to use the service at work, at home, or when traveling—whatever location is most convenient for you. America Tomorrow provides installation software for IBM-compatible or Macintosh computers, or you can use existing Prodigy software. Subscribers new to this type of communication will find the 800-assistance number reassuring.

Applications of telecommunication

Why bother with computer networking? It offers us an opportunity to communicate with and relate to colleagues, gain support, and maximize our limited resources to best serve the children we care for. Participating in a computer network is not difficult to do. I have been using networking for the past year and a half. I have integrated networking into my work as a preschool teacher and director and into my professional growth and development. I follow "threads," or paths of Internet correspondence, on topics such as mixed-age grouping, use of computers with young children, early literacy, and other topics of interest. I can ask and get feedback on questions, such as, What early childhood training delivery methods are being considered in your state (as we develop our plan in Maine)? and, I am planning a long-term garbage unit; any great resources to share?

With growing numbers of early childhood educators and parents online, computer networking offers a formidable resource pool of information and experiences available to those willing to take the leap! The children in our child care center have been involved in a book collaboration project, in which they are writing an add-on story involving groups of children ages 3 to 10 from around the world. A project in another setting involves nearly 1,000 kindergarten children collaborating on the creation of monsters, through words and graphics, in an open-ended whole language unit. It brings a reality to the concept of *world* when children do projects or exchange letters with friends in other countries. And in our global society, this is an extremely valuable experience for children to have from the earliest ages.

If this kind of communication is new to you, find someone who is already networking and who is willing to share some expertise with you. Universities, libraries, local elementary or high school volunteers, and computer user groups all are potential resources. People who are discovering this new medium for exchange are often excited about their newly developed talents and are eager to share them with a beginning colleague. So join us "online"!

Reference

InterNIC Information Services. 1994. *Fact sheet: Getting started on the Internet,* 15 August.

Daniel D. Shade

Helpful Hints on Acquiring Hardware

Once you have decided to take the plunge and become high-tech (as well as "high-touch"), there are several ways to obtain your first computer.

One temporary solution is to pick up a used computer. The Apple IIe and IIc are commonly available. Although many good programs are still available, very little new software is being released for this machine; we suggest not buying such hardware new. Lists and reviews of available software for various computers can be obtained through several sources, as noted under Resources. Comparable numbers of new software packages are constantly being released for IBM-compatible and Macintosh platforms. Do not buy—new or used—a computer that has been discontinued.

Some stores sell second-hand computers. You may be able to get a very favorable price, but sometimes prices are only marginally less than those for new equipment. A used printer is not a bargain when you can get a brand new one for $20 more at a local discount store.

You can usually find second-hand computers for reasonable prices through your local "Shopper" or "Trader" publication. The deal may include all of the software that the computer owner has collected, as well, so you might get a decent word processor in the bargain.

When parents upgrade their computer equipment, they often are willing to donate their old equipment to their child's center; small businesses might do the same for the center that serves their employees' children.

You could organize the PTA or parents of your center or school and have a fundraising event to raise money for a new computer.

You could solicit contributions or the donation of a new computer from businesses in your area. This is good public relations for them—as well as a tax deduction.

The suggestions above can be boon or bane, depending on whether someone is available to serve as a consultant. When you purchase a new computer, it generally comes with a plan for technical assistance and support. When you are given a computer out of the blue, you need someone who can tell you whether the machine is usable. Does it have enough memory to run the software you want? Does it have a hard disk drive? If so, how large is it (i.e., how many megabytes [MBs] of storage space does it have)? Can it be upgraded cheaply enough to suit your needs, or is buying a new computer a more sound economic move? Many centers and classrooms are lucky to have a computer-savvy parent who is willing to take a look at the computer and answer these questions. If your center or classroom is not so fortunate, look first for a reliable local computer repair shop. Ask the parents in your school or center where they take their computers to be fixed (just as you would ask around for referral to a good auto mechanic). Small, independent computer repair shops often will give a free estimate (or at least a cheap one, the fee for which may be applied toward future repairs or upgrades) and may be more amenable to working.

on and maintaining older computer equipment than are the national computer store chains.

If you decide to purchase a new computer, you can delay its inevitable obsolescence by buying a machine that

- has one or two expansion slots for sound boards or external disk drives;
- has at least 8 to 12 MBs of random access memory, or RAM, and provides the option of expanding to at least 32 MBs (the 4 or 5 MBs of RAM that most basic computers come with is simply not enough to run most early childhood software programs efficiently);
- is PowerPC or Intel Pentium upgradable (These are the fastest machines on the market at the time of this writing. They run at speeds of 60 to 80 MHz—two to three times faster than any other machine available—which results in, for example, being able to more quickly search for and save data, spell check, and grammar check);
- comes with, at a minimum, a 14-inch color monitor that offers a minimum of 256 colors;
- has at least one 3½-inch, 1.44 MB floppy disk drive;
- has a large (more than 100 MB) hard disk drive for permanent file storage (as early childhood software becomes better and more user-friendly, it takes up more storage space on the hard disk drive);
- contains either a built-in CD-ROM drive or an open bay or expansion slot where a CD-ROM drive could be added;
- includes a mouse or trackball (with which, research has shown, children tend to be more proficient than with a joystick or keyboard); and

• a color printer (we recommend dot matrix printers for early childhood programs because other types of color printers, as of this writing, are very expensive to purchase and to keep supplied with the colored ink or special paper required for color printouts).

You may pay a few dollars more for an expandable machine, but it will prove cost-effective in the long run. For example, we know of a preschool still running a Macintosh LC because they were able to upgrade the RAM to 10 MBs (the machine's maximum) and install a larger hard disk drive at a total cost of about $600— far less than they would have paid for a new computer.

Something must be said about peripheral devices. A good color monitor, a printer, a keyboard, and a mouse or trackball are peripheral to the computer's central processing unit (CPU), but they are not optional; they are essential to successful computing with young children. Black-and-white or color scanners, videotape interfaces, modems, external hard disk drives, and stereo speakers are other types of peripherals.

One of the most exciting developments in peripherals over the past few years has been the addition of CD-ROM technology (which uses the same compact disks that you buy for your home stereo, but the disks store other information besides digitized music). The CD-ROM drive gives the personal computer mass storage capability. A single compact disc, such as Microsoft's "Bookshelf '94," can hold the *American Heritage Dictionary, Roget's Thesaurus,* the *Columbia Book of Quotations,* the

Hammond Intermediate World Atlas, and the *World Almanac and Book of Facts 1994.* Imagine how much sound, speech, animation, and live-action video a compact disc can make available for children to explore! Also, the cost of a CD-ROM drive, for both IBM compatibles and Macintosh computers, has fallen to about $200.00 (for non–name brands). One word of warning: do not allow yourself to be talked into buying a more expensive CD version of a program that is available on floppy disk; at the time of this writing, little or no functional difference exists between the two. Software titles available only on compact disc are more likely to take advantage of CD-ROM technology and thus will probably be more interactive, colorful, and interesting to children. Be sure that you purchase at least a two-speed CD-ROM drive; single-speed drives cannot keep up with the speed with which the CPU requests information.

Choosing a computer is not an easy task, and having help can certainly ease the transition. Bear in mind that it is getting ever more difficult to distinguish between a Macintosh and an IBM-compatible computer. Software developments have brought this about, and they continue to narrow the gap. So go for the best deal you can find, and get excited! Do not let yourself be intimidated by the machine; it is just a hunk of plastic, metal, and silicon and can do nothing without commands from you. Relax and enjoy yourself. Learn about the computer with the children in your classroom. Make it a joint learning activity, and make it fun!

Software for Young Children

Adventures of Jimmy Jumper. Exceptional Children's Software/Don Johnston Developmental Equipment, Wauconda, IL.

Arthur's Teacher Troubles. Broderbund, San Rafael, CA.

A Silly Noisy House. The Voyager Company, Santa Monica, CA.

At Ease 2.0. Apple Computer, Cupertino, CA.

Bailey's Book House. Edmark Corporation, Redmond, WA.

Bald-Headed Chicken. DC Heath & Company, Lexington, MA.

Bear Jam Body Parts. Dunamis, Suwanee, GA.

Big Book Series. Queue, Fairfield, CT.

Big/Little I or II. UCLA/LAUSD Microcomputer Team, Los Angeles, CA.

Children's Writing and Publishing Center. The Learning Company, Fremont, CA.

Cinderella. Discus Knowledge Research, Buffalo, NY.

Cock-A-Doodle-Doo! What Does It Sound Like to You? Stewart, Tabori & Chang, New York, NY.

Color Me. Mindscape, Chicago, IL.

Creature Antics. Laureate Learning, Winooski, VT.

Dinosaur Game. UCLA/LAUSD Microcomputer Team, Los Angeles, CA.

Easy Street. Mind Play Methods & Solutions, Tucson, AZ.

Electronic Easel. MOBIUS Corporation, Alexandria, VA.

Explore-a-Story: The Three Little Pigs. Learningways, Acton, MA.

Facemaker. Spinnaker Software Corp, Cambridge, MA.

Farm. MOBIUS Corporation, Alexandria, VA.

First Words. Laureate Learning, Winooski, VT.

Geo-Logo. Dale Seymour, Palo Alto, CA.

Grandma and Me. Broderbund, San Rafael, CA.

Happy and You Know It. UCLA/LAUSD Microcomputer Team, Los Angeles, CA.

Hide 'N Seek with Fluffy. Playware, Kennesaw, GA.

Just Grandma and Me. Broderbund, Novato, CA.

Katie's Farm. Lawrence Productions, Galesburg, MI.

KidDesk. Edmark, Redmond, WA.

KidPix. Broderbund, Novato, CA.

Kidworks 2. Davidson and Associates, Inc., Torrance, CA.

KIDWARE2+ Learning Center. MOBIUS, Alexandria, VA.

Launch Pad. Berkeley Systems, Berkeley, CA.

LEGO Logo. Logo Computer Systems, Inc., Montreal, Quebec.

Logo. Logo Computer Systems, Inc., Montreal, Quebec.

Logo Writer. Logo Computer Systems, Inc., Montreal, Quebec.

Magic Crayon. C&C Software, Wichita, KS.

Magic Slate. Sunburst, Pleasantville, NY

McGee. Lawrence Productions, Galesburg, MI.

Mickey's ABCs. Walt Disney Software, Burbank, CA.

Microworlds. Logo Computer Systems, Inc., Montreal, Quebec.

Millie's Math House. Edmark, Redmond, WA.

Milliken Storyteller: The Ugly Duckling. Milliken, St. Louis, MO.

Mixed-up Mother Goose. Sierra On-line, Coarsegold, CA.

Neighborhoods: City. MOBIUS, Alexandria, VA.

Number Farm. DLM Teaching Resources, Allen, TX.

Number Munchers. Minnesota Educational Computing Consortium (MECC), Minneapolis, MN.

Old McDonald's Farm I. UCLA/LAUSD Microcomputer Team, Los Angeles, CA.

Peanuts Maze Marathon. Queue, Inc., Fairfield, CT.

Pelican Big Book. Queue, Inc., Fairfield, CT.

Peter Rabbit. Discus Knowledge Research, Buffalo, NY.

Playroom. Broderbund, Novato, CA.

The Pond. Sunburst, Pleasantville, NY.

Print Shop. Broderbund Software, Novato, CA.

Reader Rabbit. The Learning Co., Fremont, CA.

Rosie, the Counting Rabbit. Edmark, Redmond, WA.

Run Rabbit Run. Exceptional Children's Software/Don Johnston Developmental Equipment, Wauconda, IL.

The Rutgers Math Construction Tools: Number Blocks. Wasatch Education Systems, Salt Lake City, UT.

Stickybear Opposites. Optimum Resource/Weekly Reader Family Software, Hilton Head Island/SC

Stickybear Town Builder. Optimum Resource, Inc., Hilton Head Island/SC

Talking Animals. Orange Cherry Software, Pound Ridge, NY.

The Three Little Pigs. William K. Bradford Publishing Co., Inc., Acton, MA.

Thinkin' Things Collection 1. Edmark Corporation, Redmond, WA.

Turtle Math. Logo Computer Systems, Inc., Montreal, Quebec.

Wheels on the Bus. UCLA/LAUSD Microcomputer Team, Los Angeles, CA.

Where Did My Toothbrush Go? DC Heath & Company, Lexington, MA.

Zurk's Safari. Knowledge Adventure, Inc., LA Cresenta, CA.

Glossary

Apple IIe card[†]

An interface card or circuit board that emulates an Apple IIe computer. This card fits into several of the Macintosh models and, when emulating an Apple IIe, allows the user to run all of the software available for the Apple IIe.

assistive technology[†]

Computer attachments or peripherals that make computing more accessible to persons with differing ability. Includes but is not limited to single switches, computerized toys, and communication boards.

backup

To copy data or programs in case the original is lost or damaged.

bit

see byte

boot

The process of starting up a computer. Certain startup programs are loaded into the random access memory (RAM) of the computer and then executed. Most computers boot from either a floppy disk or a hard drive.

[†] *With the exception of these terms (marked with a* [†]*) definitions are taken from Fatouros, Downes & Blackwell,* In Control: Young Children Learning With Computers, *1994 (Wentworth Falls, New South Wales: Social Science Press), with minor adaptations for the purpose of this volume.*

bug

A programming error that causes software to malfunction.

bulletin board

An electronic means of posting general notices upon a central computer, which is accessed remotely by a number of users. To enable users to find relevant messages easily, some systems allow for a rapid search of a series of bulletin boards for all notices containing a certain word or phrase.

button[†]

An icon, picture, or box that—when identified by the cursor by clicking the mouse button— will execute a command, such as selecting a particular program from a picture menu, printing, or saving a command.

byte

A unit of data in the language understood by the computer. A byte is a group of eight bits, which are the smallest units of data and appear as "0" or "1." A byte represents one character on a computer keyboard.

CD-ROM (compact disk read-only memory)

The use of compact disc technology to permanently store large volumes of computer data and programs. One CD can store as much data as 1,000 floppy disks, and an entire encyclopedia fits easily on one CD.

central processing unit (CPU)

The chip that controls the operation of the computer, sometimes referred to as the computer's "brain." The term *CPU* is sometimes also used to describe the main box of the computer that the keyboard, monitor, etc. plug into.

character

Any symbol that can be entered into the computer from the keyboard, including spaces, tabs, carriage returns, and punctuation.

chip

A small wafer of silicon onto which are implanted millions of electrical circuits. Chips are the basic building blocks of modern computers.

clicking[†]

An action performed after the user has moved the cursor to a desired spot on the screen with the mouse or trackball and then pressed the button on the mouse. Some mice have several buttons that can be programmed to perform specific commands when clicked, such as discarding a document.

command

An instruction that the computer understands and can carry out.

communications software

Software that manages the linking together of two computers and the transfer of data and programs between them. The computers are usually connected via modems and telephone lines or directly by cable.

compatibility

The ability of two pieces of software or hardware to interact without problems. Products from one manufacturer are often incompatible with those from another unless they both adhere to an accepted standard.

computer aided design (CAD)

Refers to powerful design and drawing programs used by professional designers, such as engineers and architects, to render three-dimensional images.

computer laboratory (computer room)

A specific-purpose classroom containing a collection of hardware and software that is used for tasks involving computers. In elementary schools this room is used by the computer teacher to help children develop computer skills.

computer literacy

A minimum set of skills and knowledge deemed necessary for one to use current computer technology.

copy protection (puzzler)[†]

A scheme used by some software companies to protect their products from being illegally copied and distributed. Before the software will load and run, the user must enter a particular word or picture from a specific page in the user manual.

corrupted

Usually refers to damaged data or programs on a disk.

crash

Of computers, to suddenly cease operating. Crashes usually occur because of incompatibilities in programs running on the computer, but their unexpectedness—and the trouble they can cause—have spawned two pieces of wisdom: "Save early and save often!" and "Backitup!"

cursor

The marker on the screen that indicates where the next typed character will go. Cursors take many forms, such as a blinking underline or box or a vertical line or arrow.

debugging

The process of testing and removing errors from software before it is released for use. Also

refers to the process a computer user goes through to discover the reason for a crash, an unexplained loss of data, or a printer malfunction.

desktop

The screen environment from which programs are launched or files opened. Contains small pictures, called "icons," that represent the programs and files.

digitize[†]

The process of taking pictures and sounds and changing them from their analog state (something that bears an analogy to the real thing) to a digital representation as zeros and/or ones, which is the language computers understand. For example, the laser beam in a compact disc player reads the ones and zeros and reconstructs the music. *see* byte

disk

double-density disk

The lower capacity type of floppy disk commonly available. Double-density disks store less than 1 Mb of data.

double-sided disk

A floppy disk that increases capacity by storing information on both the top and bottom of a disk. All recent floppy disks are double sided.

floppy disk

A disk that uses a flexible, magnetic mylar plastic—similar to that on a cassette tape—for storage. Floppy disks typically store about 1 megabyte (MB) and are relatively slow compared to hard disks, but they are portable and can be safely stored away from the computer. The 5¼-inch floppy disks have a flexible case; the increasingly prevalent 3½-inch floppy disks have a durable plastic case and are sometimes mistakenly referred to as "hard disks."

hard disk (sometimes called a *fixed disk*)

A disk made from rigid material with a thin magnetic coating. Hard disks provide fast, high-capacity storage, and the sealed drive is usually mounted inside the computer (although external hard disks can be added). Many modern programs require hard disk storage because floppies are too slow and have too small a capacity. Removable hard disks provide storage for a large amount of data and are portable.

high-density disk

The higher capacity type of floppy disk commonly available. High-density disks store more than 1 Mb of data.

disk drive[†]

A permanent storage device in which data are stored on either rigid or flexible disks covered with a magnetic coating. *see also* disk

documentation

The manuals and support materials in a software package.

DOS

see system software

download

To transfer files into a computer through a modem or cable.

dragging[†]

An action performed with the cursor and mouse. Objects can be moved from one place to another on the screen by clicking the mouse, holding the button down, and dragging the object to another spot on the screen. By dragging, one can also open pull-down menus and move and size windows.

drill and practice[†]

An early and still common form of software that typically resembles a ditto or workbook page. Children respond to preprogrammed probes and often are rewarded with screen cartoons. Some early versions of drill software also punished a child for an incorrect answer with a sad tune or a frowning face.**editing**

The process of making changes to data, such as adding, deleting, or rearranging words in a word processing file.

electronic mail (or E mail)

Sending typed messages to other computer users, either through a local area network (LAN) or via modem. Messages can be easily answered, printed, or forwarded.

error message

A message indicating a problem that has occurred, usually a cryptic message, accompanied by an error number, that only someone familiar with the computer programming language would understand.

fiber optics

The use of lasers and thin glass cable to transfer data. It provides security and the capability to handle vast quantities of data.

field

The basic storage unit of a data base file. A defined part of a data base record, such as a postcode or a phone number.

file

Any set of information stored on tape or disk. Examples of files would be word processing documents, sets of data base records, computer programs, or graphics.

formatting

The process of preparing a disk for use, also known as *initializing*. Formatting also erases all data from a disk that has been previously used.

graphical user interface (GUI)

An alternative and increasingly popular method of issuing commands to a computer; one uses a mouse or pen instead of the keyboard. Popularized on the Macintosh, it uses windows, icons, and pull-down menus to simplify the operation of the computer.

graphics[†]

The images that appear on the screen of a computer monitor, such as words, numbers, and pictures. Graphics are created by causing minute dots on the screen, called *pixels,* to take on particular characteristics, such as color and position.

graphics tablet[†]

An input device consisting of a surface, or tablet, that can read the movements of a stylus that comes in contact with it.

hardware

The physical components of a computer system, such as the monitor, keyboard, and CPU.

icon[†]

A small graphic that represents a word or command, often used to make programs easier to operate. The Windows application for IBM and compatibles and the Macintosh Desk Top are icon-operated. A user points to the icon with the cursor and clicks the mouse to perform the function.

input device[†]

Any number of peripherals designed for operating computers. Input devices include keyboards, graphics tablets, disk drives, microphones, scanners, mice, joysticks, and trackballs.

integrated learning system (ILS)

A super-software package that provides a complete curriculum in a subject, such as math or reading.

integrated program

A program that combines cut-down versions of a number of software types, providing for easy sharing of data among the component functions.

interface

The junction between two parts of a computer system, one of which is usually the CPU. The interface must propagate and, where necessary, translate signals as they pass between the devices so that they can "understand" each other.

joystick

An input device used in computer game playing, with a small lever that controls cursor movement.

justify

In word processing, to align to achieve straight right and/or left margins. In full justification, such as in a newspaper column, lines of text are aligned at the right and left margins and variable spacing is placed between the letters and words. In left justification, the text is aligned with the left margin. In right justification, the right margin is straight.

K

Abbreviation for kilobyte—a unit used for computer storage; 1024 (2^{10}) bytes. *see* byte

light pen

An input device—a small pen that the user moves around directly on the computer screen.

load†

The process of copying a software program's instructions into the computer's memory, or RAM, to run the software.

local area network (LAN)

A set of computers, interconnected by cable, that can share programs, data, and peripheral devices, such as printers. A LAN commonly consists of the computers in only one room or building.

memory

Internal electronic storage using chips. *see* random access memory; read-only memory

menu

A set of related commands displayed on the screen.

menu bar

A horizontal list of menu headings, usually displayed along the top of the screen.

microcomputer†

Also called a *personal computer*, a computer that is small enough to put on a desk or a small table in the classroom.

modem

An input/output device that allows computers to communicate using telephone lines. The modem at one end converts digital data into analog form (MODulation) for transmission as sound signals. The signals are then converted back into digital form (DEModulation) by the modem on the receiving computer.

monitor

The television-like screen that displays computer output, also known as the *VDU* (video display unit).

mouse

An input device that controls a moving pointer, or cursor, on the screen. A mouse has one or more buttons that can be used to issue commands, such as "zooming in" to the image on the screen.

MSDOS

The operating system (Microsoft Disk Operating System) used in IBM-compatible computers.

multimedia

The combination of text, images, and sound.

network

A number of interconnected computers. *see* local area network; wide area network

online

With respect to telecommunications, refers to access to data bases, bulletin boards, and other users through telecommunications services. It can also mean that a printer is connected and ready to receive data from the computer.

open-ended†

Computer software is said to be open-ended when children are free to do many different things in using it. Word processing, drawing, and programming (in Logo) can all provide open-ended computer activities. Many drawing programs that purport to be open-ended are merely coloring books in disguise.

output device†

A part of the computer that responds to input from the user and results from the program's execution of the user's commands. Output can be

displayed on the screen or printed to paper (often called *hard copy*). Output can also be audio, such as the sound effects and music found in many programs for young children. Saving a file to a disk is also a form of output.

paddle

An input device used in computer game playing—a rotating knob is used to control movement on the screen.

password

A coded word or series of characters that a user must enter before gaining access to a system; similar to a credit card PIN.

peripheral

An input or output device, such as a printer, keyboard, or mouse.

piracy†

Copying software from friends and associates to avoid paying for the software. All software is fully protected under copyright law or is licensed to users for their use only. Thinking that they are being nice when they let friends copy their software, people are driving up the price of software for everyone. Pirating software is also a great way to catch a computer virus (see virus).

port

A socket, usually found at the back of the computer, into which can be plugged a cable to connect the computer to another device, e.g., a printer or a modem.

printer

continuous-feed printer

Also called *form-feed* or *tractor-feed* printer. A printer that uses continuous paper with a removable strip along each side containing holes that hold the paper in place on the printer. Pages are separated by a perforation, thus paper does not have to be loaded as separate sheets.

dot matrix printer

An output device that prints when small pins strike a ribbon and transfer dots to the page. Dot matrix printers are relatively slow and noisy but cheap.

friction-feed printer

A mechanism, such as the carriage on a typewriter, for loading single sheets into a printer.

inkjet printer

A printer that works by spraying small dots of ink onto paper. Inkjet printers are quiet, produce high-quality output on good paper, and cost less than a laser printer, but they are comparatively slow. Output is better than with a dot matrix printer but not as good as with a laser printer.

laser printer

A fast, high-quality, quiet printer that uses technology similar to that of a photocopier. Initially very expensive, laser printers are fast becoming ubiquitous.

manual-feed printer

A printer that is set up so that paper is fed one sheet at a time rather than from a cartridge or tractor feed.

printing, draft quality

High-speed output from a dot matrix or inkjet printer that produces text and images using as few dots or as little ink as possible. Draft quality is used when the document is to be previewed or proofread or when printing lists of data.

printing, letter quality

Output from a dot matrix or inkjet printer that overlaps the dots or uses more ink so that the text looks more like that produced on a typewriter or laser printer.

printer driver

Software that translates signals from a computer into signals that the printer understands. Changing the type of printer being used may require selecting a different printer driver.

program†

A set of instructions, organized in a linear manner, that cause a microcomputer to perform a particular function, such as word processing. When children draw on the screen by moving the triangle-shaped cursor, called the "turtle," in Logo, they are actually programming. A software program includes a complete set of commands or instructions.

program disk

A floppy disk that contains an application program. It may need to be inserted at different times when running the program, or it may be inserted only once to install the application onto the hard disk and then saved.

pull-down menus

Also called drop-down menus. Menu systems in which the options, which are initially hidden, display as though they were on a pull-down roller blind. Most modern software uses pull-down menus.

QWERTY keyboard

A standard keyboard, often named QWERTY because these are the first six letters on the top left-hand side of the keyboard.

random access memory (RAM)

Memory (measured in megabytes) that is used to temporarily store programs and data while the computer is running. Data in RAM are lost if the power is switched off, hence the need to save data to the disk. Some programs will not run unless there is a certain amount of RAM installed in the computer.

read-only memory (ROM)

Memory that comes with programs, notably, operating system programs. Programs in ROM cannot be changed, hence the term *read-only*. The CPU, or brain, of a computer contains ROM.

reinforcements†

Rewards embedded in a program that are released when a child gives a correct response. Sometimes the reinforcements relate to the content of the program, and sometimes they are purely entertainment. *see* drill and practice

scan mode†

Mostly used with children with special needs, the ability to have the computer scan and either blink or highlight on the screen all possible choices. When the user sees the desired event or outcome highlighted, he or she needs only to press a single key or switch. Scanning allows disabled individuals to access computers for communication, education, and fun.

scanner

An input device that allows text and images on paper to be copied directly into the computer for use in word processing or desktop publishing programs.

screen dump

To copy the screen image directly to the printer or to a disk. Screen dumps can usually be performed by pressing one or two specific keys.

screen saver[†]

A computer program that can be set to display a pleasing graphic or funny animation when the computer has been idle for a number of minutes determined by the user. This prevents the image from being burned into the phosphorus on the inside of the screen. A single keystroke or mouse click will stop the screen saver and return to the page on which the user was last working.

scrolling

Moving upwards or downwards through text in a document so that different portions of it can be viewed. Scrolling is usually accomplished using the cursor control keys or a mouse.

shareware[†]

Software, not commercially available except through clubs and certain clearinghouses, that is produced by amateurs and is very inexpensive.

simulation[†]

A program that emulates situations or conditions in the real world, such as life in an ant colony or under water, giving children opportunities to discover concepts and relationships in a context that would be difficult for them to experience in reality.

single switch[†]

A peripheral device that, when coupled with scanning equipment, allows disabled persons to operate computer software.

software

Another word for computer programs. A software package may contain one or more related programs.

speech synthesizer

A chip that can convert textual data into simulated human speech. The quality of output has so improved that synthesized speech now replaces human speech in some applications, such as telephone directory assistance.

stand-alone computer

A single computer that does not directly share data or programs with other computers through a network. Also known as a *personal computer*.

startup disk

A disk on which is stored the system programs needed for the computer to "boot." The system programs for most computers today are stored on the hard disk. *see* boot

system software

Programs needed by the computer to perform basic functions, such as starting up, putting images on the screen, and transferring data to disk drives and printers. System software is stored in ROM, on startup disks, or on the hard disk. Also referred to as operating software, disk operating system (DOS), or—in a common form—MSDOS software.

template

A spreadsheet, data base, or word processing file that has been set up and is ready for use. This setup could include layout, headings, fields, and/or formulas.

text file

Also known as an ASCII file. A file format that allows a document to be easily transferred to a different program. Any formatting, such as bolding or italicizing, is lost.

trackball[†]

An increasingly popular mechanism for interacting with the computer by means of a solid ball that sits in a hole in the keyboard or in a special box attached to the computer. Moving the ball with the hand controls the position of the cursor on the screen.

utilities

Software that combines specific commonly used functions, such as managing files or disks.

virus[†]

A computer program—written by a prankster to cause trouble for computer users—that attaches itself to other programs and thus is passed from disk to disk.

visual display unit (VDU)

Another term for monitor, screen, or display.

wide area network (WAN)

A set of computers interconnected by cable, microwaves, satellite, etc., that can share data and messages. A WAN is likely to extend across many miles and can span continents. *see* LAN

window

A screen area, displaying some of the data in a file, that overlays other screen areas. Windows can be moved, resized, and hidden.

workstation

A computer, attached to a network, that can access shared information and peripheral devices.

wrap[†]

A word processing program's ability to continue typing on succeeding lines automatically. In contrast to using a typewriter, one need not hit the RETURN or ENTER key at the end of each line.

Additional Resources

Related Organizations

Assistive Technology Resource Consortium, George Mason University Center for Human Disabilities, M.S. 1F2, Fairfax, VA 22030-4444. 800-333-7958
Provides referrals and training for educators.

Center for Applied Special Technology (CAST) 39 Cross Street, Peabody, MA 01960. 508-531-8555
Provides multiple services for people with disabilities, including evaluations, system designs, teacher training, and development of multimedia curricula.

Center for Children and Technology (CCT) Education Development Center (EDC) 96 Morton Street, 7th Floor, New York, NY 10014. 212-807-4200; fax 212-633-8804
Collaborates with schools, universities, and other institutions to do basic, applied, and formative research and technology development with the goal of improving education by altering the circumstances of teaching and learning.

Center for Technology in Education Johns Hopkins University, 2500 E. Northern Parkway, Baltimore, MD 21214. 410-254-8466
Conducts research on comprehensive inclusion programs, offers training for professionals and parents, and publishes a newsletter on assistive technology.

Closing the Gap P.O. Box 68, Henderson, MN 56044. 612-248-3294
Provides training and information on adaptive computer technologies, publishes a comprehensive list of commercially available hardware and software and a bimonthly newsletter on the use of assistive technology, and sponsors an annual conference.

Educational Resources Information Center (ERIC), Clearinghouse on Information and Technology. Syracuse University, 4-194 Center for Science and Technology, Syracuse, NY 13244-4100. 800-464-9107 or 315-443-3640. Internet: eric@ericir.syr.edu. AskERIC (Internet-based question-answering service): askeric@ericir.syr.edu
One of 16 clearinghouses in the ERIC system. Maintains a data base and provides products and services related to library and information science and educational technology.

National Center to Improve Practice, Education Development Center, 55 Chapel Street, Newton, MA 02158-1060. 617-969-7100; TTY: 617-969-4529
Runs NCIPnet telecommunications network to share information about assistive technology and effective practice.

Special Education Technology Lab, University of Connecticut. 249 Glenbrook Road, U-64, Storrs, CT 06269-2064. 203-286-0171
Provides comprehensive software evaluations and sponsors a national conference.

Technology and Media (TAM), Council for Exceptional Children. 1920 Association Drive, Reston, Virginia 22091-1598. 703-620-3660
Provides information on hardware and software and other technology for children, especially children with special needs. Produces a bimonthly newsletter and a quarterly journal on technology and special education.

Trace Research and Development Center S-151 Waisman Center. 1500 Highland Avenue, Madison, WI 53705.
Develops adaptive devices and maintains a data base of assistive technology products.

Software Evaluation Resources

Children's Software. Available from Children's Software Press, 851 President Street, Brooklyn, NY 11215. 718-622-4625. Quarterly newsletter.

Children's Software Revue. Available from Warren Buckleitner, 520 North Adams Street, Ypsilanti, MI 48197-2482. 313-480-0040; fax: 313-480-2260. Bimonthly newsletter.

Developmental Evaluations of Software for Young Children. Available from Susan W. Haugland & Daniel D. Shade. The KIDS Project, Center for Child Studies, Southeast Missouri State University, Cape Girardeau, MO 63701. 314-651-2951. Evaluation table.

High/Scope Buyer's Guide to Children's Software, 600 North River Street, Ypsilanti, MI 48198. 313-485-2000 or 800-442-4329; fax: 313-485-0704. Annual publication.

Technology and Learning, 330 Progress Road, Dayton, OH 45449. 513-847-5900. Magazine published monthly during the school year, once during the summer.

The Education Software Selector (TESS). Educational Software Information Exchange (EPIE), 103-3 West Montauk Highway, Hampton Bays, NY 11946. 516-728-9100. Data base information on floppy disk or CD-ROM updated twice a year.

Selected Readings

A to Z: The early childhood educator's guide to the Internet. 1994. Urbana, IL: ERIC Clearinghouse on Early and Elementary Childhood Education.

Benzie, D., & J.L. Wright. n.d. *Exploring a new partnership: Children, teachers and technology.* Amsterdam, Netherlands: North Holland. Distributed by Elsevier Science Ltd., 660 White Plains Rd., Tarrytown, NY 10591.

Bredekamp, S., & T. Rosegrant, eds. 1992. *Reaching potentials: Appropriate curriculum and assessment for young children,* Vol. 1. Washington, DC: NAEYC.

Brown, L.K. 1986. *Taking advantage of media: A manual for parents and teachers.* Boston: Routledge & Kegan Paul.

Bulkeley, W.M. 1994. Computers, the gender divide: A tool for women, a toy for men—Gender affects how user sees the computer. *Wall Street Journal,* 16 March.

Burns, M.S., L. Goin, & J.T. Donlon. 1990. A computer in my room. *Young Children* 45 (2): 62–67.

Campbell, P.F., & G.G Fein., eds. 1986. *Young children and microcomputers.* New York: Prentice Hall.

Clements, D.H., B.K. Nastasi, & S. Swaminathan. 1993. Research in review. Young children and computers: Crossroads and directions from research. *Young Children* 48 (2): 56–64.

The Computing Teacher, International Society for Technology in Education (ISTE), 1787 Agate St., Eugene, OR 97403-1923.

Davidson, G.V., & S.D. Ritchie. 1994. Attitudes toward integrating computers into the classroom: What parents, teachers and students report. *Journal of Computing in Childhood Education* 5 (1): 3–27.

DeVillar, R.A., & C.J. Faltis. 1991. *Computers and cultural diversity: Restructuring for school success.* Albany, NY: State University of New York Press.

Electronic Learning, Scholastic Inc., 555 Broadway, New York, NY 10012.

Elliott, A. 1993. Effects of gender on pre-schoolers' play and learning in Logo environments. *Journal of Computing in Childhood Education* 4 (2): 103–24.

Fatouros, C., T. Downes, & S. Blackwell 1994. *IN CONTROL: Young children learning with computers.* Wentworth Falls, Australia: Social Science Press.

Fite, K. 1993. A report on computer use in early childhood education. *Ed Tech Review* (Spring/ Summer): 18–24.

Forman, G., & P.B. Pufall, eds. 1998. *Constructivism in the computer age.* Hillsdale, NJ: Lawrence Erlbaum.

Guralnick, M.J. 1991. The next decade of research on the effectiveness of intervention. *Teaching Exceptional Children* 58 (2): 174–82.

Hasselbring, T., L. Goin, & J. Bransford. 1987. Developing automaticity. *Teaching Exceptional Children* 19 (3): 30–33.

Haugland, S.W., & D.D. Shade. 1988. Developmentally appropriate software for young children. *Young Children* 43 (4): 37–43.

Haugland, S.W. 1992. The effect of computer software on preschool children's developmental gains. *Journal of Computing in Childhood Education* 3 (1): 15–30.

Hohman, C. 1990. *Young children & computers.* Ypsilanti, MI: High/Scope Press.

Hoot, J.L., & S.B. Silvern. 1988. *Writing with computers in the early grades.* New York: Teachers College Press.

Jacobson, J.L. 1992. *Worldwatch paper 110— Gender bias: Roadblock to sustainable development.* Washington, DC: Worldwatch Institute.

Journal of Computing in Childhood Education, Association for the Advancement of Computing in Education (AACE), P.O. Box 2966, Charlottesville, VA 22902. (phone 804-973-3987)

Journal of Research on Computing in Education, International Society for Technology in Education (ISTE), 1787 Agate St., Eugene, OR 97403-1923.

Journal of Research on Computing in Teacher Education, International Society for Technology in Education (ISTE), 1787 Agate St., Eugene, OR 97403-1923.

Lazerson, M., J.B. McLaughlin, B. McPhearson, & S.K. Bailey. 1985. *An education of value: The purpose and practice of schools.* New York: Cambridge University Press.

McCracken, J.B. 1993. *Valuing diversity: The primary years.* Washington, DC: NAEYC.

Moxley, R.A., & B.G. Warash. 1992. Writing strategies of three prekindergarten children on the microcomputer. *Journal of Computing in Childhood Education* 3 (2): 137–79.

Moxley, R.A., B. Warash, G. Coffman, L.M. Geres, T. Roman, & L.E. Terhorst. 1994. Computer writing development in a prekindergarten class of 4 year olds. *Journal of Computing in Childhood Education* 5 (2): 211–29.

Perry, T., & J.W. Fraser, eds. 1993. *Freedom's plow: Teaching in the multicultural classroom.* New York: Routledge.

Raskin, R., & C. Ellison. 1992. *Parents, kids, and computers: An activity guide for family fun and learning.* New York: Random House.

Reyes, P., & R.R. Valencia. 1993. Educational policy and the growing Latino student population: Problems and prospects. *Hispanic Journal of Behavioral Sciences* 15 (2): 258–84.

Rowland, K.L., & D. Scott. 1992. Promoting language and literacy for young children through computers. *Journal of Computing in Childhood Education* 3 (1): 55–61.

Sadker, M., & D. Sadker. 1994. *Failing at fairness: How America's schools cheat girls.* New York: Scribner's.

Salpeter, J. 1992. *Kids & computers: A parent's handbook.* Carmel, IN: SAMS, Prentice Hall.

Shade, D.D. 1992. A developmental look at award-winning software. *Day Care & Early Education* 20 (1): 41–43.

Yager, R.E., S.M. Blunck, & E.T. Nelson. 1993. The use of computers to enhance science instruction in pre-school and K-3 classrooms. *Journal of Computing in Childhood Education* 4 (2): 125–36.

Zeece, P.D., & S.K. Graul. 1990. Learning to play: Playing to learn. *Day Care and Early Intervention* Fall: 11–15.

Information about NAEYC

NAEYC is . . .

. . . a membership-supported organization of people committed to fostering the growth and development of children from birth through age 8. Membership is open to all who share a desire to serve and act on behalf of the needs and rights of young children.

NAEYC provides . . .

. . . educational services and resources to adults who work with and for children, including

• *Young Children, the* journal for early childhood educators

• **Books, posters, brochures,** and **videos** to expand your knowledge and commitment to young children, with topics including infants, curriculum, research, discipline, teacher education, and parent involvement

• An **Annual Conference** that brings people from all over the country to share their expertise and advocate on behalf of children and families

• **Week of the Young Child** celebrations sponsored by NAEYC Affiliate Groups across the nation to call public attention to the needs and rights of children and families

• **Insurance plans** for individuals and programs

• **Public affairs information** for knowledgeable advocacy efforts at all levels of government and through the media

• The **National Academy of Early Childhood Programs,** a voluntary accreditation system for high-quality programs for children

• The **National Institute for Early Childhood Professional Development,** providing resources and services to improve professional preparation and development of early childhood educators

• The **Information Service,** a centralized source of information sharing, distribution, and collaboration

For free information about membership, publications, or other NAEYC services . . .

• call NAEYC at 202-232-8777 or 800-424-2460

• or write to NAEYC, 1509 16th St., N.W., Washington, DC 20036-1426.